Better Homes and Gardens®

15 MINUTES or LESS LOW-CARB RECIPES

Meredith® Books
Des Moines, Iowa

15 Minutes or Less Low–Carb Recipes
Editor: Tricia Laning
Contributing Editors: Spectrum Communication Services, Inc.
Associate Design Director: Chad Jewell
Copy Chief: Terri Fredrickson
Publishing Operations Manager: Karen Schirm
Edit and Design Production Coordinator: Mary Lee Gavin
Book Production Managers: Pam Kvitne, Marjorie
    J. Schenkelberg, Rick von Holdt, Mark Weaver
Contributing Proofreaders: David Craft, Susan J. Kling,
    Arianna McKinney
Indexer: Elizabeth T. Parson
Editorial Assistant: Cheryl Eckert
Test Kitchen Director: Lynn Blanchard

Meredith® Books
Editor in Chief: Linda Raglan Cunningham
Design Director: Matt Strelecki
Managing Editor: Gregory H. Kayko
Executive Editor: Jennifer Dorland Darling

Publisher: James D. Blume
Executive Director, Marketing: Jeffrey Myers
Executive Director, New Business Development:
    Todd M. Davis
Executive Director, Sales: Ken Zagor
Director, Operations: George A. Susral
Director, Production: Douglas M. Johnston
Business Director: Jim Leonard

Vice President and General Manager: Douglas J. Guendel

Better Homes and Gardens® **Magazine**
Editor in Chief: Karol DeWulf Nickell
Deputy Editor, Food and Entertaining: Nancy Hopkins

Meredith Publishing Group
President, Publishing Group: Stephen M. Lacy
Vice President-Publishing Director: Bob Mate

Meredith Corporation
Chairman and Chief Executive Officer: William T. Kerr

In Memoriam: E.T. Meredith III (1933-2003)

All of us at Meredith® Books are dedicated to providing you with the information and ideas you need to create delicious foods. We welcome your comments and suggestions. Write to us at: Meredith Books, Cookbook Editorial Department, 1716 Locust St., Des Moines, IA 50309-3023.

If you would like to purchase any of our cooking, crafts, gardening, home improvement, or home decorating and design books, check wherever quality books are sold. Or visit us at: bhgbooks.com

Pictured on front cover: Salsa–Topped Rosemary T-Bones (see recipe page 92)

Our seal assures you that every recipe in *15 Minutes or Less Low–Carb Recipes* has been tested in the Better Homes and Gardens® Test Kitchen. This means that each recipe is practical and reliable, and meets our high standards of taste appeal. We guarantee your satisfaction with this book for as long as you own it.

TABLE OF CONTENTS

INTRODUCTION 4

APPETIZERS 21

SOUPS AND SALADS 55

MAIN DISHES

BEEF AND VEAL 85

PORK AND LAMB 125

CHICKEN AND TURKEY 161

FISH AND SHELLFISH 205

SIDE DISHES 251

SNACKS 291

DESSERTS 331

HOLIDAYS 367

CARB COUNTS 401

INDEX 406

THE LOWDOWN ON LOW CARB

It's everywhere these days–at the bookstore, the grocery store, on television and the Internet, and in newspapers and magazines. Whether it's Atkins, South Beach, or the Zone–it's the Low-Carbohydrate or Low-Carb diet. The premise is simple: Cut out carbohydrates and lose weight. If you're reading this, chances are that you're one of an estimated 32 million Americans who have joined the low–carb movement.

This cookbook is for you if you're interested in cooking low carb but don't have a lot of time. Each recipe has less than 10 grams of net carbohydrates and was designed for a variety of low-carb diet plans. The majority of the recipes can be prepared in 15 minutes or less. You can't beat that for convenience–and keeping you low carb no matter which plan you are following.

Here you'll find over 200 delicious recipes– from appetizers made in a snap and sensational soups and salads that curb the carbs to fast and easy meat and fish mains and vegetable sides. We've even included delectable desserts, satisfying snacks, and special dishes for the holidays or entertaining. Before you get cooking, take a moment to get the lowdown on eating the low–carb way.

SO WHAT EXACTLY ARE CARBOHYDRATES?

Food is composed of six groups of nutrients that are necessary for health: fats, proteins, vitamins, minerals, water, and carbohydrates. Carbohydrates can be further divided into two groups: complex (starches) and simple (sugars).

Complex carbohydrates are found in foods that come from plants such as bread, pasta, cereal, rice, beans, and, to a lesser degree, fruits, and vegetables such as potatoes and corn. Simple carbohydrates are found in foods such as table sugar, honey, syrup, molasses, candy, and baked goods such as cookies, cakes, and pies.

Fiber is also a carbohydrate, but because it is not digested and absorbed by the body it is not considered a nutrient. Still, it is very important in helping to prevent heart disease, diabetes, cancer, and other chronic conditions.

In the body carbohydrates are broken down into their simplest forms, sugars called glucose, galactose, and fructose. They are then digested and move into the bloodstream where they are converted into energy. As they are transported around the body by the bloodstream, they are often referred to as "blood sugar." Carbohydrates, mainly in the form of glucose, provide about half of all the energy used by your muscles, nerves, and other body tissues. The brain prefers to rely on a steady supply of carbohydrates to function properly.

Simply speaking, as blood sugar levels rise above normal–say after you've eaten a piece of bread–the hormone insulin signals your liver, muscles, and other cells to store the extra that isn't being used immediately for energy. Stored glucose is called glycogen. Some glucose may also be converted into body fat if you've eaten more calories than your body needs.

When blood sugar levels drop below normal–for example, when you haven't eaten for a while or when you're doing something that requires more energy such as jogging–another hormone called glucagon tells your body to change the stored glycogen back into glucose. Once glucose is back in your bloodstream, it's ready to fuel your body cells. If there still isn't enough glucose, the body will start using body fat for energy.

For the complete picture, recognize that any excess calories–whether they come from carbohydrates, fat, or protein–are stored in the body as fat. Carbohydrates and protein supply 4 calories per gram, while fat more than doubles that at 9 calories per gram. Bottom line: Too much of any food will make you gain weight.

A HEALTHY APPROACH TO LOW-CARB DIETS.

Diets are nothing new. For decades people have been following one diet plan or another to drop unwanted pounds. Most diets fail because they aren't easy or enjoyable to stick to for a long period of time. They also don't take into account that most of us like to eat great-tasting and satisfying food, or that being active is very important for keeping weight off.

So where does low carb fit in? The basic premise of the low-carb diet is that by cutting down on carbs, less insulin is released by the body and fat is not stored. Replacing simple carbs with foods high in protein–such as meat, poultry, cheese, and eggs–builds muscle. As the rate of obesity continues to climb, taking a closer look at what type and how many carbohydrates we are eating may not be such a bad idea.

One way to make the most of a low-carb diet is to pay attention to the glycemic index (GI) of the carbs you are eating. This is a measure of the rate at which a food causes your blood sugar to rise. Foods are compared to pure glucose (at a GI of 100) and then ranked accordingly from 1 to 100. For example, a kaiser roll has a value of 73 while barley only rates a 25. The speed at which glucose enters your bloodstream may affect your hunger, your weight, and even your long-term health. The goal is to choose those foods with a low GI more often. Everyone–not just dieters–should avoid sugary foods and those made with refined white flour–cakes and pastries, for example. Substitute wholegrain breads, crackers, and pastas.

Another way to eat low carb in a healthy way is to opt for protein foods that are high in "good" or monounsaturated and polyunsaturated fats. Such foods–including olive oil, nuts, and fish–have been shown in studies to help lower LDL (low-density lipoprotein), or "bad" cholesterol. At the same time, they increase levels of HDL (high-density lipoprotein), or "good" cholesterol.

Look for lean cuts of meat and use low-fat cooking methods, such as broiling, baking, and grilling, instead of frying whenever possible. To make it easy, we've included all you need to know about these cooking techniques in the following introductory sections.

The amount of food you eat is also an important factor in losing weight. Eating large portions or continuing to eat even when you feel full eventually leads to your "supersizing" yourself. To help you with this, each of the recipes is 10 grams of net carb or less per serving. We've also provided meal planning tips, a pantry guide, and serving suggestions for each recipe.

TOP 10 QUESTIONS AND ANSWERS FOR EATING THE LOW-CARB WAY

Getting into the swing of a low-carb diet can be confusing. Here we've got answers to frequently asked questions.

Q. Is a low-carb diet safe for my children?
A. No. Children need lots of energy to support their rapid growth, development, and learning. To get the calories, vitamins, and minerals they require, they should be eating a wide variety of foods, including carbohydrate-rich choices such as bread, pasta, and rice. The brain prefers carbohydrates as a fuel source so it is not appropriate to restrict children's carbohydrate intake. Of course, obesity is a growing problem in children so if you are concerned about your child's weight, consult your family physician.

Q. I am the only person in my family following a low-carb diet. How do I feed my family and still eat low carb myself?
A. The easiest way to do this is to plan ahead so that meals can be altered to accommodate the needs of both your low–carb diet and your family's food preferences. Each of the recipes in the 15 Minutes or Less Low–Carb Recipes can be enjoyed by all. For example, if you are serving Pepper-Marinated Flank Steak with Down-South Green Beans, just add a small baked potato, some rice, or a whole wheat roll to the family's menu. Check out our menus and choose your favorites.

Q. How can I follow a low-carb diet plan and maintain energy for my workout?
A. When you're working out, your muscles need energy, namely in the form of glucose. During intense exercise, the body will use some fat for energy. Endurance athletes' bodies even consume a small amount of protein to keep going. It is not a good idea to work out if it's been hours since your last meal or snack. You'll find yourself flagging too fast. Again, planning ahead will make it easy. On the days you know you will be hitting the gym, plan to have something to eat an hour or so beforehand. Don't forget fluids before, during, and after exercise. Water is a great no-carb choice! If you get tired of the plain taste of water, add a squeeze of lemon or lime juice. After exercising, it's also a good idea to refuel with a snack or meal that contains some carbs.

Q. How do I eat low carb when I'm eating out?
A. More and more restaurants are offering special dishes to accommodate the low-carb customer. First ask your waiter if there are any low-carb choices on the menu, or if the chef can recommend an appropriate selection. If not, use your low-carb knowledge to guide you. Ask for salad dressings on the side and avoid the croutons. Skip the basket of bread, and choose vegetables over rice, pasta, or potato. Look for meat, poultry, or fish dishes. Drink water instead

of milk or alcoholic beverages. If you are at a fast-food restaurant, choose the low-carb option if it is available. Otherwise, banish the bun and look for items that are grilled and not breaded. Can't pass up the fries? Choose the smallest size serving. If you eat out a lot, it's a great idea to familiarize yourself with the nutrition information for your favorite spots. Most fast-food places have this information available either at the counter or on their websites.

Q. How do I entertain when I'm following a low-carb diet?
A. You have several options when deciding upon a menu for carb-consuming guests. You can serve a low-carb meal that you feel will appeal to everyone. Take a look at our holiday dishes starting on page 367 for inspiration. You can also choose to prepare a higher-carb menu and work it into your plan with smaller portions. There is also the option of providing your guests with extra foods that you don't have to eat, such as dinner rolls, pasta, or rice.

Q. If I have an existing chronic disease such as diabetes or heart disease, can I still follow a low-carb diet?
A. It is best to consult with your family physician or a registered dietitian before starting a low-carb diet. They will help you decide if low carb is appropriate for you and can help you with a diet plan personalized to accommodate any special food requirements you may have.

Q. How do I follow my low-carb diet when I'm on vacation?
A. Make choices and ask for information about the food available to you–just as you would at home when eating out or planning meals. If you are taking a road trip, have low-carb snack foods and beverages on hand in the car. If you are on a cruise or in a foreign country, stick to what you know and don't be afraid to ask questions.

Q. Is it okay to start or keep following my low-carb diet if I become pregnant or am breastfeeding?
A. No. Because your body needs extra calories, vitamins, and minerals for baby's growth and development, it is not appropriate to be restricting any particular foods. The average woman requires an extra 100–300 calories per day depending on her trimester of pregnancy. For breastfeeding, these numbers go even higher to an extra 500 calories more than prepregnancy needs. Carbohydrates should not be restricted. Consult with your family physician or a registered dietitian for assistance with your diet.

Q. Can I follow a low-carb diet if I am a vegetarian?
A. Yes, however it may be difficult considering many of the foods you would normally eat will now be restricted. Consult with a registered dietitian to help you plan a diet that meets your nutrient needs.

Q. Do I need to purchase low-carb products to follow a low-carb diet?
A. No. While they are convenient, they certainly aren't necessary. The recipes in this cookbook will provide the variety that you need to keep you motivated and on track with your weight-loss plan. No-calorie, heat-stable granular sugar substitute was used in baked products but in foods that are not heated, any non-nutritive sweetener can be used.

LOW-CARB MEAL BASICS

Use these ideas to help streamline your kitchen and your low-carb cooking.

BINDER BUDDY

For fast and easy reference use a sturdy binder and some plastic sheet protectors to get organized. Use tab sheets to divide the binder into sections that make sense to you with topics such as low-carb diet information, carb gram counter lists, glycemic index list, and favorite recipes and menu plans from the cookbook. You could also include a pantry or shopping list so that you'll know what you have and what you need on your next trip to the grocery store.

LABEL LINGO

Reading food labels is a smart way to determine how many carbohydrates a product contains. The first thing to consider when you are comparing products is the serving size. Make sure that the serving size you'll eat is equal to the amount on the Nutrition Facts label, and adjust your amount of total carbohydrates for the day if it's more or less.

The total carbs per serving will also be listed. This may be divided into grams of dietary fiber and sugar. The more fiber present, the better. Fiber causes food to be digested more slowly, thus slowing down insulin production.

ESSENTIAL EQUIPMENT

Many of our quick and easy recipes make good use of time-saving cooking techniques and appliances. If you don't already own these kitchen essentials, now is the time to treat yourself.

Blender–good for smoothing out soups, making vegetable purées

Food processor–excellent for chopping, dicing, shredding, slicing, and pureeing

Slow cooker–available in a variety of sizes

Skillets–a variety of sizes will help speed things up; nonstick makes cleanup quicker

Tabletop grill–for days when the weather isn't good for outdoor grilling

Outdoor grill–for quick, easy, and tasty meat and vegetables

MIGHTY MEALS

There are some basics to planning appetizing, nutritious, and delicious meals that will keep you satisfied and motivated.

Vary the texture. Crunchy foods offer a good contrast when served with soft foods–for example, chopped nuts in wild rice.

Vary the color. Meals that are all the same color, such as baked chicken, potatoes, and corn have little appeal. Add color to your meals and snacks with an array of low-carb vegetables.

Vary the shape. Round meatballs served with round peas or rectangular baby carrots? Choose the carrots to make the meal more interesting.

Vary the flavor. Offer foods with different flavors: sour, sweet, bitter, and salty. Each of these flavors is found naturally in food.

Vary the temperature. Nothing says everything at a meal has to be served hot or cold. A crispy salad before a sizzling steak offers appeal with different temperatures, textures, and colors.

SNACK ATTACKS

Small snacks between meals are a great way to keep your energy up and your metabolism motoring along. Use the glycemic index and your carb counter to help guide your choices. Choose snacks that have a little bit of everything in them—carbs, protein, and fat—such as low-carb whole grain crackers and some cheese.

PREPARED PANTRY

The best way to be prepared to make quick and easy low-carb meals is to have a pantry that is fully stocked with the right ingredients. Depending on which phase of the diet you are in, your pantry may vary. Here are some suggestions for foods to have on hand.

DRY GOODS

Unbleached flour

Whole wheat flour

Soy flour

Oatmeal and oat bran

Blackstrap molasses

Peanut butter

Popcorn

Sugar-free gelatin and instant pudding mix

Canned reduced-sodium beef, chicken, and vegetable broths

Canned tomato sauce and chopped tomatoes

Canned pumpkin

Tomato paste

Sundried tomatoes in oil and dry-packed

Dried mushrooms—porcini, shiitake

Wild rice

Cornmeal

Marinated artichoke hearts

Roasted red sweet peppers in the jar

Canned fish such as tuna, salmon, and sardines

Black soybeans

Nuts: almonds, walnuts, hazelnuts, pecans, sunflower and pumpkin seeds

Nut butters such as almond

Cocoa powder

Unsweetened chocolate

Sugar substitute

Flavored citrus oils

Sugar-free jams

Onions

REFRIGERATOR

Fresh fruit and vegetables— lowest GI and carb choices

Fresh lemons and limes for juicing

Eggs

Assorted cheeses

Butter

Cream

Meats such as beef, lamb, veal, and pork

Poultry—preferably skinless

Fish

Cold cuts—preferably from the deli

Tomato juice

Plain yogurt

Winter squash

FREEZER

Chopped and whole-leaf spinach

Chopped kale

Chopped collards

Snow peas

Green beans

Artichoke hearts

Asparagus spears

Chopped broccoli

Unsweetened strawberries, blueberries and/or raspberries

Rhubarb

Frozen cooked shrimp

Frozen crab meat

SPICE RACK

Vanilla and other flavor extracts

Seasonings such as black peppercorns, sea salt

Basil

Cajun spice blend

Chili powder

Chinese 5-spice powder

Cinnamon

Cumin

Curry powder

Garlic powder

Marjoram

Nutmeg

Oregano

Red pepper flakes

Rosemary

Sage

Tarragon

Thyme

When available, fresh herbs such as dill, parsley, and cilantro

CONDIMENTS

Low-sodium soy sauce

Wine vinegars such as tarragon, red and white wine

Hot pepper sauce

Worcestershire sauce

Capers

Dijon mustard

Sugar-free catsup

Sugar-free barbecue sauce

Chipotle en adobo

Chile garlic paste

Mayonnaise

QUICK COOKING METHODS

You've just come in the door from work, the kids are hungry and they've got to be at their baseball game in an hour. Fast food isn't an option. You want a healthy low-carb meal that everyone can enjoy. What can you do?

Your first line of defense is planning ahead and keeping your pantry primed so that you'll have the ingredients you need on hand. Using convenience products such as preseasoned meats can also cut down on your kitchen time. The cooking methods you use can also have a big impact on whether you're slaving by the stove or making meal time manageable.

In the previous sections we've given you our best tips on planning ahead, pantry supplies, and other timesaving pointers. Here we're taking a closer look at quick cooking methods and how they can help.

There are two basic types of meat cookery—dry and moist heat. Dry heat methods do not require any liquid, such as water, to do the job and no covers or lids are needed. These include broiling, grilling, pan-broiling, and stir-frying. Moist heat methods require some liquid and include braising, microwaving, and steaming. Covers or lids are also required to trap moisture, which helps foods cook faster and more evenly. Many of these methods may also be used for vegetables.

USING THIS BOOK

Net carbohydrates, cooking methods, serve-along suggestions, and preparation times are featured in bold type with each recipe for at-a-glance convenience. Cooking low carb couldn't be easier!

Net Grams Carbs

Ingredients/ Methods

Recipe Title

Preparation Time

Suggested Foods and/or Beverages

Cooking Method
key as follows:

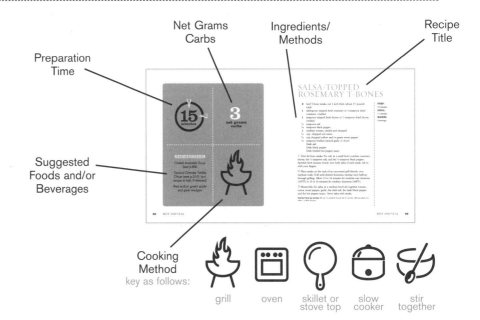

grill   oven   skillet or stove top   slow cooker   stir together

SKILLET COOKING MEAT

Select a skillet that is the correct size for the amount of meat you are cooking. (If the skillet is too large, the pan juices can burn.) Lightly coat a heavy skillet with nonstick cooking spray. (Or use a heavy nonstick skillet.) Preheat skillet over medium-high heat until very hot. Add meat. Do not add any liquid and do not cover the skillet. Reduce heat to medium and cook for the time given or until done, turning meat occasionally. If meat browns too quickly, reduce heat to medium-low.

Cut	Thickness/	Approximate Cooking Time	Doneness
Beef			
Boneless chuck eye steak	¾ inch	9 to 11 minutes	145°F med. rare to 160°F medium
	1 inch	12 to 15 minutes	145°F med. rare to 160°F medium
Boneless top sirloin steak	¾ inch	10 to 13 minutes	145°F med. rare to 160°F medium
	1 inch	15 to 20 minutes	145°F med. rare to 160°F medium
Boneless tri-tip steak (bottom sirloin)	¾ inch	6 to 9 minutes	145°F med. rare to 160°F medium
	1 inch	9 to 12 minutes	145°F med. rare to 160°F medium
Cubed steak	½ inch	5 to 8 minutes	160°F medium
Porterhouse or T-bone steak	¾ inch	11 to 13 minutes	145°F med. rare to 160°F medium
	1 inch	14 to 17 minutes	145°F med. rare to 160°F medium
Ribeye steak	¾ inch	8 to 10 minutes	145°F med. rare to 160°F medium
	1 inch	12 to 15 minutes	145°F med. rare to 160°F medium
Tenderloin steak	¾ inch	7 to 9 minutes	145°F med. rare to 160°F medium
	1 inch	10 to 13 minutes	145°F med. rare to 160°F medium
Top loin steak	¾ inch	10 to 12 minutes	145°F med. rare to 160°F medium
	1 inch	12 to 15 minutes	145°F med. rare to 160°F medium
Ground Meat			
Patties (beef, lamb, pork, or veal)	½ inch	9 to 12 minutes	160°F medium
	¾ inch	12 to 15 minutes	160°F medium
Lamb			
Chop (loin or rib)	1 inch	9 to 11 minutes	160°F medium
Pork			
Canadian-style bacon	¼ inch	3 to 4 minutes	Heated through
Chop (loin or rib) (with bone or boneless)	¾ to 1 inch	8 to 12 minutes	160°F medium
Cutlet	¼ inch	3 to 4 minutes	160°F medium
Ham slice, cooked	1 inch	14 to 16 minutes	140°F heated through
Tenderloin medallions	¼ to ½ inch	4 to 8 minutes	160°F medium
Veal			
Chop (loin or rib)	¾ to 1 inch	10 to 14 minutes	160°F medium
Cutlet	⅛ inch	2 to 4 minutes	160°F medium
	¼ inch	4 to 6 minutes	160°F medium

All cooking times are based on meat removed directly from refrigerator.

BROILING MEAT

Preheat broiler. Place meat on the unheated rack of a broiler pan. For cuts less than 1½ inches thick, broil 3 to 4 inches from the heat. For 1½-inch-thick cuts, broil 4 to 5 inches from the heat. Broil for the time given or until done, turning meat over after half of the broiling time.

Cut	Thickness/ Weight	Approximate Cooking Time	Doneness
Beef			
Boneless steak (ribeye, tenderloin, top loin)	1 inch	12 to 14 minutes	145°F medium rare
		15 to 18 minutes	160°F medium
	1½ inches	18 to 21 minutes	145°F medium rare
		22 to 27 minutes	160°F medium
Boneless top sirloin steak	1 inch	15 to 17 minutes	145°F medium rare
		20 to 22 minutes	160°F medium
	1½ inches	25 to 27 minutes	145°F medium rare
		30 to 32 minutes	160°F medium
Boneless tri-tip steak (bottom sirloin)	¾ inch	6 to 7 minutes	145°F medium rare
		8 to 9 minutes	160°F medium
	1 inch	9 to 10 minutes	145°F medium rare
		11 to 12 minutes	160°F medium
Flank steak	1¼ to 1¾ pounds	15 to 18 minutes	160°F medium
Steak with bone (porterhouse, rib, T-bone)	1 inch	12 to 15 minutes	145°F medium rare
		15 to 20 minutes	160°F medium
	1½ inches	20 to 25 minutes	145°F medium rare
		25 to 30 minutes	160°F medium
Ground Meat			
Patties (beef, lamb, pork, or veal)	½ inch	10 to 12 minutes	160°F medium
	¾ inch	12 to 14 minutes	160°F medium
Lamb			
Chop (loin or rib)	1 inch	10 to 15 minutes	160°F medium
Chop (sirloin)	1 inch	12 to 15 minutes	160°F medium
Pork			
Chop with bone (loin or rib)	¾ to 1 inch	9 to 12 minutes	160°F medium
	1¼ to 1½ inches	16 to 20 minutes	160°F medium
Chop with bone (sirloin)	3/4 to 1 inch	10 to 13 minutes	160°F medium
Chop (boneless top loin)	¾ to 1 inch	9 to 11 minutes	160°F medium
	1¼ to 1½ inches	15 to 18 minutes	160°F medium
Ham slice, cooked	1 inch	12 to 15 minutes	140°F heated through
Sausages			
Frankfurters and sausage links, cooked		3 to 7 minutes	140°F heated through
Veal			
Chop (loin or rib)	¾ to 1 inch	14 to 16 minutes	160°F medium
	1½ inches	21 to 25 minutes	160°F medium

All cooking times are based on meat removed directly from refrigerator.

DIRECT-GRILLING MEAT

For a charcoal grill, place meat on grill rack directly over medium coals. Grill, uncovered, for the time given below or to desired doneness, turning once halfway through grilling. For a gas grill, preheat grill. Reduce heat to medium. Place meat on grill rack over heat. Cover the grill. Test for doneness using a meat thermometer.

Cut	Thickness/ Weight	Grilling Temperature	Approximate Direct-Grilling Time	Doneness
Beef				
Boneless steak (ribeye, tenderloin, top loin)	1 inch	Medium	11 to 15 minutes	145°F medium rare
			14 to 18 minutes	160°F medium
	1½ inches	Medium	15 to 19 minutes	145°F medium rare
			18 to 23 minutes	160°F medium
Boneless top sirloin steak	1 inch	Medium	14 to 18 minutes	145°F medium rare
			18 to 22 minutes	160°F medium
	1½ inches	Medium	20 to 24 minutes	145°F medium rare
			24 to 28 minutes	160°F medium
Boneless tri-tip steak (bottom sirloin)	¾ inch	Medium	9 to 11 minutes	145°F medium rare
			11 to 13 minutes	160°F medium
	1 inch	Medium	13 to 15 minutes	145°F medium rare
			15 to 17 minutes	160°F medium
Flank steak	1¼ to 1¾ pounds	Medium	17 to 21 minutes	160°F medium
Steak with bone (porterhouse, rib, T-bone)	1 inch	Medium	11 to 14 minutes	145°F medium rare
			13 to 16 minutes	160°F medium
	1½ inches	Medium	18 to 21 minutes	145°F medium rare
			22 to 25 minutes	160°F medium
Ground Meat				
Patties (beef, lamb, pork, or veal)	½ inch	Medium	10 to 13 minutes	160°F medium
	¾ inch	Medium	14 to 18 minutes	160°F medium
Lamb				
Chop (loin or rib)	1 inch	Medium	12 to 14 minutes	145°F medium rare
			15 to 17 minutes	160°F medium
Chop (sirloin)	¾ to 1 inch	Medium	14 to 17 minutes	160°F medium
Pork				
Chop with bone (loin or rib)	¾ to 1 inch	Medium	11 to 14 minutes	160°F medium
	1¼ to 1½ inches	Medium	18 to 22 minutes	160°F medium
Chop (boneless top loin)	¾ to 1 inch	Medium	12 to 15 minutes	160°F medium
	1¼ to 1½ inches	Medium	17 to 21 minutes	160°F medium
Sausages, cooked (frankfurters, smoked bratwurst, etc.)		Medium	3 to 7 minutes	Heated through
Veal				
Chop (loin or rib)	1 inch	Medium	12 to 15 minutes	160°F medium

All cooking times are based on meat removed directly from refrigerator.

BROILING POULTRY

If desired, remove the skin from the poultry; sprinkle with salt and black pepper. Remove broiler pan from the oven and preheat the broiler for 5 to 10 minutes. Arrange the poultry on the unheated rack of the broiler pan with the bone side up. If desired, brush poultry with cooking oil. Place the pan under the broiler so the surface of the poultry is 4 to 5 inches from the heat; chicken and Cornish game hen halves should be 5 to 6 inches from the heat. Turn the pieces over when browned on one side, usually after half of the broiling time. Chicken halves and quarters and meaty pieces should be turned after 20 minutes. Brush again with oil. The poultry is done when the meat is no longer pink and the juices run clear. If desired, brush with a sauce the last 5 minutes of cooking.

Type of Bird	Thickness/Weight	Broiling Time
Chicken		
Broiler-fryer, half	1¼ to 1½ pounds each	28 to 32 minutes
Broiler-fryer, quarter	10 to 12 ounces	28 to 32 minutes
Kabobs (boneless breast, cut into 2 1/2-inch strips and threaded loosely onto skewers)		8 to 10 minutes
Meaty pieces (breast halves, drumsticks, and thighs with bone)	2½ to 3 pounds total	25 to 35 minutes
Skinless, boneless breast halves	4 to 5 ounces	12 to 15 minutes
Game		
Cornish game hen, half	10 to 12 ounces	25 to 35 minutes
Turkey		
Breast steak or slice	2 ounces	6 to 8 minutes
Breast tenderloin steak	4 to 6 ounces	8 to 10 minutes
Patties (ground raw turkey)	¾ inch thick ½ inch thick	14 to 18 minutes 11 to 13 minutes

MICROWAVING POULTRY

Arrange bone-in pieces in a microwave-safe baking dish with meaty portions toward edges of dish, tucking under thin boneless portions. Do not crowd the pieces in the dish. Cover with waxed paper. (Or for skinless poultry, cover with a lid or vented plastic wrap.) Microwave on 100% power (high) for the time given or until no longer pink, rearranging and turning pieces over after half of the cooking time.

Type of Bird	Amount	Power Level	Cooking Time
Chicken			
Breast halves	Two 6-ounce	100% (high)	6 to 9 minutes
	Two 8-ounce	100% (high)	8 to 11 minutes
Drumsticks	2 drumsticks	100% (high)	3½ to 5 minutes
	6 drumsticks	100% (high)	6 to 10 minutes
Meaty pieces (breast halves, drumsticks, and thighs with bone)	2½ to 3 pounds	100% (high)	9 to 17 minutes
Skinless, boneless breast halves	Two 4- to 5-ounce	100% (high)	4 to 7 minutes
	Four 4- to 5-ounce	100% (high)	5 to 8 minutes
Game			
Cornish game hen, halved	1¼ to 1½ pounds	100% (high)	7 to 10 minutes
Turkey			
Breast tenderloin steaks	Four 4-ounce	100% (high)	5 to 8 minutes
Breast tenderloins	Two 8- to 10-ounce	100% (high)	8 to 12 minutes

COOKING FISH

Minutes count when cooking fish. Weigh dressed fish or use a ruler to measure the thickness of fillets and steaks in order to better estimate when to check for doneness. Properly cooked fish is opaque, flakes easily when tested with a fork, and comes away from the bones readily; the juices should be milky white.

Cooking Method	Preparation	Fresh or Thawed Fillets or Steaks	Dressed
Bake	Place in a single layer in a greased shallow baking pan. For fillets, tuck under any thin edges. Brush with melted butter or margarine.	Bake, uncovered, in a 450°F oven for 4 to 6 minutes per ½-inch thickness.	Bake, uncovered, in a 350°F oven for 6 to 9 minutes per 8 ounces.
Broil	Preheat broiler. Place fish on greased unheated rack of a broiler pan. For fillets, tuck under any thin edges. Brush with melted butter or margarine.	Broil 4 inches from the heat for 4 to 6 minutes per ½-inch thickness. If fish is 1 inch or more thick, turn once halfway through broiling.	Not recommended.
Microwave	Arrange fish in a single layer in a shallow baking dish. For fillets, tuck under any thin edges. Cover with vented plastic wrap.	Cook on 100 percent power (high). For ½ pound of ½-inch-thick fillets, allow 1½ to 2 minutes; for 1 pound of ½-inch-thick fillets, allow 2½ to 4 minutes. For 1 pound of ¾- to 1-inch-thick steaks, allow 3 to 5 minutes.	Not recommended.
Poach	Add 1½ cups water, broth, or wine to a large skillet. Bring to boiling. Add fish. Return to boiling; reduce heat.	Simmer, uncovered, for 4 to 6 minutes per ½-inch thickness.	Simmer, covered, for 6 to 9 minutes per 8 ounces.

COOKING SHELLFISH

Refer to these directions for cooking fresh shellfish. Many types of shellfish are available partially prepared or even cooked. Ask at the fish and shellfish counter for additional information when making purchases.

Shellfish Type	Amount Per Serving	Preparing	Cooking
Clams	6 clams in the shell	Scrub live clams under cold running water. For 24 clams in shells, in an 8-quart kettle combine 4 quarts of cold water and ⅓ cup salt. Add clams and soak for 1 hour; drain and rinse. Discard water.	For 24 clams in shells, add ½ inch water to an 8-quart kettle; bring to boiling. Place clams in a steamer basket. Steam, covered, 5 to 7 minutes or until clams open. Discard any that do not open.
Crabs, hard-shell	1 pound live crabs	Grasp live crabs from behind, firmly holding the back two legs on each side. Rinse under cold running water.	To boil 3 pounds live hard-shell blue crabs, in a 12- to 16-quart kettle bring 8 quarts water and 2 teaspoons salt to boiling. Add crabs. Simmer, covered, for 10 minutes or until crabs turn pink; drain.
Crawfish	1 pound live crawfish	Rinse live crawfish under cold running water. For 4 pounds crawfish, in a 12- to 16-quart kettle combine 8 quarts cold water and ⅓ cup salt. Add crawfish. Soak for 15 minutes; rinse and drain.	For 4 pounds live crawfish, in a 12- to 16-quart kettle bring 8 quarts water and 2 teaspoons salt to boiling. Add crawfish. Simmer, covered, 5 to 8 minutes or until shells turn red; drain.
Lobster tails	One 8-ounce frozen lobster tail	Thaw frozen lobster tails in the refrigerator.	For four 8-ounce lobster tails, in a 3-quart saucepan bring 6 cups water and 1½ teaspoons salt to boiling. Add tails; simmer, uncovered, for 8 to 12 minutes or until shells turn bright red and meat is tender; drain.
Mussels	12 mussels in shells	Scrub live mussels under cold running water. Using your fingers, pull out the beards that are visible between the shells. Soak as for clams, above.	For 24 mussels, add ½ inch water to an 8-quart kettle; bring to boiling. Place mussels in a steamer basket. Steam, covered, for 5 to 7 minutes or until shells open. Discard any that do not open.
Oysters	6 oysters in shells	Scrub live oysters under cold running water. For easier shucking, bottom shells, if desired	See Oysters Broiled in Blue Cheese Butter, page 384.
Shrimp	6 ounces shrimp in shells or 3 to 4 ounces peeled, deveined shrimp	To peel shrimp, open the shell down the underside. Starting at the head end, pull back the shell. Gently pull on the tail to remove. Use a sharp knife to remove the black vein that runs along the center of the back. Rinse under cold running water .	For 1 pound shrimp, in a 3-quart saucepan bring 4 cups water and 1 teaspoon salt to boiling. Add shrimp. Simmer, uncovered, for 1 to 3 minutes or until shrimp turn opaque, stirring occasionally. Rinse under cold running water; drain and chill, if desired.

LUNCH MENUS

Each menu is 20 grams of carbs or fewer. Some of the dishes must be made ahead and reheated in the microwave at work or school. If no beverage is suggested, choose water and get your 8 to 12 glasses a day.

MENU 1: CHILLY DAY MENU

This hearty chowder is especially warming on cold days. If you don't have access to a microwave, invest in a top-quality thermos to keep the soup hot.

1 serving North Sea Chowder (page 63)	5
1 low-carb dinner roll	4
1 tablespoon butter	0
½ cup tomato juice	4.5
½ cup blueberries	4
TOTAL NET CARBS	**17.5**

MENU 2: FRESH AND FILLING MENU

Assemble the salad at home and take the dressing in a separate container. Toss when ready to eat.

1 serving Salmon Caesar Salad (page 79)	8
1 Toasted Cheese Tortilla Chips (page 311)	4
¼ cup honeydew melon	3.75
TOTAL NET CARBS	**15.75**

MENU 3: APPETIZER MENU

This menu is similar to Italian antipasto or appetizers that are often served before a meal.

6 ounces beef salami	4.8
3 marinated artichoke hearts	3
3 ounces whole milk mozzarella cheese	2
2 servings Lemony Herbed Olives (page 303)	2
½ cup cantaloupe	6
TOTAL NET CARBS	**17.8**

MENU 4: EAT-AT-YOUR-DESK MENU

This is an easy menu to pack and eat. There's no reheating required, but remember to keep the eggs in a cooler bag or in the fridge until you're ready to nosh.

2 servings Deviled Eggs with Spicy Crab (page 54)	2
2 slices low-carb rye bread	6
2 teaspoons butter	0
2 stalks celery, cut into 6 pieces	1.5
2 servings Fennel & Onion Dip (page 27)	2
TOTAL NET CARBS	**11.5**

MENU 5: FAR EAST MENU

Spice is the theme of this menu that will wake up your tastebuds.

2 servings Thai Lime Custard Soup (page 67)	8
½ cup Asian-Spiced Pecans (page 53)	2
¼ cup fresh pineapple, cubed	8.5
TOTAL NET CARBS	**18.5**

MENU 6: LEFTOVER LUNCH MENU

Make more than you need of this salad for dinner and use leftovers for lunch the next day. The salad won't be quite as fresh and crisp, but it will still be delicious.

1 serving Cabbage and Chicken with Sesame Dressing (page 75)	6
½ low-carb onion bagel	8
1 teaspoon butter	0
½ cup strawberries	4
TOTAL NET CARBS	**18**

MENU 7: LIGHT LUNCH MENU

Little bits and bites add up to a delicious lunch.

1 serving Lemon-Marinated Veggies (page 277)	6
1 low-carb sandwich roll	6
2 teaspoons butter	0
3 ounces Gouda cheese	2
1 apricot	3
TOTAL NET CARBS	**15.0**

WEEKNIGHT MENUS

This is where the quick and easy part comes in handy! These menus make use of a variety of quick cooking methods including grilling, broiling, and sautéing. All are 23 grams of carbs or fewer.

MENU 1: SUPER SALAD MENU

Chicken is dressed up with the sweet tang of raspberries. The Raspberry and Chocolate Tulips for dessert are a delectable treat. (Serves 4)

1 serving Grilled Chicken and Raspberry Salad (page 73)	6
1 low-carb dinner roll	4
2 teaspoons butter	0
1 tangerine	7
1 serving Raspberry and Chocolate Tulips (page 343)	3
TOTAL NET CARBS	**20**

MENU 2: COOL SUPPER FOR HOT DAYS

Both the soup and the eggs can be made ahead of time. This menu would be great after a hot and busy summer day. (Serves 2 with leftovers)

2 servings Chilled Avocado Soup (page 69)	8
2 servings Deviled Eggs with Spicy Crab (page 54)	2
2 servings Toasted Cheese Tortilla Chips (page 311)	4
½ cup fresh raspberries	3
2 tablespoons whipped cream	1
TOTAL NET CARBS	**18**

MENU 3: HEART-HEALTHY SUPPER

Salmon serves up a good dose of heart-healthy omega-3 fatty acids. (Serves 4)

1 serving Basil-Buttered Salmon Steaks (page 245)	0
1 serving Broiled Asparagus and Fresh Mozzarella (page 283)	1
½ cup wild rice	16
1 Orange-Cantaloupe Pop (page 341)	4
TOTAL NET CARBS	**21**

MENU 4: FAST AND FABULOUS FOR FRIENDS

Having friends for dinner on Friday? To make it easy, the steak and vegetables can be made on the grill. You can prepare the dessert ahead of time.

1 serving Herbed Tenderloin Steak and Vegetables (page 99)	4
2 servings Mesclun with Olives and Oranges (page 84)	14
1 serving Coffee and Cream Dessert (page 399)	3
TOTAL NET CARBS	**21**

MENU 5: SIMPLE SLOW-COOKER MEAL.

Let your slow cooker do most of the work when you're busy. The vegetables are ready in less than 10 minutes and the kiwi makes a quick and healthy dessert. (Serves 6)

1 serving Pot Roast with Dill (page 115)	3
½ cup tomato juice	4.5
1 serving Teeny Zucchini with Onions (page 285)	5
1 kiwi fruit	8
TOTAL NET CARBS	**20.5**

MENU 6: WEEKNIGHT MENU FOR 4

Turkey isn't just for the holidays; it makes a delicious meal anytime. (Serves 4)

1 serving Apple-Glazed Turkey (page 197)	8
½ cup broccoli, steamed	2
1 serving Saucy Skillet Mushrooms (page 255)	4
1 serving Berries with Almond Cream with Berries (page 351)	5
TOTAL NET CARBS	**19**

MENU 7: CELEBRATION MENU

This elegant menu is perfect for a special meal or celebration. (Serves 4)

1 serving Lemon Berry Fizz (page 327)	2
2 servings Warm Feta Cheese Dip (page 37)	8
1 serving (1 tail) Grilled Lobster with Rosemary Butter (page 247)	1
1 serving Lemon-Tarragon Vegetables (page 271)	6
1 serving Chocolate Mousse (page 397)	6
TOTAL NET CARBS	**23**

MENU 8: LIGHT AND LEMONY MENU

Make the veggies ahead of time and this simple dinner will be ready in a flash. (Serves 4)

1 serving Citrus Baked Halibut (page 217)	4
1 serving Lemon-Marinated Veggies (page 277)	6
¼ cup wild rice	8
1 serving Orange-Ginger Rhubarb (page 353)	5
TOTAL NET CARBS	**23**

MENU 9: PORK DINNER FOR 4

Pork is a great change from the usual chicken or beef. (Serves 4)

1 serving Country Chops and Peppers (page 153)	5
1 serving Garlicky Mushrooms (page 273)	4
2 slices low-carb rye bread	6
1 teaspoon butter	0
¼ cup grapes	6.7
TOTAL NET CARBS	**21.7**

MENU 10: VEGETARIAN MENU

Cheese and nuts replace the meat in this flavorful Asian-inspired meal. (Serves 4)

2 servings Thai Lime Custard Soup (page 67)	8
1 serving Broccoli and Peppers (page 275)	4
1 tangerine	6
1 serving Savory Nuts (page 52)	2
TOTAL NET CARBS	**20**

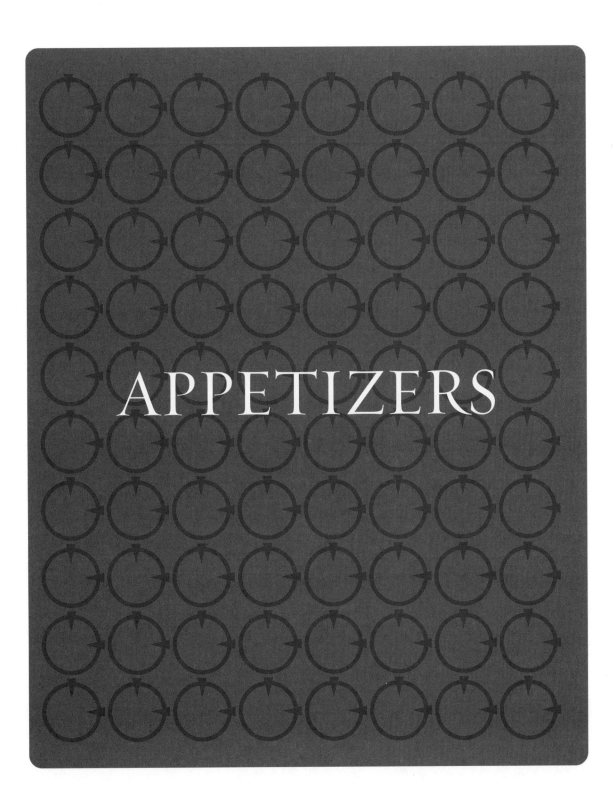

APPETIZERS

15 minutes

1 net gram carbs

SERVE-ALONG SUGGESTIONS

Nut-Crusted Turkey Breast (see p.377)

Steamed broccoli

Fruit-Topped Phyllo Cups (see p.345)

DEVILED HAM AND CHEESE BALL

2   4¼-ounce cans deviled ham
2   cups shredded cheddar cheese (8 ounces)
1   8-ounce package cream cheese, softened
½   cup finely chopped green sweet pepper
1   teaspoon ranch dry salad dressing mix
¾   cup unsalted, dry-roasted shelled sunflower seeds
     Assorted low-carb crackers (optional)

1. In a medium bowl combine deviled ham, cheddar cheese, cream cheese, sweet pepper, and salad dressing mix. Divide in half. Cover and chill for 1 to 1½ hours or until firm enough to handle.

2. Shape each portion into a ball. Roll balls in sunflower seeds to coat. Cover and chill for at least 1 hour before serving. Serve with crackers.

Nutrition Facts per serving: 129 cal., 11 g total fat (5 g sat. fat), 26 mg chol., 231 mg sodium, 2 g carbo., 1 g fiber, 5 g pro.

PREP:
15 minutes
CHILL:
2 hours
MAKES:
24 appetizer servings

15 minutes

0 net grams carbs

SERVE-ALONG SUGGESTIONS

Mixed greens tossed with bottled low-carb ranch or Caesar salad dressing and topped with toasted sunflower seeds

Coriander-Studded Tenderloin Steak (see p.103)

Spicy Baked Oranges (see p.355)

ROASTED PEPPER-CHEESE MOLD

2 3-ounce packages cream cheese, softened
3 tablespoons dairy sour cream
2 tablespoons snipped fresh cilantro
4 teaspoons finely chopped onion
¼ teaspoon bottled minced garlic (1 small clove)
   Dash cayenne pepper
   Dash ground cumin
2 tablespoons chopped bottled roasted red sweet peppers
   Assorted low-carb crackers (optional)

PREP:
15 minutes
CHILL:
4 to 24 hours
MAKES:
12 appetizer servings

1. In a small mixing bowl beat cream cheese and sour cream with an electric mixer on low to medium speed until smooth. Stir in cilantro, onion, garlic, cayenne pepper, and cumin.

2. Line a small bowl or 6- to 10-ounce custard cup or mold with plastic wrap. Spoon half of the cheese mixture into prepared bowl. Sprinkle with roasted red pepper. Spoon the remaining cheese mixture on top of roasted pepper. Cover and chill for at least 4 hours or up to 24 hours.

3. To serve, unmold cheese mixture onto a serving platter. Serve with crackers.

Nutrition Facts per serving: 50 cal., 5 g total fat (3 g sat. fat), 15 mg chol., 39 mg sodium, 0 g carbo., 0 g fiber, 1 g pro.

15 minutes

2
net grams carbs

SERVE-ALONG SUGGESTIONS

Pineapple-Glazed Pork
(see p.145)

Steamed green beans
tossed with crisp-cooked
bacon and cracked
black pepper

Coffee and Cream Dessert
(see p.399)

FENNEL AND ONION DIP

1 medium fennel bulb
1 16-ounce container dairy sour cream French onion dip
2 tablespoons finely chopped red onion
2 tablespoons thinly sliced green onion
   Vegetable dippers (optional)

1. Trim off feathery leaves from fennel. Chop enough of the leaves to make 2 tablespoons; set aside. Trim fennel bulb. Chop enough of the bulb to make 1 cup. If desired, cut remaining bulb into strips to use for dippers.

2. In a medium bowl combine the 1 cup chopped fennel, French onion dip, red onion, and green onion.

3. To serve, spoon the dip into a serving bowl. Sprinkle with the reserved 2 tablespoons fennel leaves. Serve with vegetable dippers.

Make-Ahead Tip: Prepare as directed through step 2. Cover and chill for up to 24 hours. If using fennel leaves, wrap in plastic wrap and chill separately.

Nutrition Facts per serving: 31 cal., 2 g total fat (1 g sat. fat), 0 mg chol., 105 mg sodium, 3 g carbo., 1 g fiber, 1 g pro.

START TO FINISH:
15 minutes
MAKES:
about 2¼ cups dip
(36 appetizer servings)

15 minutes

1 net gram carbs

SERVE-ALONG SUGGESTIONS

Fresh spinach leaves, sliced mushrooms and mandarin oranges tossed with low-carb bottled vinaigrette salad dressing

Papaya-Glazed Chicken (see p.163)

Vanilla whole milk yogurt topped with toasted wheat germ and macadamia nuts

SPEEDY CRAB DIP

1 10¾-ounce can condensed cream of mushroom soup
1 8-ounce package cream cheese, softened
1 cup mayonnaise or salad dressing
½ teaspoon lemon juice
    Several dashes bottled hot pepper sauce
1 6- or 8-ounce package flake- or chunk-style imitation crabmeat, finely chopped, or one 6-ounce can crabmeat, drained, flaked, and cartilage removed
1 cup finely chopped celery
½ cup finely chopped green onions
    Assorted low-carb crackers and/or vegetable dippers (optional)

1. In a medium mixing bowl combine cream of mushroom soup and cream cheese. Beat with an electric mixer on low speed until combined. Stir in mayonnaise, lemon juice, and hot pepper sauce. Fold in crabmeat, celery, and green onions.

2. Spoon the dip into a serving bowl. Cover and chill for at least 1 hour or up to 24 hours. If desired, serve with crackers and/or vegetable dippers.

Nutrition Facts per serving: 36 cal., 4 g total fat (1 g sat. fat), 5 mg chol., 69 mg sodium, 1 g carbo., 0 g fiber, 1 g pro.

PREP:
15 minutes
CHILL:
1 to 24 hours
MAKES:
about 5 cups dip
(80 appetizer servings)

15 minutes

3

net grams
carbs

SERVE-ALONG SUGGESTIONS

Chilled Avocado Soup
(see p.69)

Mixed greens with sliced
radishes, cucumber, and
green onion tossed with
bottled vinaigrette
salad dressing

Lemon Berry Fizz
(see p.327)

HOT RIBEYE BITES

¼   cup jalapeño pepper jelly
2   tablespoons steak seasoning
2   beef ribeye steaks or 1 boneless beef top sirloin steak, cut
     1-inch thick (about 1¼ pounds total)
24   pickled baby banana chile peppers or jalapeño chile peppers

PREP:
15 minutes
BROIL:
12 minutes
MAKES:
about 24 appetizers

1. Preheat broiler. For glaze, in a small saucepan stir together pepper jelly and steak seasoning. Cook and stir over low heat for 1 to 2 minutes or until jelly is melted. Set aside.

2. Trim fat from steaks. Place steaks on the unheated rack of a broiler pan. Broil 3 to 4 inches from the heat until desired doneness, turning once halfway through broiling and brushing occasionally with glaze the last 5 minutes of broiling. For ribeye steaks, allow 12 to 14 minutes for medium-rare doneness (145°F) or 15 to 18 minutes for medium doneness (160°F). For sirloin steak, allow 15 to 17 minutes for medium-rare doneness (145°F) or 20 to 22 minutes for medium doneness (160°F).

3. Cut steak into 1-inch cubes. Top each cube with a pickled chile pepper.

> **Grill Method:** Place steaks on the rack of an uncovered grill directly over medium coals. Grill until desired doneness, turning once halfway through grilling and brushing occasionally with glaze the last 5 minutes of grilling. For ribeye steaks, allow 11 to 15 minutes for medium-rare doneness (145°F) or 14 to 18 minutes for medium doneness (160°F). For sirloin steak, allow 14 to 18 minutes for medium-rare doneness (145°F) or 18 to 22 minutes for medium doneness (160°F).

Nutrition Facts per appetizer: 47 cal., 1 g total fat (1 g sat. fat), 11 mg chol., 179 mg sodium, 3 g carbo., 0 g fiber, 5 g pro.

15 minutes

4 net grams carbs

SERVE-ALONG SUGGESTIONS

Beef Steaks with Tomato-Garlic Butter (see p.101)

Sautéed sliced mushrooms and sweet onion

Napa Cabbage Slaw (see p.289)

CHILI CHICKEN APPETEASERS

4 medium nectarines or peaches
½ cup shredded cooked chicken (about 3 ounces)
2 teaspoons snipped fresh cilantro
2 teaspoons bottled Thai garlic-chili sauce or chili sauce

1. Cut nectarines into quarters; remove pits. Carefully scoop out some of the fruit, leaving ¼-inch shells. Chop the scooped-out fruit.

2. In a medium bowl combine chopped nectarines, chicken, cilantro, and chili sauce. Spoon about 1 rounded teaspoon of the chicken mixture into each nectarine shell.

Nutrition Facts per appetizer: 26 cal., 1 g total fat (0 g sat. fat), 4 mg chol., 12 mg sodium, 4 g carbo., 0 g fiber, 2 g pro.

START TO FINISH:
15 minutes
MAKES:
16 appetizers

15 minutes

4 net grams carbs

SERVE-ALONG SUGGESTIONS

Sirloin with Mustard and Chives (see p.95)

Really Hot Iced Coffee (see p.329)

Steamed or grilled asparagus

PORTOBELLO PIZZAS

4 5- to 6-ounce fresh portobello mushrooms
5 teaspoons olive oil
1 4½-ounce round Brie cheese, thinly sliced
¼ cup small arugula leaves
4 thin tomato slices

1. Cut off mushroom stems even with caps; discard stems. Lightly rinse mushroom caps; gently pat dry with paper towels. Brush mushrooms with 2 teaspoons of the oil. Sprinkle with salt and black pepper.

2. Place mushrooms, stemmed sides up, on a foil-lined baking sheet. Bake in a 400° oven for 8 to 10 minutes or until mushrooms are tender, turning once. Remove from oven.

3. Turn mushroom caps, stemmed sides up; top with Brie cheese and arugula leaves. Drizzle with the remaining 3 teaspoons oil; top with tomato slices.

Nutrition Facts per appetizer: 181 cal., 16 g total fat (6 g sat. fat), 28 mg chol., 257 mg sodium, 5 g carbo., 1 g fiber, 10 g pro.

PREP:
15 minutes
BAKE:
8 minutes
OVEN:
400°F
MAKES:
4 appetizers

20 minutes

4
net grams
carbs

SERVE-ALONG SUGGESTIONS

Turkey Tenderloins with Cilantro Pesto (see p.201)

Lemon-Marinated Veggies (see p.277)

Sliced fresh nectarines and/or peaches

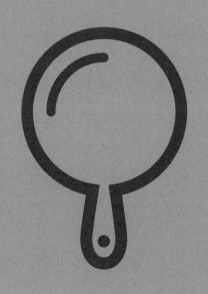

WARM FETA CHEESE DIP

2	teaspoons olive oil or cooking oil
1	small onion, finely chopped (⅓ cup)
1½	teaspoons bottled minced garlic (3 cloves)
1	8-ounce package cream cheese, cut up
1	cup crumbled feta cheese (4 ounces)
½	cup chopped pitted kalamata olives or ripe olives
¼	cup chopped bottled roasted red sweet peppers
1	teaspoon dried dill
1	recipe homemade or purchased low-carb tortilla chips (see recipe, below) (optional)

START TO FINISH:
20 minutes
MAKES:
8 appetizer servings

1. In a medium skillet heat olive oil over medium heat. Add onion and garlic; cook for 4 to 5 minutes or until onion is tender. Reduce heat to low. Add cream cheese and feta cheese; stir until mixture is nearly smooth. Stir in olives, roasted peppers, and dill. Serve warm with low-carbohydrate tortilla chips, if desired.

Homemade low-carb tortilla chips: Preheat broiler. Cut four 7- to 8-inch low-carbohydrate multigrain or whole wheat flour tortillas into 8 wedges each. Place tortilla wedges in a single layer on a large baking sheet. Broil 3 to 4 inches from the heat for 1 to 2 minutes or until tortillas are lightly toasted.

Nutrition Facts per 1/4 cup dip: 51 cal., 4 g total fat (2 g sat. fat), 10 mg chol., 101 mg sodium, 4 g carbo., 0 g fiber, 1 g pro.

15
minutes

1
net gram
carbs

SERVE-ALONG SUGGESTIONS

Baby greens tossed with bottled low-carb balsamic vinaigrette salad dressing and toasted pine nuts

Salmon Fillets Bathed in Garlic (see p.239)

Tiramisu Cream (see p.359)

ENDIVE LEAVES WITH ARTICHOKE CAVIAR

1   6-ounce jar marinated artichoke hearts
½   cup finely chopped zucchini
1   medium tomato, peeled, seeded, and finely chopped
1   green onion, chopped
2   tablespoons snipped fresh basil or 1 teaspoon dried basil, crushed
1   teaspoon bottled minced garlic (2 cloves)
1   teaspoon lemon juice
3   heads Belgian endive

PREP:
15 minutes
MARINATE:
2 to 6 hours
MAKES:
about 36 appetizers

1. Drain artichokes, reserving marinade (about ⅓ cup). Set aside. Finely chop artichokes.

2. In a medium bowl combine artichokes, zucchini, tomato, and green onion. In a small bowl whisk together the reserved artichoke marinade, basil, garlic, and lemon juice. Pour over artichoke mixture; toss gently to combine. Cover and marinate in the refrigerator for 2 to 6 hours, stirring occasionally.

3. To serve, remove core from Belgian endive. Separate endive into leaves. Drain artichoke mixture. Spoon about 2 teaspoons of the artichoke mixture onto each endive leaf.

Nutrition Facts per appetizer: 6 cal., 0 g total fat (0 g sat. fat), 0 mg chol., 15 mg sodium, 1 g carbo., 0 g fiber, 0 g pro.

15 minutes

5 net grams carbs

SERVE-ALONG SUGGESTIONS

Herbed Tenderloin Steaks and Vegetables (see p.99)

Sliced fresh strawberries and chopped fresh pineapple

Decaf iced tea served with lemon and/or lime wedges

CHEESY SPINACH QUESADILLAS

1½   cups coarsely chopped spinach leaves
3   tablespoons purchased basil pesto
2   teaspoons snipped oil-packed dried tomatoes
1½   cups shredded Colby Jack or cheddar cheese (6 ounces)
⅓   cup finely chopped pine nuts or pecans, toasted
6   8-inch low-carb whole wheat flour tortillas

1. In a medium bowl stir together spinach, pesto, and dried tomatoes. Stir in 1 cup of the cheese and half of the nuts.

2. Spread cheese mixture evenly over 3 of the tortillas; top with remaining tortillas. Transfer to a very large baking sheet. Sprinkle with the remaining ½ cup cheese and the remaining nuts.

3. Bake in a 450° oven for 5 to 6 minutes or until tortillas are lightly browned and crisp. Cut each quesadilla into 8 wedges.

Nutrition Facts per appetizer: 78 cal., 5 g total fat (2 g sat. fat), 8 mg chol., 109 mg sodium, 5 g carbo., 0 g fiber, 3 g pro.

PREP:
15 minutes
BAKE:
5 minutes
OVEN:
450°F
MAKES:
24 appetizers

15 minutes

1
net gram
carbs

SERVE-ALONG SUGGESTIONS

Chopped romaine lettuce served with sweet pepper strips, shredded cheese, and bottled low-carb ranch salad dressing

Pepper-Marinated Flank Steak (see p.119)

Strawberry-Citrus Slush (see p.365)

CLASSIC BUFFALO WINGS

12 chicken wings (about 2 pounds total)
2   to 3 tablespoons bottled hot pepper sauce
2   tablespoons margarine or butter, melted
1   teaspoon paprika
½   cup dairy sour cream
½   cup mayonnaise or salad dressing
½   cup crumbled blue cheese (2 ounces)
1   tablespoon white wine vinegar or white vinegar
½   teaspoon bottled minced garlic (1 clove)
    Celery sticks (optional)

1. Cut off and discard tips of chicken wings. Cut wings at joints to make 24 pieces. Place chicken in a shallow nonmetal dish.

2. For marinade, in a small bowl stir together hot pepper sauce, melted margarine, and paprika. Pour over chicken; stir to coat. Cover and marinate at room temperature for 30 minutes.

3. Preheat broiler. Drain chicken, reserving marinade. Place chicken on the unheated rack of a broiler pan. If desired, sprinkle chicken with salt and black pepper. Brush with some of the reserved marinade.

4. Broil 4 to 5 inches from the heat for 20 to 25 minutes or until chicken is tender and no longer pink, turning and brushing once with remaining reserved marinade halfway through broiling.

5. Meanwhile, for dip, in blender or food processor combine sour cream, mayonnaise, blue cheese, vinegar, and garlic. Cover and blend or process until smooth. Transfer to a small serving bowl. If desired, sprinkle with additional crumbled blue cheese. Serve chicken wings with dip and celery sticks.

Nutrition Facts per serving: 178 cal., 17 g total fat (4 g sat. fat), 39 mg chol., 183 mg sodium, 1 g carbo., 0 g fiber, 6 g pro.

PREP:
15 minutes
MARINATE:
30 minutes
BROIL:
20 minutes
MAKES:
12 appetizer servings

15 minutes

1
net gram
carbs

SERVE-ALONG SUGGESTIONS

Cumberland Pork
Medallions (see p.135)

Assorted mixed berries
such as strawberries,
raspberries, and/or
blackberries

Chocolate Mousse
(see p.397)

SAVORY BAKED BRIE

1 13½-ounce round Brie cheese
¼ cup pine nuts, toasted
2 tablespoons snipped fresh thyme or oregano
3 slices provolone cheese (about 2½ ounces)
  Apple and/or pear slices (optional)

1. Unwrap Brie cheese. Using a sharp knife, slice off the top rind. Place Brie round in a 9-inch glass pie plate. Sprinkle with pine nuts and thyme.

2. Overlap provolone cheese slices over top of Brie round, covering the nuts and thyme. If necessary, tuck ends of provolone cheese under Brie round.

3. Place pie plate in a cool oven. Turn oven to 325°. Bake for 20 to 25 minutes or until cheese is softened. If desired, serve with apple and/or pear slices.

Nutrition Facts per serving: 217 cal., 18 g total fat (10 g sat. fat), 54 mg chol., 378 mg sodium, 1 g carbo., 0 g fiber, 13 g pro.

PREP:
15 minutes
BAKE:
20 minutes
OVEN:
325°F
MAKES:
8 appetizer servings

15 minutes

3 net grams carbs

SERVE-ALONG SUGGESTIONS

Fresh baby spinach leaves with chopped hard-cooked egg and oil and vinegar

Mustard Baked Chicken (see p.165)

Spiced Cantaloupe (see p.347)

GREEK-STYLE PARTY PIZZETTAS

4   7- to 8-inch low-carb multigrain or whole wheat flour tortillas

½   of a 7-ounce container hummus (about ⅓ cup)

½   cup bottled roasted red sweet peppers, drained and chopped

½   cup crumbled feta cheese (2 ounces)

½   cup shredded mozzarella cheese (2 ounces)

8   pitted kalamata olives, halved

1   teaspoon snipped fresh oregano

1. Arrange tortillas in an even layer on a very large baking sheet. Bake in a 425° oven for 3 to 4 minutes or until crisp.

2. Spread tortillas with hummus; top with roasted peppers, feta cheese, and mozzarella cheese. Bake about 6 minutes more or until cheese is melted and edges are lightly browned. Top with olives and oregano. Quarter each pizzetta to serve.

Nutrition Facts per appetizer: 52 cal., 3 g total fat (1 g sat. fat), 5 mg chol., 151 mg sodium, 5 g carbo., 2 g fiber, 2 g pro.

PREP:
15 minutes
BAKE:
9 minutes
OVEN:
425°F
MAKES:
16 appetizers

12 minutes

2 net grams carbs

SERVE-ALONG SUGGESTIONS

Swordfish with Spicy Tomato Sauce (see p.233)

Assorted fresh melon such as honeydew and/or cantaloupe

Low-calorie lemonade flavored drink mix served with sliced lemon

ROMAS WITH CHÈVRE AND BASIL PESTO

10   roma tomatoes (about 2 pounds), halved lengthwise
¼   teaspoon dried thyme, crushed
¼   cup purchased basil pesto
¼   cup soft goat cheese (chèvre)
2   tablespoons snipped fresh parsley or basil

1. Sprinkle cut sides of tomato halves with thyme; season with salt and black pepper. Place tomatoes, cut sides up, in a greased shallow baking pan. Bake in a 400° oven about 5 minutes or until nearly tender.

2. Spoon about 1 teaspoon of the pesto onto each tomato half. Top each half with about 1 teaspoon of the goat cheese. Bake about 2 minutes more or until cheese is softened. Sprinkle with parsley.

Nutrition Facts per appetizer: 39 cal., 3 g total fat (0 g sat. fat), 2 mg chol., 67 mg sodium, 3 g carbo., 1 g fiber, 1 g pro.

PREP:
12 minutes
BAKE:
7 minutes
OVEN:
400°F
MAKES:
20 appetizers

HOT AND SWEET COCKTAIL WIENERS

PREP:
10 minutes
COOK:
4 hours
MAKES:
16 appetizer servings

1	16-ounce package cocktail wieners or small cooked smoked sausage links
1	8-ounce can tomato sauce
¼	cup low-sugar orange marmalade or apricot spread
1	to 2 tablespoons canned chipotle chile pepper in adobo sauce, chopped

1. In a 1½-quart slow cooker* combine cocktail wieners, tomato sauce, orange marmalade, and chipotle pepper.

2. Cover and cook for 4 hours. Serve wieners with toothpicks.

Note: The 1½-quart slow cooker does not have a low or high setting. It cooks on one heat setting only.

Nutrition Facts per serving: 105 cal., 8 g total fat (3 g sat. fat), 20 mg chol., 343 mg sodium, 3 g carbo., 0 g fiber, 3 g pro.

3
net grams carbs

SERVE-ALONG SUGGESTIONS

Sesame-Ginger Barbecued Chicken (see p.169)

Grilled or sautéed sweet pepper halves

Peppered Strawberries (see p.337)

ITALIAN COCKTAIL MEATBALLS

1   16-ounce package (32) frozen cooked meatballs, thawed
½   cup bottled roasted red and/or yellow sweet peppers, drained and cut into 1-inch pieces
⅛   teaspoon crushed red pepper
1½   cups bottled onion-garlic pasta sauce

1. In a 1½-quart slow cooker* combine meatballs and roasted peppers. Sprinkle with crushed red pepper. Pour pasta sauce over meatball mixture in slow cooker.

2. Cover and cook for 4 to 5 hours. Skim fat from sauce. Stir gently before serving.

> **Note:** The 1½-quart slow cooker does not have a low or high setting. It cooks on one heat setting only.

Nutrition Facts per serving: 99 cal., 8 g total fat (3 g sat. fat), 10 mg chol., 322 mg sodium, 4 g carbo., 1 g fiber, 4 g pro.

PREP:
10 minutes
COOK:
4 to 5 hours
MAKES:
16 appetizer servings

3
net grams carbs

SERVE-ALONG SUGGESTIONS

Grilled Turkey Piccata (see p.203)

Lemon-Marinated Veggies (see p.277)

Wedges of fresh pineapple

SAVORY NUTS

PREP:
10 minutes
BAKE:
12 minutes
OVEN:
350°F
MAKES:
2 cups
(8 appetizer servings)

2
net grams
carbs

SERVE-ALONG SUGGESTIONS

Grilled Beef, Red Onion, and Blue Cheese Salad (see p.71)

Fresh strawberries tossed with orange juice and snipped fresh mint

Orange-Cantaloupe Pops (see p.341)

2   cups macadamia nuts, broken walnuts, and/or unblanched almonds
2   tablespoons white wine Worcestershire sauce
1   tablespoon olive oil
2   teaspoons snipped fresh thyme or ½ teaspoon dried thyme, crushed
1   teaspoon snipped fresh rosemary or ¼ teaspoon dried rosemary, crushed
¼   teaspoon salt
⅛   teaspoon cayenne pepper

1. Place nuts in a 13×9×2-inch baking pan. In a small bowl combine Worcestershire sauce, oil, thyme, rosemary, salt, and cayenne pepper. Drizzle over nuts; toss gently to coat. Spread nuts in a single layer.

2. Bake in a 350° oven for 12 to 15 minutes or until nuts are toasted, stirring occasionally. Spread in a single layer on a large piece of foil to cool.

Nutrition Facts per serving: 259 cal., 27 g total fat (4 g sat. fat), 0 mg chol., 191 mg sodium, 5 g carbo., 3 g fiber, 3 g pro.

ASIAN-SPICED PECANS

1   pound pecan halves, toasted (4 cups)
¼   cup butter or margarine, melted
2   tablespoons soy sauce
1   teaspoon five-spice powder
½   teaspoon garlic powder
½   teaspoon ground ginger
¼   teaspoon cayenne pepper

1. Place pecans in a 3½- or 4-quart slow cooker. In a small bowl combine melted butter, soy sauce, five-spice powder, garlic powder, ginger, and cayenne pepper. Pour over nuts; toss gently to coat.

2. Cover and cook on low-heat setting for 2 hours. Stir nuts. Spread in a single layer on a large piece of foil to cool. (Nuts appear soft after cooking, but will crisp upon cooling.)

Nutrition Facts per serving: 225 cal., 23 g total fat (4 g sat. fat), 8 mg chol., 146 mg sodium, 4 g carbo., 3 g fiber, 3 g pro.

PREP:
10 minutes
COOK:
2 hours
(low-heat setting)
MAKES:
4 cups
(16 appetizer servings)

1
net gram carbs

SERVE-ALONG SUGGESTIONS

Soy and Sesame Pork
(see p.149)

Steamed sugar
snap peas

Strawberries with
Orange Cream Dip
(see p.333)

DEVILED EGGS

WITH SPICY CRAB

PREP:
15 minutes
CHILL:
1 to 2 hours
MAKES:
16 appetizers

1
net gram carbs

SERVE-ALONG SUGGESTIONS

Dijon-Rosemary Roast
Leg of Lamb
(see p.375)

Broiled Asparagus and
Fresh Mozzarella
(see p.283)

Raspberry and
Chocolate Tulips
(see p.343)

8	hard-cooked eggs
¼	cup mayonnaise or salad dressing
1	tablespoon finely chopped green onion
1	to 2 teaspoons flavored mustard (such as Dijon-style mustard or horseradish mustard)
¼	teaspoon salt
¼	teaspoon cayenne pepper
1	to 2 tablespoons mango chutney
3	tablespoons mayonnaise or salad dressing
½	teaspoon curry powder
½	cup cooked crabmeat (about 3 ounces)

1. Cut hard-cooked eggs in half lengthwise; remove yolks. Set whites aside. In a quart-size, resealable plastic bag combine egg yolks, the ¼ cup mayonnaise, green onion, mustard, ⅛ teaspoon of the salt, and ⅛ teaspoon of the cayenne pepper. Seal bag. Gently squeeze the bag to combine ingredients. Snip one corner of the bag; pipe egg yolk mixture into egg white halves.

2. Cut up any large pieces of chutney. In a small bowl combine chutney, the 3 tablespoons mayonnaise, curry powder, remaining ⅛ teaspoon salt, and remaining ⅛ teaspoon cayenne pepper. Gently fold in crabmeat. Top each deviled egg with a spoonful of the crabmeat mixture. Cover and chill for at least 1 hour or up to 2 hours.

Nutrition Facts per appetizer: 91 cal., 8 g total fat (1 g sat. fat), 113 mg chol., 119 mg sodium, 1 g carbo., 0 g fiber, 4 g pro.

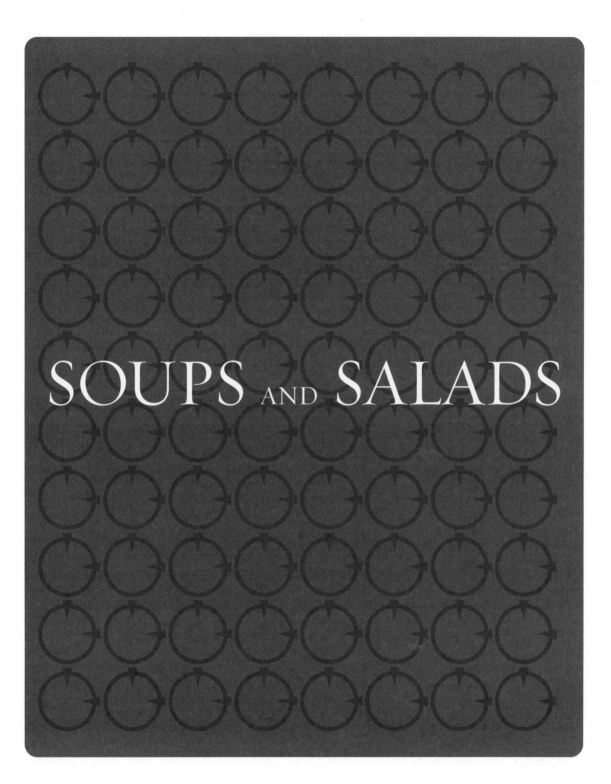

SOUPS AND SALADS

15 minutes

7

net grams
carbs

SERVE-ALONG SUGGESTIONS

Toasted Cheese Tortilla Chips (see p.311)

Mixed greens tossed with bottled low-carb balsamic vinaigrette salad dressing and garnished with chopped hard-cooked egg and chopped tomato, if desired

Strawberries with Orange Cream Dip (see p.333)

FAST ITALIAN-STYLE CHICKEN SOUP

1   15-ounce container refrigerated marinara sauce
1   cup water
2   5-ounce cans or one 10-ounce can chunk-style chicken, undrained
½   teaspoon dried sage, crushed

1. In a medium saucepan stir together marinara sauce and the water. Bring to boiling; reduce heat.

2. Stir in chicken and sage. Simmer, uncovered, for 5 to 8 minutes or until mixture is heated through.

Nutrition Facts per serving: 159 cal., 6 g total fat (1 g sat. fat), 35 mg chol., 604 mg sodium, 9 g carbo., 2 g fiber, 18 g pro.

PREP:
15 minutes
COOK:
5 minutes
MAKES:
4 main-dish servings

15 minutes

6 net grams carbs

SERVE-ALONG SUGGESTIONS

Tomatillo Guacamole
(see p.296)

Grilled ribeye steak

Peppered Strawberries
(see p.337)

CORN AND CHICKEN SOUP

6 ounces skinless, boneless chicken breast halves, finely chopped

¼ cup water

1 tablespoon rice wine or dry white wine

2 teaspoons soy sauce

1 teaspoon grated fresh ginger

1 teaspoon toasted sesame oil

2½ cups chicken broth

1 cup loose-pack frozen corn

1 beaten egg

1. In a small bowl combine chicken, the water, rice wine, soy sauce, ginger, and sesame oil. Cover and let stand at room temperature for 20 minutes.

2. In a wok or large saucepan combine chicken broth and corn. Bring to boiling. Add chicken mixture, stirring constantly to separate chicken pieces. Return to boiling; reduce heat. Simmer, uncovered, about 2 minutes or until chicken is no longer pink, stirring often.

3. Pour beaten egg into hot chicken mixture in a steady stream while stirring 2 or 3 times to create shreds. Remove from heat. Cover and let stand for 1 minute.

Nutrition Facts per serving: 98 cal., 3 g total fat (1 g sat. fat), 54 mg chol., 466 mg sodium, 7 g carbo., 1 g fiber, 11 g pro.

PREP:
15 minutes
STAND:
20 minutes
MAKES:
6 side-dish servings

10 minutes

6
net grams
carbs

SERVE-ALONG SUGGESTIONS

Herbed Steak (see p.89)

Braised Seasoned
Brussels Sprouts
(see p.269)

Sugar-free cherry-flavored
gelatin topped with
whipped cream

PRONTO BEEFY MUSHROOM SOUP

2	tablespoons butter or margarine
1	8-ounce package sliced fresh mushrooms
1	small red or yellow onion, thinly sliced
1	14-ounce can beef broth
1½	cups water
1	envelope (½ of a 1.8- to 2.2-ounce package) onion-mushroom soup mix or beefy onion soup mix
1	to 2 tablespoons dry sherry (optional)

PREP:

10 minutes

COOK:

10 minutes

MAKES:

4 side-dish servings

1. In a medium saucepan melt butter over medium-high heat. Add mushrooms and onion; cook about 5 minutes or until tender. Stir in beef broth, the water, and dry soup mix. Cook and stir until bubbly.

2. Reduce heat. Simmer, uncovered, for 5 minutes. If desired, stir in sherry.

Nutrition Facts per serving: 104 cal., 8 g total fat (4 g sat. fat), 16 mg chol., 861 mg sodium, 7 g carbo., 1 g fiber, 3 g pro.

15 minutes

5
net grams
carbs

SERVE-ALONG SUGGESTIONS

Halved red and/or yellow cherry tomatoes tossed with red wine vinegar or bottled low-carb red wine vinaigrette salad dressing

Roasted Asparagus Parmesan (see p.267)

Orange-Ginger Rhubarb (see p.353)

NORTH SEA CHOWDER

1	pound fresh or frozen skinless, boneless sea bass, red snapper, and/or catfish fillets
1	tablespoon butter or olive oil
1	medium onion, chopped
1	teaspoon bottled minced garlic (2 cloves)
4	cups water
1	tablespoon lemon juice
1	bay leaf
2	fish bouillon cubes or 2 teaspoons instant chicken bouillon granules
½	teaspoon instant chicken bouillon granules
½	teaspoon dried thyme, crushed
¼	teaspoon fennel seeds
	Dash ground saffron (optional)
4	roma tomatoes, halved lengthwise and thinly sliced

PREP:
15 minutes
COOK:
10 minutes
MAKES:
4 to 6 main-dish
servings

1. Thaw fish, if frozen. Rinse fish; pat dry with paper towels. Cut fish into ¾-inch pieces; set aside.

2. In a large saucepan melt butter over medium heat. Add onion and garlic; cook until tender. Stir in the water, lemon juice, bay leaf, fish bouillon cubes, the ½ teaspoon chicken bouillon granules, the thyme, fennel seeds, and, if desired, saffron. Bring to boiling.

3. Add fish and tomatoes. Return to boiling; reduce heat. Simmer, covered, for 10 minutes. Discard bay leaf.

Nutrition Facts per serving: 160 cal., 5 g total fat (2 g sat. fat), 55 mg chol., 683 mg sodium, 6 g carbo., 1 g fiber, 22 g pro.

15 minutes

9
net grams
carbs

SERVE-ALONG SUGGESTIONS

Assorted low-carb
crackers

Lemon-Marinated Veggies
(see p.277)

Double Berry Delight
(see p.361)

EFFORTLESS SHRIMP CHOWDER

1 10¾-ounce can condensed cream of shrimp soup
1 cup half-and-half or light cream
¼ cup cream sherry or dry sherry
1 tablespoon butter or margarine (optional)
8 ounces fresh or frozen peeled and deveined small shrimp

START TO FINISH:
15 minutes
MAKES:
4 main-dish servings

1. In a medium saucepan combine cream of shrimp soup, half-and-half, and sherry. Bring just to boiling. If desired, add butter. Reduce heat. Simmer, uncovered, for 5 minutes, stirring often.

2. Meanwhile, rinse shrimp; pat dry with paper towels. If desired, chop shrimp. Stir shrimp into soup mixture. Return to boiling; reduce heat. Simmer, uncovered, for 1 to 2 minutes more or until shrimp are opaque.

Nutrition Facts per serving: 214 cal., 11 g total fat (6 g sat. fat), 118 mg chol., 702 mg sodium, 9 g carbo., 0 g fiber, 15 g pro.

15 minutes

4 net grams carbs

SERVE-ALONG SUGGESTIONS

Salmon with Fruit Salsa (see p.219)

Low-carb tortillas, cut into wedges, brushed with melted butter and minced garlic, toasted

Steamed snow peas

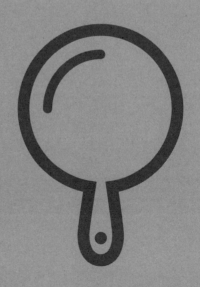

THAI LIME CUSTARD SOUP

1   tablespoon vegetable oil
2   baby eggplants or Japanese eggplants (about 1 pound), halved lengthwise and sliced
1   tablespoon grated fresh ginger
1   to 1½ teaspoons bottled minced garlic (2 to 3 cloves) (optional)
¼   teaspoon crushed red pepper
2   14-ounce cans vegetable broth
3   eggs
2   cups chopped fresh spinach
¼   cup finely shredded fresh basil
¼   cup lime juice

PREP:
15 minutes
COOK:
10 minutes
MAKES:
5 side-dish servings

1. In a large saucepan heat oil over medium-high heat. Add eggplant, ginger, garlic (if desired), and crushed red pepper; cook for 2 minutes. Add vegetable broth. Bring to boiling; reduce heat. Simmer, covered, for 5 minutes.

2. In a small bowl beat eggs with a fork. Gradually stir about ½ cup of the hot broth mixture into eggs. Return egg mixture to the remaining broth mixture in saucepan. Add spinach.

3. Cook and stir over medium-low heat about 2 minutes or until mixture is slightly thickened and spinach is wilted. Stir in basil and lime juice; heat through.

Nutrition Facts per serving: 109 cal., 7 g total fat (2 g sat. fat), 128 mg chol., 294 mg sodium, 7 g carbo., 3 g fiber, 5 g pro.

**15
minutes**

**4
net grams
carbs**

SERVE-ALONG SUGGESTIONS

Classic Buffalo Wings
(see p.43)

Lime-Cilantro Flank Steak
(see p.117)

Skewers of kiwi fruit, fresh
pineapple, and mango

CHILLED AVOCADO SOUP

3 ripe avocados, seeded and peeled (about 1¼ pounds)
1 cup chicken broth
¼ cup water
1 cup half-and-half or light cream
¼ teaspoon salt
⅛ teaspoon onion powder
Dash white pepper
1 tablespoon lemon juice

1. In a blender container or food processor bowl combine avocados, chicken broth, and the water. Cover and blend or process until smooth. Add half-and-half, salt, onion powder, and white pepper. Cover and blend or process until combined.

2. Transfer avocado mixture to a glass serving bowl. Stir in lemon juice. Cover and chill for at least 3 hours or up to 24 hours. Stir before serving.

Nutrition Facts per serving: 167 cal., 15 g total fat (5 g sat. fat), 15 mg chol., 287 mg sodium, 7 g carbo., 3 g fiber, 3 g pro.

PREP:
15 minutes
CHILL:
3 to 24 hours
MAKES:
6 side-dish servings

15 minutes

7 net grams carbs

SERVE-ALONG SUGGESTIONS

Herbed Soy Snacks
(see p.320)

Spicy Baked Oranges
(see p.355)

Low calorie peach-iced
tea-flavored drink mix

GRILLED BEEF, RED ONION, AND BLUE CHEESE SALAD

3 tablespoons balsamic vinegar
2 tablespoons olive oil
½ teaspoon salt
½ teaspoon black pepper
½ teaspoon bottled minced garlic (1 clove)
1 12-ounce boneless beef top sirloin steak, cut 1 inch thick
1 tablespoon snipped fresh thyme
2 teaspoons snipped fresh rosemary
4 ¼-inch slices red onion
6 cups lightly packed mesclun or torn mixed salad greens
8 yellow and/or red pear-shaped tomatoes, halved
2 tablespoons crumbled blue cheese

PREP:
15 minutes
GRILL:
14 minutes
MAKES:
4 main-dish servings

1. For vinaigrette, in a screw-top jar combine balsamic vinegar, oil, salt, pepper, and garlic. Cover and shake well. Trim fat from steak. Remove 1 tablespoon of the vinaigrette from jar and brush onto both sides of steak. Press thyme and rosemary onto both sides of steak. Brush some of the remaining vinaigrette onto both sides of onion slices, reserving the rest. Set aside.

2. Place steak on the rack of an uncovered grill directly over medium coals. Grill until desired doneness, turning once halfway through grilling. Allow 14 to 18 minutes for medium-rare doneness (145°F) or 18 to 22 minutes for medium doneness (160°F). For the last 10 minutes of grilling, place onion slices on grill rack next to steak; grill until tender and browned, turning once.

3. Divide mesclun among 4 dinner plates. Thinly slice steak across the grain; separate onion slices into rings. Arrange steak slices and onion rings on top of greens. Drizzle with reserved vinaigrette. Top with tomatoes and cheese.

Nutrition Facts per serving: 266 cal., 16 g total fat (5 g sat. fat), 59 mg chol., 373 mg sodium, 9 g carbo., 2 g fiber, 22 g pro.

15 minutes

6 net grams carbs

SERVE-ALONG SUGGESTIONS

Napa Cabbage Slaw
(see p.289)

Sliced nectarines
and/or peaches

Really Hot Iced Coffee
(see p.329)

GRILLED CHICKEN AND RASPBERRY SALAD

¼ cup raspberry vinegar
3 tablespoons cooking oil
½ teaspoon poppy seeds
¼ teaspoon salt
¼ teaspoon black pepper
1 pound skinless, boneless chicken breast halves
6 cups torn mixed salad greens
½ of a small red onion, thinly sliced and separated into rings
1 cup raspberries

PREP:
15 minutes
GRILL:
12 minutes
MAKES:
4 main-dish servings

1. For dressing, in a screw-top jar combine raspberry vinegar, oil, poppy seeds, salt, and pepper. Cover and shake well. Set aside.

2. Place chicken on the rack of an uncovered grill directly over medium coals. Grill for 12 to 15 minutes or until chicken is tender and no longer pink (170°F), turning once halfway through grilling.

3. Place salad greens and onion on a large serving platter. Thinly slice chicken diagonally; arrange on top of greens mixture. Drizzle with dressing; sprinkle with raspberries.

Broiler Method: Preheat broiler. Place chicken on the unheated rack of a broiler pan. Broil 4 to 5 inches from the heat for 12 to 15 minutes or until chicken is tender and no longer pink (170°F), turning once halfway through broiling.

Nutrition Facts per serving: 244 cal., 14 g total fat (2 g sat. fat), 59 mg chol., 190 mg sodium, 8 g carbo., 2 g fiber, 23 g pro.

15 minutes

6 net grams carbs

SERVE-ALONG SUGGESTIONS

Romas with Chèvre and Basil Pesto (see p. 49)

Red and/or green seedless grapes

Lemon-Berry Fizz (see p.327)

CABBAGE AND CHICKEN WITH SESAME DRESSING

¼ cup bottled Italian salad dressing
1 tablespoon soy sauce
1 teaspoon toasted sesame oil
⅛ to ¼ teaspoon crushed red pepper
3 cups packaged shredded cabbage with carrot (coleslaw mix)
2 cups chopped cooked chicken (about 10 ounces)
2 tablespoons snipped fresh cilantro
1 head Boston lettuce, separated into leaves
¼ cup slivered almonds, toasted

PREP:
15 minutes
MAKES:
4 main-dish servings

1. For dressing, in a small bowl combine Italian salad dressing, soy sauce, sesame oil, and crushed red pepper. Set aside.

2. In a large bowl toss together cabbage, chicken, and cilantro. Drizzle with dressing; toss gently to coat.

3. Line 4 dinner plates with lettuce leaves. Place chicken mixture on top of lettuce. Sprinkle with almonds.

Nutrition Facts per serving: 298 cal., 18 g total fat (3 g sat. fat), 68 mg chol., 457 mg sodium, 9 g carbo., 3 g fiber, 25 g pro.

15 minutes

6 net grams carbs

SERVE-ALONG SUGGESTIONS

Asian-Spiced Pecans (see p.53)

Cranberry Coleslaw (see p.391)

Low-calorie citrus carbonated beverage

TERIYAKI PORK SALAD

4	boneless pork loin chops, cut ¾ inch thick
⅓	cup rice vinegar
⅓	cup orange juice
2	tablespoons light teriyaki sauce
1	tablespoon peanut oil or salad oil
1	teaspoon sesame seeds, toasted
1	teaspoon bottled minced garlic (2 cloves)
6	cups torn mixed salad greens
¾	cup sliced red radishes
¼	cup thinly sliced green onions

PREP:
15 minutes
GRILL:
12 minutes
MARINATE:
20 minutes to 8 hours
MAKES:
4 main-dish servings

1. Trim fat from chops. Place chops in a resealable plastic bag set in a shallow dish. For marinade, in a small bowl whisk together vinegar, orange juice, teriyaki sauce, oil, sesame seeds, and garlic. Reserve half of the marinade for dressing. Pour remaining marinade over chops. Seal bag; turn to coat chops. Marinate in the refrigerator for at least 20 minutes or up to 8 hours, turning bag occasionally.

2. Drain chops, reserving marinade. Place chops on the rack of an uncovered grill directly over medium coals. Grill for 12 to 15 minutes or until chops are slightly pink in center and juices run clear (160°F), turning and brushing once with marinade halfway through grilling. Discard any remaining marinade.

3. Divide salad greens, radishes, and green onions among 4 dinner plates. Thinly slice chops diagonally; arrange on top of greens mixture. Drizzle with dressing.

Nutrition Facts per serving: 199 cal., 11 g total fat (3 g sat. fat), 51 mg chol., 172 mg sodium, 7 g carbo., 1 g fiber, 18 g pro.

15 minutes

8 net grams carbs

SERVE-ALONG SUGGESTIONS

Lemony Herbed Olives
(see p.303)

Grapefruit halves sprinkled
with sugar substitute

Strawberry-Citrus Slush
(see p.365)

SALMON CAESAR SALAD

1 10-ounce package Caesar salad kit (includes lettuce, dressing, croutons, and cheese)
1 small sweet pepper, cut into thin strips
1 small cucumber, quartered lengthwise and sliced
6 ounces smoked, poached, or canned salmon, skinned, boned, and broken into chunks (1 cup)
½ of a lemon, cut into 3 wedges

START TO FINISH:
15 minutes
MAKES:
3 main-dish servings

1. In a large bowl combine lettuce and dressing from packaged salad, sweet pepper, and cucumber; toss gently to coat. Add croutons and cheese from packaged salad and salmon; toss gently to combine.

2. Divide salmon mixture among 3 dinner plates. Serve with lemon wedges to squeeze over each salad.

Nutrition Facts per serving: 251 cal., 18 g total fat (3 g sat. fat), 23 mg chol., 826 mg sodium, 11 g carbo., 3 g fiber, 14 g pro.

15 minutes

3
net grams carbs

SERVE-ALONG SUGGESTIONS

Chili Chicken Appeteasers (see p.33)

Crème Fraîche Fool with Berries (see p.400)

Decaf iced tea served with orange wedges, if desired

ASIAN GRILLED SALMON SALAD

4 6- to 8-ounce fresh or frozen salmon fillets or steaks, about 1 inch thick
1 pound asparagus spears
1 tablespoon salad oil
1 teaspoon fennel seeds, crushed
1 head Bibb lettuce, separated into leaves
1 cup fresh enoki mushrooms
1 medium tomato, cut into thin wedges
1 recipe Asian Dressing (see recipe, below)

1. Thaw fish, if frozen. Rinse fish; pat dry with paper towels. Snap off and discard woody bases from asparagus.

2. Lightly brush both sides of fish and the asparagus with oil. Press fennel seeds onto both sides of fish.

3. Place fish on the greased rack of an uncovered grill directly over medium coals. Place asparagus on a piece of heavy foil on grill rack next to fish. Grill for 8 to 12 minutes or until fish flakes easily when tested with a fork and asparagus is crisp-tender, turning fish and asparagus once halfway through grilling.

4. Line 4 dinner plates with lettuce leaves. Place fish on top of lettuce. Arrange asparagus, mushrooms, and tomato around fish. Shake Asian Dressing; drizzle over salads.

> **Asian Dressing:** In a screw-top jar combine 1 tablespoon salad oil, 1 tablespoon rice vinegar, 1 tablespoon soy sauce, 1 teaspoon toasted sesame oil, and ¼ teaspoon grated fresh ginger or ½ teaspoon chopped pickled ginger. Cover and shake well.

Nutrition Facts per serving: 422 cal., 27 g total fat (5 g sat. fat), 99 mg chol., 346 mg sodium, 5 g carbo., 2 g fiber, 38 g pro.

PREP:
15 minutes
GRILL:
8 minutes
MAKES:
4 main-dish servings

15 minutes

0 net grams carbs

SERVE-ALONG SUGGESTIONS

Orange-Mustard Lamb Chops (see p.159)

Mixed fresh berries

Macadamia-White Chocolate Dessert (see p.363)

WARM ASPARAGUS, FENNEL, AND SPINACH SALAD

1   medium fennel bulb
2   tablespoons water
2   tablespoons olive oil
¼   teaspoon finely shredded lemon peel
4   teaspoons lemon juice
¼   teaspoon salt
⅛   teaspoon black pepper
8   ounces asparagus spears, trimmed
4   cups fresh spinach leaves
¼   cup finely grated Parmesan cheese (1 ounce)
1   tablespoon finely shredded fresh basil

PREP:
15 minutes
GRILL:
8 minutes
MAKES:
4 side-dish servings

1. Trim off stem end of fennel; quarter fennel but do not remove core. Place fennel in a small microwave-safe dish or pie plate; add the water. Cover with vented plastic wrap. Microwave on 100% power (high) about 4 minutes or until nearly tender; drain.

2. Meanwhile, for dressing, in a small bowl whisk together oil, lemon peel, lemon juice, salt, and pepper. Brush fennel and asparagus with 1 tablespoon of the dressing; reserve remaining dressing.

3. Place fennel and asparagus on the rack of an uncovered grill directly over medium coals (lay asparagus spears perpendicular to wires on grill rack so they won't fall into coals). Grill about 8 minutes or until vegetables are crisp-tender and lightly browned, turning occasionally.

4. Cut fennel into ¼- to ½-inch slices, discarding core. Divide fennel and asparagus among 4 salad plates. Arrange spinach on top of vegetables. Drizzle with remaining dressing. Top with Parmesan cheese and basil.

Nutrition Facts per serving: 111 cal., 9 g total fat (1 g sat. fat), 5 mg chol., 231 mg sodium, 5 g carbo., 7 g fiber, 4 g pro.

MESCLUN

WITH OLIVES AND ORANGES

PREP:

15 minutes

MAKES:

8 side-dish servings

7

net grams carbs

12 cups mesclun or other mild salad greens
3 tablespoons olive oil
2 tablespoons blood orange juice or orange juice
2 tablespoons balsamic vinegar
2 cups blood orange and/or orange sections (8 blood oranges or 6 oranges)
8 thin slices red onion, separated into rings
⅔ cup pitted kalamata olives
⅛ teaspoon salt
⅛ teaspoon black pepper

1. Place mesclun in a large salad bowl. For dressing, in a small bowl whisk together oil, orange juice, and balsamic vinegar. Pour over mesclun; toss gently to coat.

2. Divide mesclun mixture among 8 salad plates. Top with orange sections, onion rings, and olives. Sprinkle with salt and pepper.

Nutrition Facts per serving: 103 cal., 7 g total fat (1 g sat. fat), 0 mg chol., 151 mg sodium, 10 g carbo., 3 g fiber, 1 g pro.

SERVE-ALONG SUGGESTIONS

Thyme and Garlic Chicken Breasts (see p.185)

Cooked acorn squash sprinkled with ground cinnamon and finely shredded orange peel

Assorted cheeses, cut into cubes and served with low-carb crackers, if desired

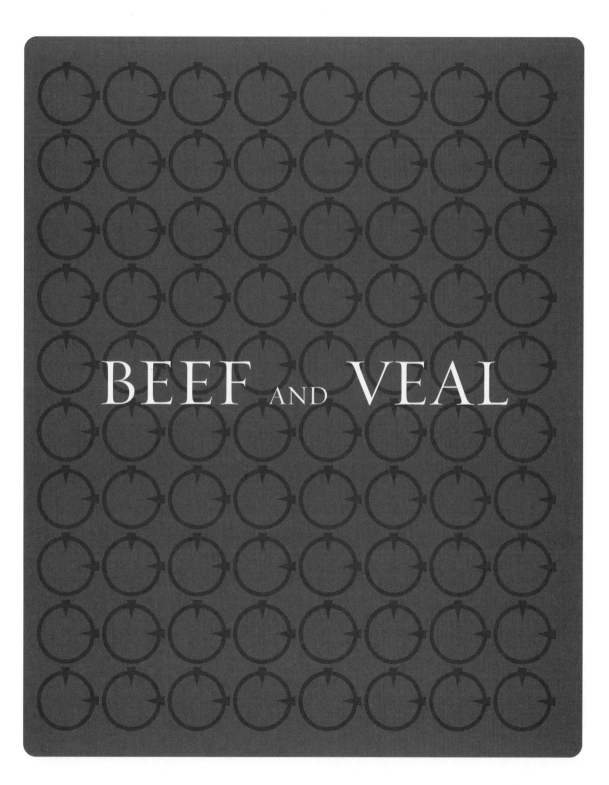

BEEF AND VEAL

10 minutes

2
net grams carbs

SERVE-ALONG SUGGESTIONS

Sautéed sliced button, crimini, and/or shiitake mushrooms

Roasted Asparagus Parmesan (see p.267)

Chocolate Mousse (see p.397)

BEEF TENDERLOINS

WITH WINE SAUCE

4	beef tenderloin steaks, cut 1 inch thick (about 1 pound total)
½	teaspoon cracked black pepper
1	tablespoon butter or margarine
¼	cup chopped onion
¼	cup beef broth
¼	cup dry red wine
1	teaspoon dried marjoram, crushed

PREP:
10 minutes
COOK:
15 minutes
MAKES:
4 servings

1. Trim fat from steaks. Press pepper onto both sides of each steak. In a large heavy skillet melt butter over medium-high heat. Add steaks; reduce heat to medium. Cook for 10 to 13 minutes for medium-rare (145°F) to medium (160°F) doneness, turning once. Transfer steaks to a serving platter, reserving drippings in skillet. Cover steaks; keep warm.

2. For sauce, stir onion into reserved drippings in skillet. Cook until onion is tender. Remove from heat. Carefully add beef broth, wine, and marjoram to onion in skillet, scraping up any browned bits from bottom of skillet. Return to heat. Bring to boiling; reduce heat. Boil gently, uncovered, about 2 minutes or until reduced to about ¼ cup. Serve sauce over steaks.

Nutrition Facts per serving: 315 cal., 15 g total fat (6 g sat. fat), 120 mg chol., 176 mg sodium, 2 g carbo., 0 g fiber, 38 g pro.

10 minutes

2 net grams carbs

SERVE-ALONG SUGGESTIONS

Green and/or red leaf lettuce tossed with cherry tomatoes, chopped hard-cooked egg and bottled low-carb Italian salad dressing

Steamed sugar snap peas

Spicy Baked Oranges (see p.355)

HERBED STEAK

2	boneless beef top loin steaks, cut ¾ inch thick (about 1¼ pounds total)
1	tablespoon butter or margarine
⅓	cup sliced green onions
1½	teaspoons snipped fresh thyme or basil or ½ teaspoon dried thyme or basil, crushed
¼	teaspoon salt
⅛	teaspoon black pepper
1	medium tomato, chopped

PREP:
10 minutes
COOK:
12 minutes
MAKES:
4 servings

1. Trim fat from steaks. Cut each steak in half. In a large heavy skillet melt butter over medium-high heat. Add steaks; reduce heat to medium. Cook for 10 to 12 minutes for medium-rare (145°F) to medium (160°F) doneness, turning once. Transfer steaks to a serving platter, reserving drippings in skillet. Cover steaks; keep warm.

2. Stir green onions, thyme, salt, and pepper into reserved drippings in skillet. Cook for 1 to 2 minutes or until green onions are tender. Stir in tomato; heat through. Serve tomato mixture over steaks.

Nutrition Facts per serving: 207 cal., 9 g total fat (4 g sat. fat), 89 mg chol., 230 mg sodium, 2 g carbo., 0 g fiber, 28 g pro.

15 minutes

2 net grams carbs

SERVE-ALONG SUGGESTIONS

Mediterranean Walnut Spread (see p.324)

Relish tray of baby dill pickles, stuffed green olives, ripe black olives, radishes, jicama and/or celery sticks

Mixed fresh berries such as strawberries, raspberries, and blackberries

GARLICKY STEAK AND ASPARAGUS

2 boneless beef top loin steaks, cut ¾ inch thick (1½ to 1¾ pounds total)

1 to 2 teaspoons bottled minced garlic (2 to 4 cloves)

1 teaspoon cracked or coarsely ground black pepper

½ teaspoon salt

16 to 20 thin asparagus spears, trimmed (about 12 ounces)

4 teaspoons garlic-flavored olive oil or plain olive oil

1 cup beef broth

2 tablespoons dry white wine or

½ teaspoon Dijon-style mustard

PREP:
15 minutes
COOK:
4 minutes
BROIL:
8 minutes
MAKES:
4 servings

1. Preheat broiler. Trim fat from steaks. For rub, in a small bowl combine garlic, pepper, and salt. Sprinkle garlic mixture evenly over both sides of each steak; rub in with your fingers. Place asparagus in a shallow dish; drizzle with oil.

2. For sauce, in a medium skillet combine beef broth and wine. Cook over high heat for 4 to 5 minutes or until mixture is reduced to about ½ cup. Whisk in mustard. Cover sauce; keep warm.

3. Place steaks on the unheated rack of a broiler pan. Broil 3 to 4 inches from the heat until desired doneness, turning once halfway through broiling. Allow 8 to 10 minutes for medium-rare doneness (145°F) or 11 to 14 minutes for medium doneness (160°F). For the last 2 minutes of broiling, place asparagus on the broiler rack next to steaks; broil until crisp-tender.

4. Cut each steak in half. Spoon sauce onto 4 dinner plates. Top with steaks and asparagus.

Nutrition Facts per serving: 458 cal., 32 g total fat (11 g sat. fat), 110 mg chol., 549 mg sodium, 3 g carbo., 1 g fiber, 37 g pro.

15 minutes

2
net grams
carbs

SERVE-ALONG SUGGESTIONS

Chilled Avocado Soup
(see p.69)

Toasted Cheese Tortilla
Chips (see p.311)

Red and/or green apple
and pear wedges

SALSA-TOPPED ROSEMARY T-BONES

2   beef T-bone steaks, cut 1 inch thick (about 1½ pounds total)
1   tablespoon snipped fresh rosemary or 1 teaspoon dried rosemary, crushed
1   teaspoon snipped fresh thyme or ¼ teaspoon dried thyme, crushed
¼   teaspoon salt
⅛   teaspoon black pepper
1   medium tomato, seeded and chopped
¼   cup chopped red onion
¼   cup chopped yellow and/or green sweet pepper
½   teaspoon bottled minced garlic (1 clove)
    Dash salt
    Dash black pepper
    Dash bottled hot pepper sauce

PREP:
15 minutes
GRILL:
11 minutes
MAKES:
4 servings

1. Trim fat from steaks. For rub, in a small bowl combine rosemary, thyme, the ¼ teaspoon salt, and the ⅛ teaspoon black pepper. Sprinkle herb mixture evenly over both sides of each steak; rub in with your fingers.

2. Place steaks on the rack of an uncovered grill directly over medium coals. Grill until desired doneness, turning once halfway through grilling. Allow 11 to 14 minutes for medium-rare doneness (145°F) or 13 to 16 minutes for medium doneness (160°F).

3. Meanwhile, for salsa, in a medium bowl stir together tomato, onion, sweet pepper, garlic, the dash salt, the dash black pepper, and the hot pepper sauce. Serve salsa with steaks.

Nutrition Facts per serving: 255 cal., 10 g total fat (3 g sat. fat), 81 mg chol., 268 mg sodium, 3 g carbo., 1 g fiber, 36 g pro.

10 minutes

2 net grams carbs

SERVE-ALONG SUGGESTIONS

Chili Chicken Appeteasers (see p.33)

Grilled or sautéed strips of red, yellow, orange, and/or green sweet peppers

Decaf iced tea with sugar substitute and lime wedges

SIROIN

WITH MUSTARD AND CHIVES

4   boneless beef top sirloin or ribeye steaks, cut ¾ inch thick (about 1½ pounds total)
2   teaspoons garlic-pepper seasoning
½   cup dairy sour cream
2   tablespoons Dijon-style mustard
1   tablespoon snipped fresh chives

PREP:
10 minutes
GRILL:
9 minutes
MAKES:
4 servings

1. Trim fat from steaks. Sprinkle 1½ teaspoons of the seasoning evenly over both sides of each steak. Place steaks on the rack of an uncovered grill directly over medium coals. Grill until desired doneness, turning once halfway through grilling. Allow 9 to 11 minutes for medium-rare doneness (145°F) or 11 to 13 minutes for medium doneness (160°F). Transfer steaks to a serving platter.

2. Meanwhile, in a small bowl combine sour cream, mustard, chives, and the remaining ½ teaspoon seasoning. Spoon sour cream mixture on top of steaks.

Nutrition Facts per serving: 277 cal., 12 g total fat (5 g sat. fat), 114 mg chol., 619 mg sodium, 2 g carbo., 0 g fiber, 37 g pro.

10 minutes

4 net grams carbs

SERVE-ALONG SUGGESTIONS

Curried Apple Spread
(see p.330)

Steamed broccoli and
cauliflower with melted
pepper-jack
cheese, if desired

Orange-Ginger Rhubarb
(see p.353)

STEAK WITH CREAMY ONION SAUCE

4 beef ribeye steaks, cut 1 inch thick (about 1½ pounds total)
1 tablespoon Mediterranean seasoning blend or lemon-pepper seasoning
1 medium sweet onion (such as Vidalia, Maui, or Walla Walla), thinly sliced
1 8-ounce carton dairy sour cream
2 tablespoons drained capers

PREP:
10 minutes
BROIL:
12 minutes
MAKES:
4 servings

1. Preheat broiler. Trim fat from steaks. Sprinkle 1½ teaspoons of the seasoning blend over both sides of each steak. Place steaks on the unheated rack of a broiler pan. Broil 3 to 4 inches from the heat until desired doneness, turning once halfway through broiling. Allow 12 to 14 minutes for medium-rare doneness (145°F) or 15 to 18 minutes for medium doneness (160°F). For the last 10 minutes of broiling, place onion slices on broiler rack next to steaks; broil until tender and browned, turning once.

2. For sauce, coarsely chop broiled onion. In a small saucepan combine onion, sour cream, capers, and the remaining 1½ teaspoons seasoning blend. Cook over medium-low heat until heated through, but do not boil. Serve sauce over steaks.

Nutrition Facts per serving: 398 cal., 22 g total fat (11 g sat. fat), 106 mg chol., 472 mg sodium, 4 g carbo., 0 g fiber, 39 g pro.

15
minutes

4
net grams
carbs

SERVE-ALONG SUGGESTIONS

Cheesy Pecan Quesadillas
(see p.295)

Mixed greens tossed with
thin wedges of red onion,
crisp-cooked crumbled
bacon, and bottled low-
carb ranch salad dressing

Grapefruit halves sprinkled
with sugar substitute

HERBED TENDERLOIN STEAKS AND VEGETABLES

2 cloves garlic
¼ cup loosely packed fresh basil leaves
2 tablespoons fresh thyme leaves
1 tablespoon fresh rosemary leaves
1 tablespoon fresh mint leaves
2 tablespoons olive oil
½ teaspoon salt
½ teaspoon black pepper
4 beef tenderloin steaks, cut 1 inch thick (about 1 pound total)
2 large yellow tomatoes, halved crosswise
1 pound asparagus spears, trimmed

PREP:
15 minutes
GRILL:
11 minutes
MAKES:
4 servings

1. With food processor or blender running, add garlic through feed tube or lid. Process or blend until garlic is finely chopped. Add basil, thyme, rosemary, and mint. Cover and process or blend until herbs are chopped. With food processor or blender running, add oil in a thin steady stream. (When necessary, stop food processor or blender and use a rubber spatula to scrape sides of bowl or container.) Stir in salt and pepper.

2. Trim fat from steaks. Spread some of the herb mixture evenly over both sides of each steak and over cut sides of each tomato; set aside. Fold an 18×12-inch piece of heavy foil in half to make a double thickness of foil that measures 12×9 inches. Place asparagus in center of foil. Add remaining herb mixture, turning asparagus to coat evenly.

3. Place steaks on the rack of an uncovered grill directly over medium coals. Grill until desired doneness, turning once halfway through grilling. Allow 11 to 15 minutes for medium-rare doneness (145°F) or 14 to 18 minutes for medium doneness (160°F). For the last 8 minutes of grilling, place asparagus (on foil) on grill rack next to steaks; grill until crisp-tender. For the last 3 minutes of grilling, place tomatoes on grill rack; grill until heated through.

Nutrition Facts per serving: 245 cal., 14 g total fat (4 g sat. fat), 65 mg chol., 322 mg sodium, 6 g carbo., 2 g fiber, 24 g pro.

10 minutes

0 net grams carbs

SERVE-ALONG SUGGESTIONS

Sliced cucumber tossed with olive oil, cider vinegar, and your favorite snipped fresh herb

Steamed snow pea pods (serve with remaining tomato-garlic butter from steaks, if desired)

Vanilla Cream-Topped Raspberries (see p.335)

BEEF STEAKS

WITH TOMATO-GARLIC BUTTER

½ cup butter, softened
1 tablespoon snipped oil-packed dried tomatoes
1 tablespoon chopped kalamata olives
1 tablespoon finely chopped green onion
½ teaspoon bottled minced garlic (1 clove)
4 boneless beef top loin steaks, cut 1 inch thick (about 1½ pounds total)

PREP:
10 minutes
GRILL:
11 minutes
MAKES:
4 servings

1. For flavored butter, in a small bowl stir together softened butter, dried tomatoes, olives, green onion, and garlic. Set aside.

2. Trim fat from steaks. Place steaks on the rack of an uncovered grill directly over medium coals. Grill until desired doneness, turning once halfway through grilling. Allow 11 to 15 minutes for medium-rare doneness (145°F) or 14 to 18 minutes for medium doneness (160°F). If desired, sprinkle lightly with salt and black pepper.

3. To serve, spread 1 tablespoon of the flavored butter over each steak. Cover and chill the remaining flavored butter for another time.

Nutrition Facts per serving: 383 cal., 22 g total fat (11 g sat. fat), 161 mg chol., 227 mg sodium, 0 g carbo., 0 g fiber, 45 g pro.

10 minutes

1

net gram
carbs

SERVE-ALONG SUGGESTIONS

Fresh spinach leaves tossed with balsamic vinegar and olive oil and topped with crisp-cooked crumbled bacon

Broiled Eggplant with Cheese (see p.257)

Fresh sliced strawberries and/or peaches topped with heavy cream and toasted pecans or walnuts

CORIANDER-STUDDED TENDERLOIN STEAK

4 beef tenderloin steaks, cut 1 inch thick (about 1 pound total)
⅛ teaspoon salt
1 tablespoon salt reduced-sodium soy sauce
1 tablespoon olive oil
1 tablespoon snipped fresh chives
1 teaspoon bottled minced garlic (2 cloves)
½ teaspoon coriander seeds or cumin seeds, crushed
½ teaspoon celery seeds
½ teaspoon coarsely ground black pepper

1. Preheat broiler. Trim fat from steaks. Sprinkle lightly with salt. In a small bowl combine soy sauce, oil, chives, garlic, coriander seeds, celery seeds, and pepper. Brush soy mixture onto both sides of each steak.

2. Place steaks on the unheated rack of a broiler pan. Broil 3 to 4 inches from the heat until desired doneness, turning once halfway through broiling. Allow 12 to 14 minutes for medium-rare doneness (145°F) or 15 to 18 minutes for medium doneness (160°F).

Nutrition Facts per serving: 219 cal., 12 g total fat (4 g sat. fat), 56 mg chol., 341 mg sodium, 1 g carbo., 0 g fiber, 24 g pro.

PREP:
10 minutes
BROIL:
12 minutes
MAKES:
4 servings

15 minutes

3
net grams
carbs

SERVE-ALONG SUGGESTIONS

Savory Baked Brie
(see p.45)

Steamed haricots verts or
green beans with butter
and crushed red pepper

Ruby and Gold Grapefruit
(see p.313)

FILET MIGNON
WITH PORTOBELLO SAUCE

4	beef tenderloin steaks, cut 1 inch thick (about 1¼ pounds total)
1	teaspoon olive oil
¼	teaspoon black pepper
1	tablespoon butter or margarine
2	large fresh portobello mushrooms, halved and sliced
8	green onions, cut into 1-inch pieces
⅓	cup reduced-sodium beef broth
2	tablespoons Madeira or port wine

PREP:
15 minutes
GRILL:
11 minutes
MAKES:
4 servings

1. Trim fat from steaks. Rub both sides of each steak with oil and pepper. Place steaks on the rack of an uncovered grill directly over medium coals. Grill until desired doneness, turning once halfway through grilling. Allow 11 to 15 minutes for medium-rare doneness (145°F) or 14 to 18 minutes for medium doneness (160°F).

2. For sauce, in a large skillet melt butter over medium heat. Add mushrooms and green onions; cook about 5 minutes or until vegetables are tender. Stir in beef broth and Madeira. Bring to boiling. Remove from heat. Thinly slice steaks diagonally; serve with sauce.

Nutrition Facts per serving: 260 cal., 13 g total fat (5 g sat. fat), 88 mg chol., 160 mg sodium, 4 g carbo., 1 g fiber, 29 g pro.

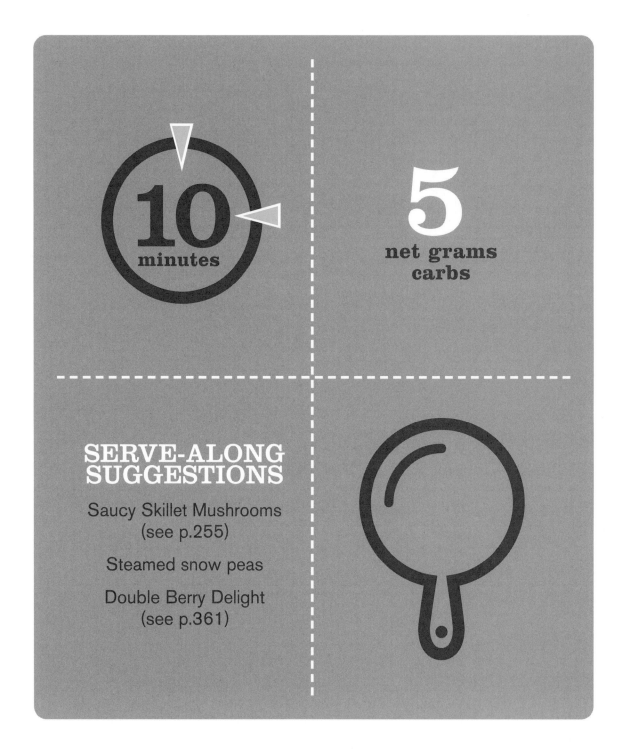

10 minutes

5 net grams carbs

SERVE-ALONG SUGGESTIONS

Saucy Skillet Mushrooms
(see p.255)

Steamed snow peas

Double Berry Delight
(see p.361)

HERBED TOP LOIN STEAK

WITH BALSAMIC SAUCE

2	boneless beef top loin steaks, cut ¾ inch thick (about 1 pound total)
1	tablespoon cracked black pepper
1½	teaspoons dried basil, crushed
1½	teaspoons dried oregano, crushed
1	teaspoon garlic powder
1	tablespoon olive oil
¼	cup balsamic vinegar
¼	cup beef broth
1	tablespoon butter or whipping cream
¼	cup snipped fresh parsley

PREP:
10 minutes
COOK:
14 minutes
MAKES:
4 servings

1. Trim fat from steaks. For rub, in a small bowl stir together pepper, basil, oregano, and garlic powder. Sprinkle pepper mixture evenly over both sides of each steak; rub in with your fingers.

2. In a large heavy skillet heat oil over medium-high heat. Add steaks; reduce heat to medium. Cook for 10 to 12 minutes for medium-rare (145°F) to medium (160°F) doneness, turning once. Remove steaks from skillet, reserving drippings in skillet. Cover steaks; keep warm.

3. For sauce, carefully add balsamic vinegar and beef broth to drippings in skillet, scraping up any browned bits from bottom of skillet. Bring to boiling; reduce heat. Boil gently, uncovered, about 4 minutes or until sauce is reduced by half. Remove from heat; stir in butter.

4. Thinly slice steaks diagonally. Spoon sauce onto 4 dinner plates. Top with steak slices and sprinkle with parsley.

Nutrition Facts per serving: 346 cal., 26 g total fat (10 g sat. fat), 84 mg chol., 134 mg sodium, 5 g carbo., 0 g fiber, 23 g pro.

10 minutes

0 net grams carbs

SERVE-ALONG SUGGESTIONS

Asparagus with Sorrel Dressing (see p.259)

Spiced Cantaloupe (see p.347)

Decaf iced tea

CHILI-RUBBED STEAKS

2	beef ribeye steaks, cut 1 inch thick (about 1½ pounds total)
1	tablespoon chili powder
1	tablespoon olive oil
1½	teaspoons dried oregano, crushed
½	teaspoon salt
½	teaspoon ground cumin

1. Trim fat from steaks. Place steaks in a single layer in a shallow dish. For rub, in a small bowl combine chili powder, oil, oregano, salt, and cumin. Sprinkle spice mixture evenly over both sides of each steak; rub in with your fingers. Cover and marinate in the refrigerator for at least 1 hour or up to 2 hours.

2. Place steaks on the rack of an uncovered grill directly over medium coals. Grill until desired doneness, turning once halfway through grilling. Allow 11 to 15 minutes for medium-rare doneness (145°F) or 14 to 18 minutes for medium doneness (160°F). Cut each steak in half.

Nutrition Facts per serving: 323 cal., 16 g total fat (5 g sat. fat), 92 mg chol., 376 mg sodium, 1 g carbo., 1 g fiber, 42 g pro.

PREP:
10 minutes
MARINATE:
1 to 2 hours
GRILL:
11 minutes
MAKES:
4 servings

10
minutes

4
net grams
carbs

SERVE-ALONG SUGGESTIONS

Warm Asparagus, Fennel,
and Spinach Salad
(see p.83)

Cottage cheese with
snipped fresh chives

Sugar-free strawberry-
flavored gelatin topped with
whipped cream, if desired

ROUND STEAK

WITH HERBS

2 pounds beef round steak, cut ¾ inch thick
1 medium onion, sliced
1 10¾-ounce can condensed cream of celery soup
½ teaspoon dried oregano, crushed
¼ teaspoon dried thyme, crushed
¼ teaspoon black pepper

1. Trim fat from steak. Cut steak into 6 serving-size pieces. Place onion in a 3½- or 4-quart slow cooker; place steak on top of onion. In a small bowl combine cream of celery soup, oregano, thyme, and pepper; pour over steak.

2. Cover and cook on low-heat setting for 10 to 12 hours or on high-heat setting for 5 to 6 hours.

Nutrition Facts per serving: 249 cal., 9 g total fat (3 g sat. fat), 78 mg chol., 475 mg sodium, 5 g carbo., 1 g fiber, 34 g pro.

PREP:
10 minutes
COOK:
10 to 12 hours (low-heat setting) or 5 to 6 hours (high-heat setting)
MAKES:
6 servings

15 minutes

3 net grams carbs

SERVE-ALONG SUGGESTIONS

Cheesy Spinach Quesadillas (see p.41)

Sautéed marinated artichoke hearts tossed with toasted pine nuts and chopped tomato

Warm Spiced Peaches (see p.357)

SWEET-PEPPER STEAK

4 boneless beef top loin steaks, cut 1 inch thick (about 3 pounds total)

2 teaspoons cracked black pepper

2 tablespoons butter or cooking oil

½ of a medium red sweet pepper, cut into thin strips

½ of a medium yellow sweet pepper, cut into thin strips

½ of a medium green sweet pepper, cut into thin strips

1 0.6-ounce envelope au jus gravy mix

PREP:
15 minutes
BROIL:
12 minutes
MAKES:
4 servings

1. Preheat broiler. Trim fat from steaks. Press cracked black pepper into one side of each steak.

2. Place steaks on the unheated rack of a broiler pan. Broil 3 to 4 inches from the heat until desired doneness, turning once halfway through broiling. Allow 12 to 14 minutes for medium-rare doneness (145°F) or 15 to 18 minutes for medium doneness (160°F). Remove from broiler. Cover steaks; keep warm.

3. In a medium skillet melt butter over medium heat. Add sweet peppers; cook until tender. Remove from heat. In a small saucepan prepare au jus gravy mix according to package directions.

4. Transfer steaks to 4 dinner plates. Top with sweet peppers and au jus gravy.

> **Grill Method:** Place steaks on the rack of an uncovered grill directly over medium coals. Grill until desired doneness, turning once halfway through grilling. Allow 11 to 15 minutes for medium-rare doneness (145°F) or 14 to 18 minutes for medium doneness (160°F).

Nutrition Facts per serving: 533 cal., 30 g total fat (13 g sat. fat), 160 mg chol., 910 mg sodium, 4 g carbo., 1 g fiber, 58 g pro.

15 minutes

3 net grams carbs

SERVE-ALONG SUGGESTIONS

Saucy Skillet Mushrooms (see p.255)

Steamed green peas

Mandarin oranges tossed with fresh berries

POT ROAST WITH DILL

1	2½- to 3-pound boneless beef chuck pot roast
1	tablespoon cooking oil
½	cup water
1	teaspoon dried dill
½	teaspoon coarse salt (kosher) or ¼ teaspoon regular salt
½	teaspoon black pepper
½	cup plain yogurt
2	tablespoons unbleached all-purpose flour

1. Trim fat from meat. If necessary, cut meat to fit into a 3½- or 4-quart slow cooker. In a large skillet heat oil over medium-high heat. Add meat; cook on all sides until brown. Transfer meat to slow cooker; add the water. Sprinkle meat with ¾ teaspoon of the dried dill, the salt, and pepper.

2. Cover and cook on low-heat setting for 10 to 12 hours or on high-heat setting for 5 to 6 hours. Transfer meat to a serving platter, reserving juices. Cover meat; keep warm.

3. For sauce, pour cooking juices into a glass measuring cup; skim off fat. Measure 1 cup juices. In a small saucepan stir together yogurt and flour. Stir in the 1 cup juices and remaining ¼ teaspoon dried dill. Cook and stir over medium heat until thickened and bubbly. Cook and stir for 1 minute more.

4. To serve, pour some of the sauce over meat; pass the remaining sauce.

Nutrition Facts per serving: 275 cal., 10 g total fat (3 g sat. fat), 113 mg chol., 302 mg sodium, 3 g carbo., 0 g fiber, 42 g pro.

PREP:
15 minutes
COOK:
10 to 12 hours (low-heat setting) or 5 to 6 hours (high-heat setting)
MAKES:
6 servings

15 minutes

1
net gram
carbs

SERVE-ALONG SUGGESTIONS

Italian-Style Chips
(see p.309)

Napa Cabbage Slaw
(see p.289)

Fresh pineapple

LIME-CILANTRO FLANK STEAK

1 1½-pound beef flank steak
2 limes
1 cup loosely packed fresh cilantro leaves
1½ teaspoons bottled minced garlic (3 cloves)
½ teaspoon salt
¼ to ½ teaspoon cayenne pepper

PREP:
15 minutes
MARINATE:
2 hours
GRILL:
17 minutes
MAKES:
6 servings

1. Trim fat from steak. Score both sides of steak in a diamond pattern by making shallow diagonal cuts at 1-inch intervals. Place steak in a resealable plastic bag set in a shallow dish. Finely shred enough lime peel to make 1 tablespoon. Cut limes in half; squeeze enough juice to make 3 tablespoons.

2. For marinade, in a blender container or food processor bowl combine the 1 tablespoon lime peel, the 3 tablespoons lime juice, cilantro, garlic, salt, and cayenne pepper. Cover and blend or process until nearly smooth. Pour over steak. Seal bag; turn to coat steak. Marinate in the refrigerator for 2 hours, turning bag occasionally.

3. Drain steak, discarding marinade. Place steak on the rack of an uncovered grill directly over medium coals. Grill for 17 to 21 minutes or until medium doneness (160°F), turning once halfway through grilling. Thinly slice steak diagonally across the grain.

Nutrition Facts per serving: 177 cal., 8 g total fat (3 g sat. fat), 56 mg chol., 271 mg sodium, 2 g carbo., 1 g fiber, 23 g pro.

15 minutes

2 net grams carbs

SERVE-ALONG SUGGESTIONS

Garlicky Mushrooms (see p.273)

Steamed snow peas

Fresh sliced strawberries topped with a little heavy cream and ground cinnamon, if desired

PEPPER-MARINATED FLANK STEAK

1	1- to 1½-pound beef flank steak
½	cup dry red wine
⅓	cup finely chopped onion
2	tablespoons lime juice
1	tablespoon cooking oil
1	tablespoon reduced-sodium soy sauce
1½	teaspoons bottled minced garlic (3 cloves)
1	teaspoon crushed red pepper
½	teaspoon coarsely ground black pepper
½	teaspoon dried whole green peppercorns, crushed
1	tablespoon snipped fresh parsley

PREP:
15 minutes
MARINATE:
6 to 24 hours
GRILL:
17 minutes
MAKES:
4 to 6 servings

1. Trim fat from steak. Score both sides of steak in a diamond pattern by making shallow diagonal cuts at 1-inch intervals. Place steak in a resealable plastic bag set in a shallow dish.

2. For marinade, in a small bowl stir together wine, onion, lime juice, oil, soy sauce, garlic, crushed red pepper, black pepper, and green peppercorns. Pour over steak. Seal bag; turn to coat steak. Marinate in the refrigerator for at least 6 hours or up to 24 hours, turning bag occasionally.

3. Drain steak, reserving marinade. Place steak on the rack of an uncovered grill directly over medium coals. Grill for 17 to 21 minutes or until medium doneness (160°F), turning and brushing once with reserved marinade halfway through grilling. Discard any remaining marinade.

4. Thinly slice steak diagonally across the grain. Sprinkle with parsley.

Nutrition Facts per serving: 199 cal., 10 g total fat (4 g sat. fat), 53 mg chol., 145 mg sodium, 2 g carbo., 0 g fiber, 22 g pro.

15 minutes

3 net grams carbs

SERVE-ALONG SUGGESTIONS

Portobello Pizzas (see p.35)

Strawberries with Orange Cream Dip (see p.333)

Low-calorie raspberry-flavored drink mix served with small skewers of orange wedges and fresh raspberries

GARLIC-STUDDED VEAL CHOPS AND ASPARAGUS

1 pound asparagus spears
2 tablespoons dry sherry
2 tablespoons olive oil
½ teaspoon bottled minced garlic (1 clove)
4 boneless veal top loin chops, cut ¾ inch thick
3 or 4 cloves garlic, peeled and cut into thin slivers
1 tablespoon snipped fresh thyme or 1 teaspoon dried thyme, crushed
⅛ teaspoon salt
⅛ teaspoon black pepper

PREP:
15 minutes
MARINATE:
30 minutes
GRILL:
9 minutes
MAKES:
4 servings

1. Snap off and discard woody bases from asparagus. In a medium skillet bring a small amount of water to boiling; add asparagus. Simmer, covered, about 3 minutes or until crisp-tender; drain. Place asparagus in a resealable plastic bag; add sherry, 1 tablespoon of the oil, and the minced garlic. Seal bag; turn to coat asparagus. Marinate at room temperature for 30 minutes.

2. Meanwhile, trim fat from chops. Using the tip of a sharp knife, make a few small slits in each chop; insert garlic slivers in slits. In a small bowl combine the remaining 1 tablespoon oil, the thyme, salt, and pepper; brush over both sides of each chop.

3. Place chops on the rack of an uncovered grill directly over medium coals. Grill for 9 to 11 minutes or until medium doneness (160°F), turning once halfway through grilling. For the last 3 to 4 minutes of grilling, place asparagus on grill rack next to chops (lay spears perpendicular to wires on grill rack so they won't fall into coals). Grill until crisp-tender and lightly browned, turning occasionally. Serve asparagus with chops.

Nutrition Facts per serving: 237 cal., 11 g total fat (3 g sat. fat), 92 mg chol., 131 mg sodium, 5 g carbo., 2 g fiber, 27 g pro.

10 minutes

3 net grams carbs

SERVE-ALONG SUGGESTIONS

Peppers Stuffed with Goat Cheese (see p.263)

Wedges of fresh watermelon

Tiramisu Cream (see p.359)

GRILLED VEAL CHOPS WITH PESTO MUSHROOMS

4 veal loin chops with bone, cut ¾ inch thick
¼ cup dry white wine
1 tablespoon snipped fresh sage or thyme
1 tablespoon white wine Worcestershire sauce
1 tablespoon olive oil
1½ to 2 teaspoons bottled minced garlic (3 to 4 cloves)
8 large fresh mushrooms (each 2 to 2½ inches in diameter)
2 to 3 tablespoons purchased pesto

PREP:
10 minutes
MARINATE:
6 to 24 hours
GRILL:
9 minutes
MAKES:
4 servings

1. Trim fat from chops. Place chops in a resealable plastic bag set in a shallow dish. For marinade, in a small bowl combine wine, sage, Worcestershire sauce, oil, and garlic. Pour over chops. Seal bag; turn to coat chops. Marinate in the refrigerator for at least 6 hours or up to 24 hours, turning bag occasionally.

2. Drain chops, reserving marinade. Sprinkle chops with freshly ground black pepper. Place chops on the rack of an uncovered grill directly over medium coals. Grill for 9 to 11 minutes or until medium doneness (160°F), turning and brushing once with reserved marinade halfway through grilling.

3. Meanwhile, cut off mushroom stems even with caps; discard stems. Lightly rinse mushroom caps; gently pat dry with paper towels. Brush mushrooms with reserved marinade.

4. Place mushrooms, stemmed sides down, on grill rack next to chops. Grill for 4 minutes. Turn mushrooms, stemmed sides up; spoon pesto into mushroom caps. Grill about 4 minutes more or until heated through. Serve mushrooms with chops.

Nutrition Facts per serving: 285 cal., 16 g total fat (2 g sat. fat), 100 mg chol., 157 mg sodium, 4 g carbo., 1 g fiber, 28 g pro.

VEAL

WITH APPLE-MARSALA SAUCE

PREP:
10 minutes

COOK:
12 minutes

MAKES:
4 servings

6
net grams carbs

Nonstick cooking spray

12	ounces veal scaloppine, boneless veal round steak, or boneless beef top round steak,* cut ¼ inch thick
1	apple, thinly sliced
½	teaspoon bottled minced garlic (1 clove)
½	cup dry Marsala
⅓	cup reduced-sodium chicken broth
1	tablespoon snipped fresh parsley

1. Coat a large skillet with cooking spray; heat skillet over medium-high heat. Add meat, half at a time; cook for 4 to 5 minutes or until no longer pink, turning once. Transfer to a serving platter. Cover meat; keep warm.

2. Add apple and garlic to skillet. Stir in Marsala and chicken broth. Bring to boiling; reduce heat. Boil gently, uncovered, for 4 to 5 minutes or until mixture is reduced by half. Spoon over meat. Sprinkle with parsley.

*Note: If using veal or beef round steak, trim fat from steak. Cut steak into 8 pieces. Place each piece between 2 pieces of plastic wrap. Working from center to edges, pound with the flat side of a meat mallet to an even ⅛-inch thickness. Remove plastic wrap.

Nutrition Facts per serving: 167 cal., 4 g total fat (1 g sat. fat), 69 mg chol., 100 mg sodium, 7 g carbo., 1 g fiber, 19 g pro.

SERVE-ALONG SUGGESTIONS

Broiled Asparagus and Fresh Mozzarella (see p.283)

Sautéed sweet onion slices

Fruit-Topped Phyllo Cups (see p.345)

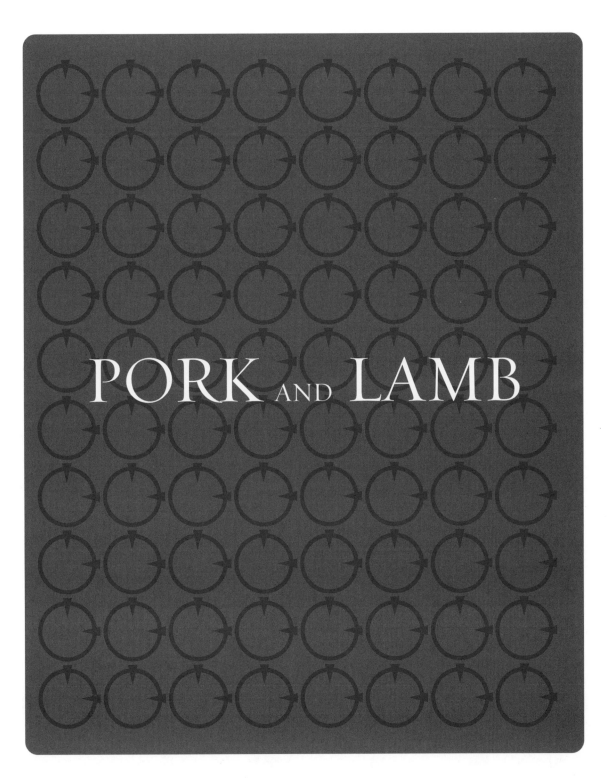

PORK AND LAMB

15 minutes

3 net grams carbs

SERVE-ALONG SUGGESTIONS

Steamed sugar snap peas

Whole milk vanilla-flavored yogurt topped with mixed nuts

Skewered fresh strawberries, sliced kiwi fruit and pineapple chunks

GRILLED PORK CHOPS

WITH MUSHROOM STUFFING

2	teaspoons olive oil
2	tablespoons thinly sliced green onion
1	8-ounce package fresh mushrooms, coarsely chopped
2	teaspoons snipped fresh rosemary or oregano
1/8	teaspoon salt
1/8	teaspoon black pepper
4	boneless pork loin chops, cut 3/4 to 1 inch thick
2	teaspoons Worcestershire sauce

PREP:
15 minutes
COOK:
3 minutes
GRILL:
12 minutes
MAKES:
4 servings

1. For stuffing, in a large skillet heat oil over medium heat. Add green onion; cook for 1 minute. Stir in mushrooms, rosemary, salt, and pepper. Cook and stir for 2 to 3 minutes more or until mushrooms are tender. Remove from heat.

2. Trim fat from chops. To cut a pocket in each chop, use a sharp knife to make a 3-inch-long slit in the fatty side. Work the knife inside, cutting almost to the other side. Divide stuffing among pockets in chops. If necessary, secure openings with toothpicks.

3. Brush chops with Worcestershire sauce. Lightly sprinkle chops with additional salt and black pepper. Place chops on the rack of an uncovered grill directly over medium coals. Grill for 12 to 15 minutes or until chops are slightly pink in center and juices run clear (160°F), turning once halfway through grilling. Remove toothpicks from chops.

Nutrition Facts per serving: 241 cal., 14 g total fat (4 g sat. fat), 77 mg chol., 218 mg sodium, 4 g carbo., 1 g fiber, 25 g pro.

10 minutes

2
net grams carbs

SERVE-ALONG SUGGESTIONS

Spanish Olive Spread
(see p.305)

Cooked green beans

No-sugar-added ice cream
topped with fresh
raspberries and chopped
toasted almonds, if desired

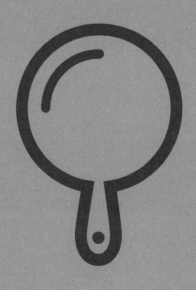

PEPPERED PORK

WITH CHIVE SAUCE

4 boneless pork loin chops, cut ¾ inch thick
1 teaspoon coarsely ground tri-colored peppercorns or coarsely ground black pepper
2 teaspoons cooking oil
¼ cup water
3 tablespoons dry sherry or chicken broth
1 3-ounce package cream cheese with chives, cut up

PREP:
10 minutes
COOK:
15 minutes
MAKES:
4 servings

1. Trim fat from chops. Sprinkle pepper evenly over both sides of each chop; rub in with your fingers. In a large skillet heat oil over medium-high heat. Add chops; reduce heat to medium. Cook for 8 to 12 minutes or until chops are slightly pink in center and juices run clear (160°F), turning once. Remove from skillet. Cover chops; keep warm.

2. For sauce, carefully add the water and sherry to skillet. Cook and stir until bubbly. Add cream cheese. Using a wire whisk, heat and whisk over medium heat until cream cheese is melted. Serve sauce over chops.

Nutrition Facts per serving: 291 cal., 20 g total fat (8 g sat. fat), 92 mg chol., 117 mg sodium, 2 g carbo., 0 g fiber, 23 g pro.

15 minutes

5 net grams carbs

SERVE-ALONG SUGGESTIONS

Mesclun with Oranges and Olives (see p.84)

Cooked spaghetti squash

Fresh assorted melon

INDIAN PORK PATTIES

⅓ cup plain low-fat yogurt
¼ cup chopped seeded cucumber
¼ cup finely chopped onion
1 medium fresh jalapeño chile pepper, seeded and chopped,* or 2 tablespoons canned diced green chile peppers
1 tablespoon snipped fresh mint or 1 teaspoon dried mint, crushed
½ teaspoon ground cumin
½ teaspoon bottled minced garlic (1 clove) or ⅛ teaspoon garlic powder
½ teaspoon salt
8 ounces lean ground pork, beef, or lamb

PREP:
15 minutes
GRILL:
14 minutes
MAKES:
2 servings

1. For sauce, in a small bowl stir together yogurt and cucumber. Cover and chill until ready to serve.

2. In a medium bowl combine onion, jalapeño pepper, mint, cumin, garlic, and salt. Add ground meat; mix well. Shape meat mixture into two ¾-inch-thick patties.

3. Place patties on the rack of an uncovered grill directly over medium coals. Grill for 14 to 18 minutes or until done (160°F),** turning once halfway through grilling. Serve sauce over meat patties.

> ***Note:** Because chile peppers contain volatile oils that can burn your skin and eyes, avoid direct contact with them as much as possible. When working with chile peppers, wear plastic or rubber gloves. If your bare hands do touch the peppers, wash your hands and nails well with soap and warm water.

> ****Note:** The internal color of a burger is not a reliable doneness indicator. A pork, beef, or lamb patty cooked to 160°F is safe, regardless of color. To measure the doneness of a patty, insert an instant-read thermometer through the side of the patty to a depth of 2 to 3 inches.

Nutrition Facts per serving: 264 cal., 16 g total fat (6 g sat. fat), 78 mg chol., 384 mg sodium, 6 g carbo., 1 g fiber, 22 g pro.

15 minutes

3
net grams carbs

SERVE-ALONG SUGGESTIONS

Blue Cheese-Walnut Dip
(see p.325)

Steamed snow peas

Raspberry and Chocolate
Tulips (see p.343)

PORK AU POIVRE

WITH MUSTARD AND SAGE

4	boneless pork loin butterfly chops
1	to 2 teaspoons whole black peppercorns
1	to 2 teaspoons whole pink peppercorns
1	to 2 teaspoons whole white peppercorns
⅔	cup whipping cream
3	tablespoons dry white wine
2	tablespoons snipped fresh sage
2	tablespoons Dijon-style mustard
1	tablespoon whole green peppercorns in brine, rinsed and drained

PREP:
15 minutes
COOK:
12 minutes
MAKES:
4 servings

1. Trim fat from chops. Coarsely crack black, pink, and white peppercorns;* stir together. Press peppercorn mixture onto one side of each chop.

2. In a 12-inch skillet cook chops, peppered sides down, over medium-high heat for 5 minutes. Turn chops; cook for 5 to 7 minutes more or until chops are slightly pink in center and juices run clear (160°F). (If chops brown too quickly, reduce heat to medium.) Transfer chops to a serving platter. Cover chops; keep warm. Discard any burnt peppercorns from bottom of skillet.

3. For sauce, add cream, wine, sage, mustard, and green peppercorns to skillet. Bring to boiling; reduce heat. Simmer, uncovered, about 2 minutes or until reduced to about ½ cup. Serve sauce over chops.

*Note: The best way to crack peppercorns is with a rolling pin. Place them in a small plastic bag, squeeze out all the air, and seal it. Roll the pin over the peppercorns while pressing down firmly until they're coarsely cracked.

Nutrition Facts per serving: 416 cal., 25 g total fat (13 g sat. fat), 148 mg chol., 128 mg sodium, 4 g carbo., 1 g fiber, 39 g pro.

15
minutes

8
net grams
carbs

SERVE-ALONG SUGGESTIONS

Corn and Chicken Soup
(see p.59)

Broiled Asparagus and
Fresh Mozzarella
(see p.283)

Orange-Ginger Rhubarb
(see p.353)

CUMBERLAND PORK MEDALLIONS

1   pound pork tenderloin
1   tablespoon cooking oil or olive oil
¼   cup sliced green onions
½   cup dry red wine, dry white wine, or apple juice
½   cup chicken broth
2   tablespoons currant jelly
1   teaspoon Dijon-style mustard
1   tablespoon chicken broth or water

PREP:
15 minutes
COOK:
15 minutes
MAKES:
4 servings

1. Trim fat from meat. Cut meat crosswise into ¾-inch slices. In a large skillet heat oil over medium-high heat. Add meat; reduce heat to medium. Cook for 6 to 8 minutes or until meat is slightly pink in center and juices run clear (160°F), turning once. Remove from skillet. Cover meat; keep warm.

2. For sauce, add green onions to skillet; cook just until tender. Add wine and the ½ cup chicken broth. Bring to boiling; reduce heat. Boil gently, uncovered, about 4 minutes or until reduced to about ½ cup. Add jelly and mustard, stirring until jelly is melted.

3. Stir the 1 tablespoon chicken broth into wine mixture. Cook and stir over medium heat until heated through. Serve sauce over meat.

Nutrition Facts per serving: 221 cal., 7 g total fat (2 g sat. fat), 73 mg chol., 221 mg sodium, 8 g carbo., 0 g fiber, 24 g pro.

15 minutes

1
net gram
carbs

SERVE-ALONG SUGGESTIONS

Sautéed fresh spinach leaves topped with toasted pine nuts

Go-With-Anything Tomato Sauté (see p.287)

Almond Cream with Berries (see p.351)

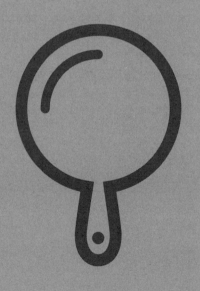

PORK DIANE

1 tablespoon water
1 tablespoon white wine Worcestershire sauce
1 teaspoon lemon juice
1 teaspoon Dijon-style mustard
1 pound boneless pork top loin roast (single loin)
1 teaspoon lemon-pepper seasoning
2 tablespoons butter or margarine
1 tablespoon snipped fresh chives or parsley

PREP:
15 minutes
COOK:
6 minutes
MAKES:
4 servings

1. For sauce, in a small bowl stir together the water, Worcestershire sauce, lemon juice, and mustard. Set aside.

2. Trim fat from meat. Cut meat crosswise into ¾- to 1-inch slices. Sprinkle lemon-pepper seasoning evenly over both sides of each meat slice. In a large skillet melt butter over medium-high heat. Add meat; reduce heat to medium. Cook for 6 to 10 minutes or until meat is slightly pink in center and juices run clear (160°F), turning once. Remove from heat. Remove meat from skillet. Cover meat; keep warm.

3. Add sauce to skillet; stir until combined. Serve sauce over meat. Sprinkle with chives.

Nutrition Facts per serving: 192 cal., 13 g total fat (6 g sat. fat), 66 mg chol., 441 mg sodium, 1 g carbo., 0 g fiber, 16 g pro.

15
minutes

2
net grams
carbs

SERVE-ALONG SUGGESTIONS

Toasted Almonds with Rosemary (see p.323)

Broiled Eggplant with Cheese (see p.257)

Strawberries with Orange Cream Dip (see p.333)

SHERRIED PORK

12	ounces pork tenderloin
1	beaten egg
1	tablespoon water
1¾	cups pork rinds (about 1¼ ounces), finely crushed
⅛	teaspoon garlic powder
2	tablespoons butter or margarine
¼	cup water
¼	cup dry sherry, dry Marsala, or water
½	teaspoon instant chicken bouillon granules
	Dash ground black pepper
1	tablespoon snipped fresh parsley

PREP:
15 minutes
COOK:
15 minutes
MAKES:
4 servings

1. Trim fat from meat. Cut meat crosswise into 4 slices. Place each slice, cut side up, between 2 pieces of plastic wrap. Using the flat side of a meat mallet, pound meat lightly to an even ½-inch thickness. Remove plastic wrap.

2. In a shallow dish combine egg and the 1 tablespoon water. In another shallow dish combine pork rinds and garlic powder. Dip each meat slice into egg mixture; dip into crumb mixture to coat.

3. In a large skillet melt butter over medium-high heat. Add meat; cook for 6 to 7 minutes or until meat is slightly pink in center and juices run clear (160°F), turning once. (If meat browns too quickly, reduce heat to medium.) Remove skillet from heat. Transfer meat to a serving platter, reserving drippings in skillet. Cover meat; keep warm.

4. For sauce, stir the ¼ cup water, sherry, bouillon granules, and pepper into reserved drippings in skillet, scraping up any browned bits from bottom of skillet. Return to heat. Bring to boiling. Boil, uncovered, for 1 to 2 minutes or until reduced to about ¼ cup. Pour sauce over meat. Sprinkle with parsley.

Nutrition Facts per serving: 234 cal., 12 g total fat (6 g sat. fat), 128 mg chol., 384 mg sodium, 2 g carbo., 0 g fiber, 24 g pro.

15 minutes

6 net grams carbs

SERVE-ALONG SUGGESTIONS

Cheesy Spinach Quesadillas (see p.41)

Dancing Mushrooms (see p.261)

Whole milk lemon- or vanilla-flavored yogurt sprinkled with finely shredded lemon peel and fresh blackberries

BROILED CHOPS

WITH ITALIAN VEGETABLES

1	tablespoon dry white wine
½	teaspoon bottled minced garlic (1 clove)
⅛	teaspoon black pepper
4	pork loin chops with bone, cut ½ inch thick
	Nonstick cooking spray
2	medium zucchini and/or yellow summer squash, cut into thin bite-size strips
1	small green or red sweet pepper, cut into strips
1	small onion, sliced
¾	teaspoon dried basil, crushed
½	teaspoon dried oregano, crushed
⅛	teaspoon salt
8	cherry tomatoes, halved

PREP:
15 minutes
BROIL:
9 minutes
MAKES:
4 servings

1. Preheat broiler. In a small bowl combine wine, garlic, and black pepper. Set aside.

2. Trim fat from chops. Place chops on the unheated rack of a broiler pan. Broil 3 to 4 inches from the heat for 5 minutes. Brush with wine mixture; turn chops. Broil about 4 to 5 minutes more or until chops are slightly pink in center and juices run clear (160°F). Brush with remaining wine mixture.

3. Meanwhile, coat a large skillet with cooking spray; heat skillet over medium-high heat. Add zucchini, sweet pepper, onion, basil, oregano, and salt. Cook and stir about 4 minutes or until vegetables are crisp-tender. Stir in tomatoes; reduce heat. Cover and cook for 1 minute more. Serve chops with vegetable mixture.

Nutrition Facts per serving: 201 cal., 8 g total fat (3 g sat. fat), 71 mg chol., 138 mg sodium, 8 g carbo., 2 g fiber, 24 g pro.

12 minutes

2 net grams carbs

SERVE-ALONG SUGGESTIONS

Sautéed sweet onion slices with butter and fresh ground pepper

Mixed greens tossed with snipped fresh chives, shredded cheese and toasted soy nuts

Sugar-free instant banana pudding

PECAN-GLAZED PORK CHOPS

4 boneless pork loin chops, cut ¾ inch thick
Salt
Black pepper
¼ cup butter, softened
2 tablespoons controlled-carb sugar-free maple-flavored syrup
⅓ cup chopped pecans, toasted

PREP:
12 minutes
COOK:
8 minutes
MAKES:
4 servings

1. Trim fat from chops. Lightly sprinkle salt and pepper over both sides of each chop. In a 12-inch skillet melt 1 tablespoon of the butter over medium-high heat. Add chops; reduce heat to medium. Cook for 8 to 12 minutes or until chops are slightly pink in center and juices run clear (160°F), turning once. Transfer chops to a serving platter. Cover chops; keep warm.

2. In a small bowl combine the remaining 3 tablespoons butter and the maple syrup. Spread maple mixture evenly over chops. Let stand about 1 minute or until maple mixture is melted. Sprinkle with pecans.

Nutrition Facts per serving: 382 cal., 27 g total fat (11 g sat. fat), 110 mg chol., 194 mg sodium, 3 g carbo., 1 g fiber, 32 g pro.

15 minutes

2
net grams
carbs

SERVE-ALONG SUGGESTIONS

Chilled Avocado Soup
(see p.69)

Down-South Green Beans
(see p.253)

Low-calorie lemon-lime-flavored drink mix served with small skewers of fresh pineapple chunks and strawberries

PINEAPPLE-GLAZED PORK

½ of a 6-ounce can (⅓ cup) frozen pineapple juice concentrate
1 tablespoon Dijon-style mustard
1 teaspoon snipped fresh rosemary or ¼ teaspoon dried
   rosemary, crushed
½ teaspoon bottled minced garlic (1 clove)
2 12-ounce pork tenderloins

1. For sauce, in a small saucepan combine juice concentrate, mustard, rosemary, and garlic. Cook over medium heat about 5 minutes or until slightly thickened, stirring once. Remove from heat.

2. Trim fat from meat. In a grill with a cover, arrange hot coals around a drip pan. Test for medium-hot heat above the pan. Place meat on the grill rack over drip pan. Brush with sauce. Cover and grill for 30 to 35 minutes or until meat is slightly pink in center and juices run clear (155°F), brushing once with sauce the last 10 minutes of grilling.

3. Transfer meat to a serving platter. Cover with foil; let stand for 10 minutes before slicing. Temperature of the meat after standing should be 160°F.

Nutrition Facts per serving: 154 cal., 4 g total fat (1 g sat. fat), 81 mg chol., 121 mg sodium, 2 g carbo., 0 g fiber, 25 g pro.

PREP:
15 minutes
GRILL:
30 minutes
STAND:
10 minutes
MAKES:
6 servings

15 minutes

2
net grams
carbs

SERVE-ALONG SUGGESTIONS

Roasted Asparagus
Parmesan (see p.267)

Spiced Cantaloupe
(see p.347)

Flavored decaf coffee,
served over ice, if desired

PORK

WITH APPLE BRANDY AND CREAM

1   12-ounce pork tenderloin
2   tablespoons butter
½   cup whipping cream
½   of a 4½-ounce jar (drained weight) whole mushrooms, drained
2   tablespoons Calvados, brandy, or apple juice

PREP:
15 minutes
COOK:
15 minutes
MAKES:
4 servings

1. Trim fat from meat. Cut meat crosswise into 1-inch slices. Place each slice between 2 pieces of plastic wrap. Press with the palm of your hand to an even ½-inch thickness. Remove plastic wrap.

2. In a large skillet melt butter over medium-high heat. Add meat, half at a time; cook for 5 to 6 minutes or until meat is slightly pink in center and juices run clear (160°F), turning once. (If meat browns too quickly, reduce heat to medium.) Transfer meat to a serving platter. Cover meat; keep warm.

3. For sauce, add cream, mushrooms, and Calvados to skillet, scraping up any browned bits from bottom of skillet. Bring to boiling; reduce heat. Simmer, uncovered, for 3 to 5 minutes or until slightly thickened. Serve sauce over meat.

Nutrition Facts per serving: 279 cal., 20 g total fat (12 g sat. fat), 112 mg chol., 183 mg sodium, 2 g carbo., 0 g fiber, 19 g pro.

10 minutes

1
net gram
carbs

SERVE-ALONG SUGGESTIONS

Asian-Spiced Pecans
(see p.53)

Warm Asparagus, Fennel,
and Spinach Salad
(see p.83)

Almond-Sauced Berries
(see p.349)

SOY AND SESAME PORK

1   1-pound pork tenderloin
¼   cup reduced-sodium soy sauce
1   tablespoon low-carb catsup
¼   teaspoon garlic powder
2   to 3 tablespoons sesame seeds, toasted

PREP:
10 minutes
MARINATE:
4 to 24 hours
ROAST:
25 minutes
OVEN:
425°F
MAKES:
4 servings

1. Trim fat from meat. Place meat in a resealable plastic bag set in a shallow dish. For marinade, in a small bowl combine soy sauce, catsup, and garlic powder. Pour over meat. Seal bag; turn to coat meat. Marinate in the refrigerator for at least 4 hours or up to 24 hours, turning bag occasionally.

2. Drain meat, discarding marinade. Place meat on a rack in a shallow roasting pan. Roast in a 425° oven for 25 to 35 minutes or until meat is slightly pink in center and juices run clear (160°F). Sprinkle sesame seeds on a piece of foil; carefully roll meat in sesame seeds to coat.

Nutrition Facts per serving: 162 cal., 6 g total fat (2 g sat. fat), 73 mg chol., 355 mg sodium, 1 g carbo., 0 g fiber, 25 g pro.

10 minutes

2
net grams carbs

SERVE-ALONG SUGGESTIONS

Feta-Stuffed Mushrooms (see p.319)

Fresh spinach leaves tossed with cherry tomato halves and bottled low-carb Italian salad dressing

Warm Spiced Peaches (see p.357)

PEPPERY PORK CHOPS

4	pork loin chops with bone, cut ¾ inch thick
2	teaspoons paprika
1	teaspoon garlic salt
½	teaspoon black pepper
½	cup dairy sour cream

1. Preheat broiler. Trim fat from chops. For rub, in a small bowl stir together paprika, garlic salt, and pepper. Sprinkle paprika mixture evenly over both sides of each chop; rub in with your fingers.

2. Place chops on the unheated rack of a broiler pan. Broil 3 to 4 inches from the heat for 9 to 12 minutes or until chops are slightly pink in center and juices run clear (160°F), turning once halfway through broiling. Serve chops with sour cream.

Nutrition Facts per serving: 246 cal., 12 g total fat (5 g sat. fat), 87 mg chol., 310 mg sodium, 2 g carbo., 0 g fiber, 31 g pro.

PREP:
10 minutes
BROIL:
9 minutes
MAKES:
4 servings

10 minutes

5
net grams
carbs

SERVE-ALONG SUGGESTIONS

Curried Apple Spread
(see p. 330)

Green leaf lettuce tossed
with sliced celery, sliced
mushrooms, and bottled
low-carb ranch salad
dressing

Macadamia-White
Chocolate Dessert
(see p.363)

COUNTRY CHOPS AND PEPPERS

4 pork loin chops with bone, cut ¾ inch thick
Seasoned salt
Black pepper
Nonstick cooking spray
1 medium sweet pepper, cut into strips
1 tablespoon butter or margarine
⅓ cup white wine Worcestershire sauce or 2 tablespoons Worcestershire sauce plus ¼ cup water

1. Trim fat from chops. Lightly sprinkle seasoned salt and black pepper over both sides of each chop; rub in with your fingers.

2. Coat a large skillet with cooking spray; heat skillet over medium-high heat. Add chops; reduce heat to medium. Cook for 4 minutes. Turn chops; add sweet pepper. Cover and cook for 4 to 6 minutes more or until chops are slightly pink in center and juices run clear (160°F). Remove from skillet. Cover chops and sweet pepper; keep warm.

3. For sauce, add butter to skillet. Cook over medium heat until butter is melted, scraping up any browned bits from bottom of skillet. Add Worcestershire sauce. Cook and stir until slightly thickened.

4. Place chops on 4 dinner plates; top with sweet pepper. Serve sauce over chops and sweet pepper.

Nutrition Facts per serving: 282 cal., 11 g total fat (5 g sat. fat), 101 mg chol., 282 mg sodium, 6 g carbo., 1 g fiber, 38 g pro.

PREP:
10 minutes
COOK:
13 minutes
MAKES:
4 servings

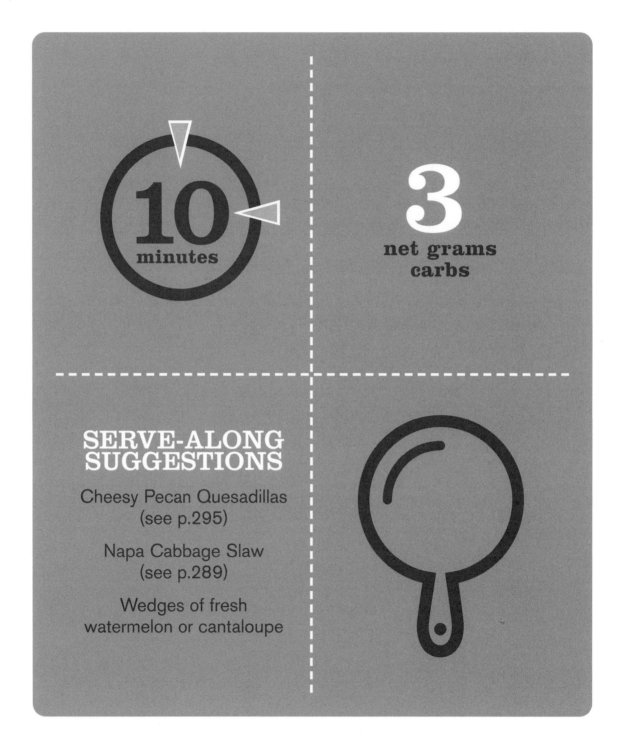

10 minutes

3 net grams carbs

SERVE-ALONG SUGGESTIONS

Cheesy Pecan Quesadillas
(see p.295)

Napa Cabbage Slaw
(see p.289)

Wedges of fresh
watermelon or cantaloupe

PORK CHOPS DIJON

3 tablespoons Dijon-style mustard
2 tablespoons bottled reduced-calorie Italian salad dressing
¼ teaspoon black pepper
4 pork loin chops with bone, cut ½ inch thick
  Nonstick cooking spray
1 medium onion, halved lengthwise and sliced

PREP:
10 minutes
COOK:
25 minutes
MAKES:
4 servings

1. In a small bowl combine mustard, Italian dressing, and pepper; set aside. Trim fat from chops. Coat a large skillet with cooking spray; heat skillet over medium-high heat. Add chops; cook on both sides until brown. Remove chops from skillet.

2. Add onion to skillet. Cook and stir over medium heat for 3 minutes. Push onion aside; return chops to skillet. Spread mustard mixture over chops. Cover and cook over medium-low heat about 15 minutes or until chops are slightly pink in center and juices run clear (160°F). Serve onion over chops.

Nutrition Facts per serving: 153 cal., 5 g total fat (2 g sat. fat), 58 mg chol., 218 mg sodium, 4 g carbo., 1 g fiber, 21 g pro.

10 minutes

0
net grams carbs

SERVE-ALONG SUGGESTIONS

Pear-Chutney Salsa to serve with the chops (see p.383)

Cooked green beans with crisp-cooked bacon or diced cooked ham and butter

Chocolate Mousse (see p.397)

THYME PORK CHOPS

6   pork loin center-cut chops with bone, cut 1½ inches thick
     Salt
     Black pepper
2   tablespoons olive oil
1   tablespoon snipped fresh thyme or ½ teaspoon dried thyme, crushed

1. Trim fat from chops. Lightly sprinkle salt and black pepper over both sides of each chop. In a small bowl stir together oil and thyme; brush over all sides of each chop.

2. Place chops on a rack in a shallow roasting pan. Roast in a 350° oven for 45 to 50 minutes or until chops are slightly pink in center and juices run clear (160°F).

Nutrition Facts per serving: 391 cal., 19 g total fat (6 g sat. fat), 129 mg chol., 108 mg sodium, 0 g carbo., 0 g fiber, 51 g pro.

PREP:
10 minutes
ROAST:
45 minutes
OVEN:
350°F
MAKES:
6 servings

10
minutes

4
net grams
carbs

SERVE-ALONG SUGGESTIONS

Portobello Pizzas
(see p.35)

Zucchini alla Romana
(see p.281)

Sliced mango
and/or papaya

ORANGE-MUSTARD LAMB CHOPS

8 lamb loin or rib chops with bone, cut 1 inch thick
3 tablespoons sugar-free orange marmalade
4 teaspoons Dijon-style mustard

1. Preheat broiler. Trim fat from chops. Place chops on the unheated rack of a broiler pan. Broil 3 to 4 inches from the heat for 10 to 15 minutes for medium doneness (160°F), turning once halfway through broiling.

2. Meanwhile, in a small saucepan stir together marmalade and mustard. Cook and stir over medium heat until heated through. Spoon over chops.

Nutrition Facts per serving: 140 cal., 5 g total fat (2 g sat. fat), 60 mg chol., 168 mg sodium, 4 g carbo., 0 g fiber, 19 g pro.

PREP:
10 minutes
BROIL:
10 minutes
MAKES:
4 servings

MINTED LAMB CHOPS

PREP:

15 minutes

MARINATE:

4 to 24 hours

GRILL:

12 minutes

MAKES:

4 servings

1
net gram carbs

SERVE-ALONG SUGGESTIONS

Asparagus with Sorrel Dressing (see p.259)

Almond-Sauced Berries (see p.349)

Iced herbal tea served with lemon and/or orange wedges

8	lamb rib chops with bone, cut 1 inch thick
¼	cup snipped fresh mint
¼	cup lemon juice
2	tablespoons cooking oil
2	tablespoons water
1	tablespoon grated fresh ginger
1½	teaspoons paprika
1	teaspoon ground cumin
½	to 1 teaspoon bottled minced garlic (1 to 2 cloves)
½	teaspoon salt
⅛	teaspoon cayenne pepper
1	to 2 tablespoons finely shredded fresh mint

1. Trim fat from chops. Place chops in a resealable plastic bag set in a shallow dish. For marinade, in a small bowl combine the snipped mint, lemon juice, oil, the water, ginger, paprika, cumin, garlic, salt, and cayenne pepper. Pour over chops. Seal bag; turn to coat chops. Marinate in the refrigerator for at least 4 hours or up to 24 hours, turning bag occasionally.

2. Drain chops, discarding marinade. Place chops on the rack of an uncovered grill directly over medium coals. Grill until desired doneness, turning once halfway through grilling. Allow 12 to 14 minutes for medium-rare doneness (145°F) or 15 to 17 minutes for medium doneness (160°F).

3. Transfer chops to a serving platter. Sprinkle with the shredded mint.

Broiler Method: Place chops on the unheated rack of a broiler pan. Broil 3 to 4 inches from the heat until desired doneness, turning once halfway through broiling. Allow 7 to 9 minutes for medium-rare doneness (145°F) or 10 to 15 minutes for medium doneness (160°F).

Nutrition Facts per serving: 236 cal., 14 g total fat (4 g sat. fat), 80 mg chol., 234 mg sodium, 1 g carbo., 0 g fiber, 25 g pro.

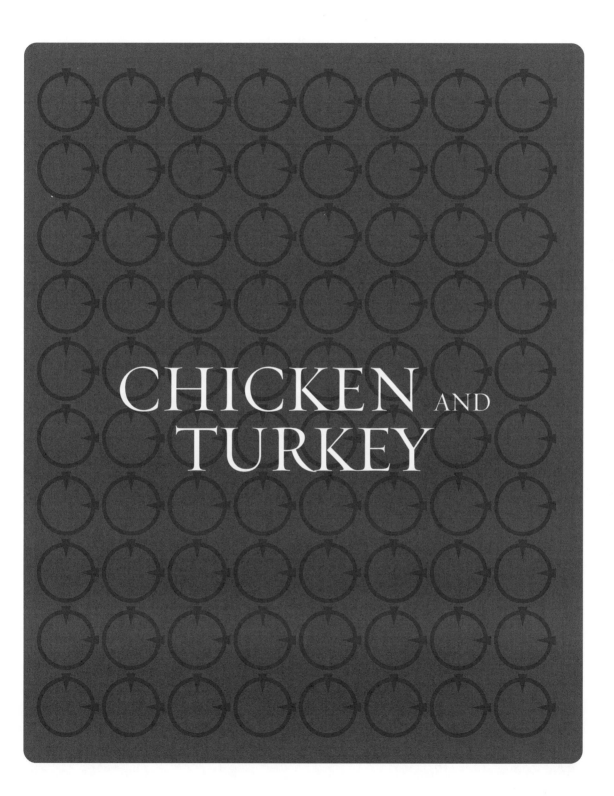

CHICKEN AND TURKEY

10 minutes

4 net grams carbs

SERVE-ALONG SUGGESTIONS

Mixed greens with shaved Parmesan cheese, toasted pine nuts, and bottled low-carb raspberry vinaigrette salad dressing

Lemon-Marinated Veggies (see p.277)

Wedges of fresh pineapple

PAPAYA-GLAZED CHICKEN

2½ to 3 pounds meaty chicken pieces (breast halves, thighs, and drumsticks)
½ teaspoon seasoned salt
1 cup chopped peeled papaya
1 tablespoon frozen orange juice concentrate
1 tablespoon water
½ to 1 teaspoon curry powder

PREP:
10 minutes
BAKE:
35 minutes
OVEN:
425°F
MAKES:
6 servings

1. If desired, remove skin from chicken. Place chicken in a 3-quart rectangular baking dish. Sprinkle with seasoned salt. Bake in a 425° oven for 20 minutes.

2. Meanwhile, in a blender container or food processor bowl combine papaya, juice concentrate, the water, and curry powder. Cover and blend or process until smooth.

3. Remove chicken from oven. Generously brush papaya mixture over chicken. Bake for 15 to 20 minutes more or until chicken is tender and no longer pink (170°F for breasts; 180°F for thighs and drumsticks), brushing occasionally with papaya mixture.

Nutrition Facts per serving: 228 cal., 11 g total fat (3 g sat. fat), 86 mg chol., 204 mg sodium, 4 g carbo., 0 g fiber, 28 g pro.

10 minutes

4 net grams carbs

SERVE-ALONG SUGGESTIONS

Thinly sliced cucumber and sweet onion tossed with coarse salt and white wine vinegar

Down-South Green Beans (see p.253)

Sugar-free instant chocolate fudge pudding topped with whipped cream, if desired

MUSTARD BAKED CHICKEN

2½ to 3 pounds meaty chicken pieces (breast halves, thighs, and drumsticks)
⅓ cup brown mustard
1 tablespoon cooking oil
1 tablespoon soy sauce
2 teaspoons heat-stable granular sugar substitute

1. If desired, remove skin from chicken. Place chicken in a greased 3-quart rectangular baking dish. Bake in a 425° oven for 15 minutes.

2. Meanwhile, in a small bowl stir together mustard, oil, soy sauce, and sugar substitute.

3. Remove chicken from oven. Generously brush mustard mixture over chicken. Bake for 20 to 25 minutes more or until chicken is tender and no longer pink (170°F for breasts; 180°F for thighs and drumsticks), brushing occasionally with mustard mixture.

Nutrition Facts per serving: 259 cal., 14 g total fat (3 g sat. fat), 86 mg chol., 409 mg sodium, 4 g carbo., 0 g fiber, 29 g pro.

PREP:
10 minutes
BAKE:
35 minutes
OVEN:
425°F
MAKES:
6 servings

10 minutes

4 net grams carbs

SERVE-ALONG SUGGESTIONS

Thai Lime Custard Soup
(see p.67)

Cubes of fresh melon such
as crenshaw, cantaloupe,
honeydew, and/or
watermelon

Iced herbal tea

CHICKEN AND PEA PODS

2 teaspoons lemon-pepper seasoning
4 skinless, boneless chicken breast halves (about 1¼ pounds total)
3 tablespoons butter or margarine
2 cups fresh sugar snap peas

PREP:
10 minutes
COOK:
10 minutes
MAKES:
4 servings

1. Sprinkle 1½ teaspoons of the lemon-pepper seasoning evenly over both sides of each chicken piece. In a large skillet melt 2 tablespoons of the butter over medium-high heat. Add chicken; cook for 8 to 10 minutes or until chicken is tender and no longer pink (170°F), turning once. Transfer chicken to a serving platter. Cover chicken; keep warm.

2. Add the remaining 1 tablespoon butter to skillet. Add snap peas and the remaining ½ teaspoon lemon-pepper seasoning. Cook and stir over medium heat for 2 to 3 minutes or until snap peas are crisp-tender. Serve snap pea mixture over chicken.

Nutrition Facts per serving: 259 cal., 11 g total fat (6 g sat. fat), 107 mg chol., 716 mg sodium, 5 g carbo., 1 g fiber, 34 g pro.

15 minutes

9
net grams
carbs

SERVE-ALONG SUGGESTIONS

Zucchini Bites (see p.317)

Orange-Cantaloupe Pops
(see p.341)

Sugar-free instant coconut
cream-flavored pudding

SESAME-GINGER BARBECUED CHICKEN

⅓	cup bottled plum sauce or sweet-and-sour sauce
¼	cup water
3	tablespoons bottled hoisin sauce
1½	teaspoons sesame seeds (toasted, if desired)
1	teaspoon grated fresh ginger or ¼ teaspoon ground ginger
½	teaspoon bottled minced garlic (1 clove)
¼	to ½ teaspoon Oriental chile sauce or several dashes bottled hot pepper sauce
6	skinless, boneless chicken breast halves and/or thighs (about 2 pounds total)

PREP:
15 minutes
GRILL:
12 minutes
MAKES:
6 servings

1. For sauce, in a small saucepan combine plum sauce, the water, hoisin sauce, sesame seeds, ginger, garlic, and chile sauce. Bring to boiling over medium heat, stirring often; reduce heat. Cover and simmer for 3 minutes. Remove from heat.

2. Place chicken on the rack of an uncovered grill directly over medium coals. Grill for 12 to 15 minutes or until chicken is tender and no longer pink (170°F), turning once and brushing with some of the sauce the last half of grilling.

3. To serve, reheat the remaining sauce until bubbly; pass with chicken.

Nutrition Facts per serving: 209 cal., 5 g total fat (1 g sat. fat), 81 mg chol., 237 mg sodium, 9 g carbo., 0 g fiber, 31 g pro.

10 minutes

1 net gram carbs

SERVE-ALONG SUGGESTIONS

Greek-Style Party Pizzettas (see p.47)

Steamed green beans tossed with butter and sprinkled with snipped fresh chives

Chunks of fresh pineapple skewered with small fresh strawberries

LEMON-MUSTARD CHICKEN

2½	to 3 pounds meaty chicken pieces (breast halves, thighs, and drumsticks)
2	tablespoons cooking oil
1	tablespoon Dijon-style mustard
1	tablespoon lemon juice
1½	teaspoons lemon-pepper seasoning
1	teaspoon dried oregano or basil, crushed
⅛	teaspoon cayenne pepper

PREP:
10 minutes
BROIL:
25 minutes
MAKES:
6 servings

1. Preheat broiler. Remove skin from chicken. Place chicken, bone sides up, on the unheated rack of a broiler pan. Broil 4 to 5 inches from the heat for 20 minutes, turning once.

2. Meanwhile, for glaze, in a small bowl stir together oil, mustard, lemon juice, lemon-pepper seasoning, oregano, and cayenne pepper.

3. Brush chicken with glaze. Turn chicken; brush with remaining glaze. Broil for 5 to 15 minutes more or until chicken is tender and no longer pink (170°F for breasts; 180°F for thighs and drumsticks).

Nutrition Facts per serving: 207 cal., 11 g total fat (2 g sat. fat), 77 mg chol., 355 mg sodium, 1 g carbo., 0 g fiber, 25 g pro.

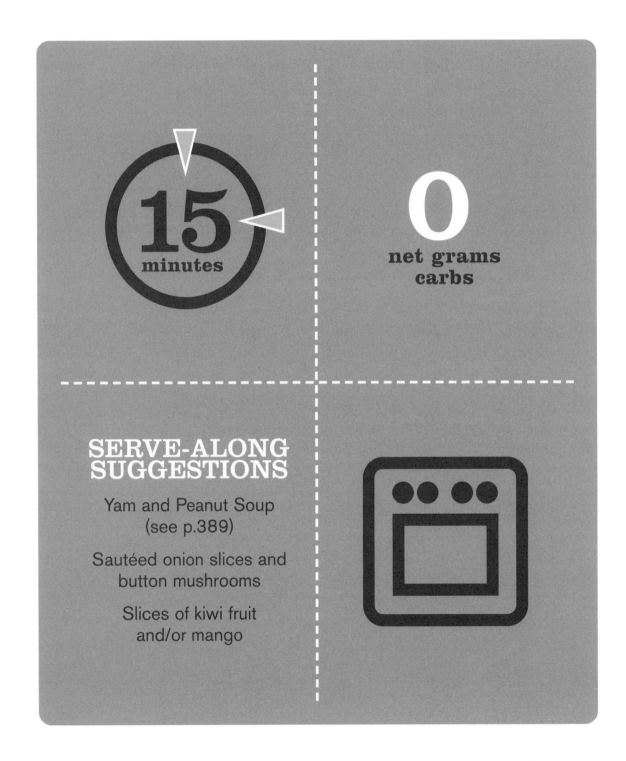

15 minutes

0 net grams carbs

SERVE-ALONG SUGGESTIONS

Yam and Peanut Soup
(see p.389)

Sautéed onion slices and
button mushrooms

Slices of kiwi fruit
and/or mango

CHICKEN WITH NEW MEXICAN-STYLE RUB

2 teaspoons New Mexican Rub (see recipe, below)
4 skinless, boneless chicken breast halves (about 1¼ pounds)

1. Preheat broiler. Prepare New Mexican-Style Rub. Sprinkle herb mixture evenly over both sides of each chicken piece; rub in with your fingers.

2. Place chicken on the unheated rack of a broiler pan. Broil 4 to 5 inches from the heat for 12 to 15 minutes or until chicken is tender and no longer pink (170°F), turning once halfway through broiling.

> **New Mexican-Style Rub:** Using a mortar and pestle, grind together 1 tablespoon dried oregano, 1 tablespoon dried thyme, 1 teaspoon coriander seeds, and 1 teaspoon anise seeds. Transfer to a small bowl. Stir in ¼ cup chile powder, 1 teaspoon paprika, ½ teaspoon cracked black pepper, and ¼ teaspoon salt. Store, covered, in a cool dry place for up to 6 months. Makes about 7 tablespoons.

Nutrition Facts per serving: 155 cal., 3 g total fat (1 g sat. fat), 75 mg chol., 103 mg sodium, 0 g carbo., 0 g fiber, 29 g pro.

PREP:
15 minutes
BROIL:
12 minutes
MAKES:
4 servings

15 minutes

7 net grams carbs

SERVE-ALONG SUGGESTIONS

Sliced red and/or yellow tomatoes sprinkled with black pepper, coarse salt, and white balsamic vinegar

Pistachios with a Kick (see p.326)

Sliced mango served with half-and-half and a little finely chopped crystallized ginger, if desired

MIDDLE-EASTERN GRILLED CHICKEN

1 8-ounce carton plain fat-free yogurt
1 small onion, finely chopped
1 tablespoon snipped fresh oregano or savory or 1 teaspoon dried oregano or savory, crushed
1 to 1½ teaspoons bottled minced garlic (2 to 3 cloves)
1 teaspoon sesame seeds, toasted
½ teaspoon ground cumin
¼ teaspoon ground turmeric (optional)
⅛ teaspoon salt
1 small cucumber, seeded and chopped (about ⅔ cup)
4 skinless, boneless chicken breast halves (about 1¼ pounds total)

PREP:
15 minutes
GRILL:
15 minutes
MAKES:
4 servings

1. In a medium bowl combine yogurt, onion, oregano, garlic, sesame seeds, cumin, turmeric (if desired), and salt. Transfer half of the yogurt mixture to a small bowl; stir in cucumber. Cover and chill until ready to serve. Reserve the remaining yogurt mixture.

2. In a grill with a cover, arrange medium-hot coals around a drip pan. Test for medium heat above the pan. Place chicken on the grill rack over drip pan. Spoon the reserved yogurt mixture over chicken. Cover and grill for 15 to 18 minutes or until chicken is tender and no longer pink (170°F).

3. Serve chicken with cucumber mixture.

Nutrition Facts per serving: 201 cal., 4 g total fat (1 g sat. fat), 76 mg chol., 181 mg sodium, 7 g carbo., 0 g fiber, 33 g pro.

10 minutes

2 net grams carbs

SERVE-ALONG SUGGESTIONS

Savory Baked Brie
(see p.45)

Vegetables in Spicy Sour
Cream (see p.290)

Mint Julep Melon
(see p.339)

PEPPER-LIME CHICKEN

2½ to 3 pounds meaty chicken pieces (breast halves, thighs, and drumsticks)
1 teaspoon finely shredded lime peel
¼ cup lime juice
1 tablespoon cooking oil
1 teaspoon dried thyme or basil, crushed
1 teaspoon bottled minced garlic (2 cloves)
½ to 1 teaspoon black pepper
¼ teaspoon salt

1. Preheat broiler. If desired, remove skin from chicken. Place chicken, bone sides up, on the unheated rack of a broiler pan. Broil 4 to 5 inches from the heat for 20 minutes.

2. Meanwhile, for glaze, in a small bowl stir together lime peel, lime juice, oil, thyme, garlic, pepper, and salt.

3. Brush chicken with glaze. Turn chicken; brush with more glaze. Broil for 5 to 15 minutes more or until chicken is tender and no longer pink (170°F for breasts; 180°F for thighs and drumsticks), brushing with the remaining glaze the last 5 minutes of broiling.

Nutrition Facts per serving: 242 cal., 13 g total fat (3 g sat. fat), 86 mg chol., 173 mg sodium, 2 g carbo., 0 g fiber, 28 g pro.

PREP:
10 minutes
BROIL:
25 minutes
MAKES:
6 servings

10 minutes

9 net grams carbs

SERVE-ALONG SUGGESTIONS

Shredded radicchio and romaine lettuce tossed with bottled low-carb creamy Italian salad dressing

Broiled Eggplant with Cheese (see p.257)

Sliced seedless red and/or green grapes

PLUM-SAUCED CHICKEN

1 tablespoon butter or margarine
4 skinless, boneless chicken breast halves (about 1¼ pounds total)
1 small onion, chopped
⅓ cup bottled plum sauce
1 tablespoon vinegar
1 tablespoon water
¼ teaspoon five-spice powder
⅛ teaspoon garlic powder

1. In a large skillet melt butter over medium-high heat. Add chicken; cook for 8 to 10 minutes or until chicken is tender and no longer pink (170°F), turning once. Transfer chicken to a serving platter, reserving drippings in skillet. Cover chicken; keep warm.

2. For sauce, add onion to reserved drippings in skillet; cook over medium heat until tender. (If necessary, add more butter.) Stir in plum sauce, vinegar, the water, five-spice powder, and garlic powder. Cook and stir until heated through. Serve sauce over chicken.

Nutrition Facts per serving: 214 cal., 6 g total fat (2 g sat. fat), 83 mg chol., 109 mg sodium, 9 g carbo., 0 g fiber, 29 g pro.

PREP:
10 minutes
COOK:
15 minutes
MAKES:
4 servings

15 minutes

4
net grams carbs

SERVE-ALONG SUGGESTIONS

Roasted Pepper-Cheese Mold (see p.25)

Torn romaine lettuce tossed with bottled low-carb Caesar salad dressing and grated Parmesan or Romano cheese

Teeny Zucchini with Onions (see p.285)

KEYS-STYLE CITRUS CHICKEN

1 tablespoon butter or margarine

4 skinless, boneless chicken breast halves (about 1¼ pounds total)

2 to 3 cloves garlic, peeled and thinly sliced

1 teaspoon finely shredded lime peel

2 tablespoons lime juice

¼ teaspoon ground ginger

⅛ teaspoon crushed red pepper

1 orange

PREP:
15 minutes
COOK:
9 minutes
MAKES:
4 servings

1. In a large skillet melt butter over medium-high heat. Add chicken and garlic; cook for 8 to 10 minutes or until chicken is tender and no longer pink (170°F), turning chicken once and stirring garlic occasionally.

2. Meanwhile, in a small bowl combine lime peel, lime juice, ginger, and crushed red pepper; set aside. Peel orange, reserving juice. Cut orange in half lengthwise; cut crosswise into slices. Add lime juice mixture and any reserved orange juice to chicken in skillet. Place orange slices on top of chicken. Cover and cook for 1 to 2 minutes or until heated through. Serve any reserved drippings over chicken.

Nutrition Facts per serving: 199 cal., 6 g total fat (3 g sat. fat), 83 mg chol., 99 mg sodium, 5 g carbo., 1 g fiber, 29 g pro.

10 minutes

6 net grams carbs

SERVE-ALONG SUGGESTIONS

Cooked spaghetti squash

Cooked green beans with crisp-cooked crumbled bacon

Sugar-free raspberry-flavored gelatin topped with whipped cream, if desired

CHICKEN WITH CREAMY CHIVE SAUCE

6 skinless, boneless chicken breast halves (about 2 pounds total)
¼ cup butter
1 0.7-ounce envelope Italian dry salad dressing mix
1 10¾-ounce can condensed golden mushroom soup
½ of an 8-ounce tub cream cheese with chives and onion
½ cup dry white wine

PREP:
10 minutes
COOK:
4 to 5 hours
(low-heat setting)
MAKES:
6 servings

1. Place chicken in a 3½- or 4-quart slow cooker. In a medium saucepan melt butter over medium heat. Stir in dry salad dressing mix. Stir in golden mushroom soup, cream cheese, and wine. Pour over chicken.

2. Cover and cook on low-heat setting for 4 to 5 hours. Serve chicken with sauce.

Nutrition Facts per serving: 353 cal., 18 g total fat (9 g sat. fat), 132 mg chol., 1,064 mg sodium, 6 g carbo., 0 g fiber, 37 g pro.

15 minutes

3 net grams carbs

SERVE-ALONG SUGGESTIONS

Mixed baby greens topped with sliced mushrooms, mandarin oranges, and oil and fruit-flavored vinegar

Roasted Asparagus Parmesan (see p.267)

Vanilla whole milk yogurt sprinkled with toasted wheat germ and chopped peaches

THYME AND GARLIC CHICKEN BREASTS

3 to 4 pounds whole chicken breasts with bone, halved lengthwise
1 tablespoon bottled minced garlic (6 cloves)
1½ teaspoons dried thyme, crushed
¼ cup orange juice
1 tablespoon balsamic vinegar

1. Remove skin from chicken. Place chicken in a 3½- or 4-quart slow cooker. Sprinkle with garlic and thyme. Pour orange juice and balsamic vinegar over chicken.

2. Cover and cook on low-heat setting for 5 to 6 hours or on high-heat setting for 2½ to 3 hours. Transfer chicken to a serving platter, reserving juices. Cover chicken; keep warm.

3. For sauce, skim off fat from cooking juices. Strain juices into a small saucepan. Bring to boiling; reduce heat. Boil gently, uncovered, about 10 minutes or until reduced to about 1 cup. Pass sauce with chicken.

Nutrition Facts per serving: 178 cal., 2 g total fat (0 g sat. fat), 85 mg chol., 78 mg sodium, 3 g carbo., 0 g fiber, 34 g pro.

PREP:
15 minutes
COOK:
5 to 6 hours (low-heat setting) or 2½ to 3 hours (high-heat setting) plus 10 minutes
MAKES:
6 to 8 servings

12 minutes

3 net grams carbs

SERVE-ALONG SUGGESTIONS

Ruby and Gold Grapefruit (see p.313)

Go-With-Anything Tomato Sauté (see p.287)

Almond Cream with Berries (see p.351)

PESTO CHICKEN BREASTS

WITH SUMMER SQUASH

2	tablespoons purchased pesto
4	skinless, boneless chicken breast halves (about 1¼ pounds total)
2	cups chopped zucchini and/or yellow summer squash
2	tablespoons finely shredded Asiago or Parmesan cheese

1. Skim off 1 tablespoon oil from pesto (or substitute 1 tablespoon olive oil). In a large nonstick skillet heat oil over medium-high heat. Add chicken; cook for 4 minutes.

2. Turn chicken; add zucchini and/or yellow summer squash. Cook for 4 to 6 minutes more or until chicken is tender and no longer pink (170°F) and squash is crisp-tender, stirring squash gently once or twice. Divide chicken and squash among 4 dinner plates. Spread pesto over chicken; sprinkle with Asiago cheese.

Nutrition Facts per serving: 233 cal., 9 g total fat (1 g sat. fat), 81 mg chol., 189 mg sodium, 4 g carbo., 1 g fiber, 32 g pro.

PREP:
12 minutes
COOK:
8 minutes
MAKES:
4 servings

15 minutes

4

net grams
carbs

SERVE-ALONG SUGGESTIONS

Mesclun with Olives
and Oranges
(see p.84)

Steamed sugar snap peas

Double Berry Delight
(see p.361)

CHICKEN ALFREDO

8 skinless, boneless chicken breast halves (about 2½ pounds total)
⅛ teaspoon salt
⅛ teaspoon black pepper
2 tablespoons cooking oil
1 10-ounce container refrigerated Alfredo sauce
1 7-ounce jar roasted red sweet peppers, drained and cut into strips
¼ cup finely shredded fresh basil
¼ cup finely shredded Parmesan cheese (1 ounce)

PREP:
15 minutes
BAKE:
10 minutes
OVEN:
350°F
MAKES:
8 servings

1. Sprinkle chicken with salt and pepper. In a 12-inch skillet heat oil over medium-high heat. Add chicken; cook for 8 to 10 minutes or until chicken is tender and no longer pink (170°F), turning once. Transfer chicken to a 2-quart rectangular baking dish.

2. Spread Alfredo sauce over chicken; top with roasted peppers. Bake in a 350° oven for 10 to 15 minutes or until peppers and sauce are heated through.

3. To serve, sprinkle chicken with basil and Parmesan cheese.

Nutrition Facts per serving: 347 cal., 20 g total fat (1 g sat. fat), 113 mg chol., 288 mg sodium, 4 g carbo., 0 g fiber, 38 g pro.

15 minutes

6 net grams carbs

SERVE-ALONG SUGGESTIONS

Savory Nuts (see p.52)

Mixed berries such as fresh blueberries, raspberries, and/or blackberries

Iced hazelnut-flavored decaf coffee

BALSAMIC CHICKEN OVER GREENS

4 skinless, boneless chicken breast halves (about 1¼ pounds total)
1 cup bottled balsamic vinaigrette salad dressing
1½ teaspoons bottled minced garlic (3 cloves)
¼ teaspoon crushed red pepper
8 cups torn mixed salad greens

1. Place chicken in a resealable plastic bag set in a shallow dish. For marinade, in a small bowl combine ½ cup of the vinaigrette dressing, the garlic, and crushed red pepper. Pour over chicken. Seal bag; turn to coat chicken. Marinate in the refrigerator for 1 to 4 hours, turning bag occasionally.

2. Drain chicken, reserving marinade. Place chicken on the rack of an uncovered grill directly over medium coals. Grill for 12 to 15 minutes or until chicken is tender and no longer pink (170°F), turning and brushing once with reserved marinade halfway through grilling. Discard any remaining marinade.

3. Divide salad greens among dinner plates. Cut chicken into strips. Arrange chicken strips on top of greens. Serve with the remaining ½ cup vinaigrette dressing.

> **Broiler Method:** Preheat broiler. Place chicken on the unheated rack of a broiler pan. Broil 4 to 5 inches from the heat for 12 to 15 minutes or until chicken is tender and no longer pink (170°F), turning and brushing once with reserved marinade halfway through broiling. Discard any remaining marinade.

Nutrition Facts per serving: 284 cal., 13 g total fat (2 g sat. fat), 82 mg chol., 525 mg sodium, 7 g carbo., 1 g fiber, 34 g pro.

PREP:
15 minutes
GRILL:
12 minutes
MARINATE:
1 to 4 hours
MAKES:
4 servings

15 minutes

1 net gram carbs

SERVE-ALONG SUGGESTIONS

Tomatillo Guacamole (see p.296)

Slices of fresh mango, papaya, and kiwi fruit

Decaf iced tea with a splash of lemon or lime juice

OVEN-FRIED COCONUT CHICKEN

2½ to 3 pounds meaty chicken pieces (breast halves, thighs, and drumsticks)

1 cup unsweetened flaked coconut

¾ cup finely crushed pork rinds (about 1½ ounces)

¼ cup butter or margarine, melted

1. Remove skin from chicken. In a shallow dish stir together coconut and pork rinds. Brush chicken with melted butter; sprinkle with salt and black pepper. Dip into coconut mixture to coat.

2. In a 15×10×1-inch baking pan arrange chicken pieces, bone sides down, so the pieces aren't touching. Drizzle any remaining melted butter over chicken.

3. Bake in a 375° oven for 45 to 55 minutes or until chicken is tender and no longer pink (170°F for breasts; 180°F for thighs and drumsticks). Do not turn chicken pieces while baking.

Nutrition Facts per serving: 318 cal., 21 g total fat (12 g sat. fat), 105 mg chol., 382 mg sodium, 2 g carbo., 1 g fiber, 29 g pro.

PREP:
15 minutes
BAKE:
45 minutes
OVEN:
375°F
MAKES:
6 servings

15 minutes

1
net gram
carbs

SERVE-ALONG SUGGESTIONS

Fresh spinach leaves tossed with crisp-cooked crumbled bacon, sliced celery, shredded cheese, and bottled low-carb Italian salad dressing

Orange and/or tangerine slices

Lemon Berry Fizz (see p.327)

CHILI POWDER NUGGETS

WITH CILANTRO CREAM

¼ cup finely crushed pork rinds (about ½ ounce)
1 tablespoon chili powder
¼ teaspoon salt
¼ teaspoon black pepper
⅛ teaspoon cayenne pepper
1 pound skinless, boneless chicken breast halves, cut into 1-inch pieces
2 tablespoons butter or margarine, melted
½ cup dairy sour cream
2 tablespoons snipped fresh cilantro

PREP:
15 minutes
BAKE:
8 minutes
OVEN:
400°F
MAKES:
4 servings

1. In a plastic bag combine pork rinds, chili powder, salt, black pepper, and cayenne pepper. In a medium bowl combine chicken pieces and melted butter; toss gently to coat. Add chicken pieces to pork rind mixture; shake to coat.

2. Place chicken pieces in a single layer on a lightly greased baking sheet. Bake in a 400° oven for 8 to 10 minutes or until chicken is tender and no longer pink, turning pieces once.

3. Meanwhile, for cilantro cream, in a small bowl stir together sour cream and cilantro. Serve chicken with cilantro cream.

Nutrition Facts per serving: 259 cal., 14 g total fat (8 g sat. fat), 96 mg chol., 367 mg sodium, 2 g carbo., 1 g fiber, 30 g pro.

10 minutes

8 net grams carbs

SERVE-ALONG SUGGESTIONS

Mixed greens with sliced pear, toasted soy nuts, and bottled low-carb red wine vinaigrette salad dressing

Cooked frozen peas with pearl onions

Coffee and Cream Dessert (see p.399)

APPLE-GLAZED TURKEY

2 turkey breast tenderloins (about 1 pound total)
1 tablespoon lemon juice
1 tablespoon olive oil or cooking oil
2 teaspoons bottled minced garlic (4 cloves)
½ teaspoon seasoned salt
½ teaspoon dried sage, crushed
2 tablespoons apple jelly, melted

1. Preheat broiler. Split each turkey tenderloin in half horizontally. Place turkey on the unheated rack of a broiler pan. In a small bowl combine lemon juice, oil, garlic, seasoned salt, and sage. Brush lemon mixture on both sides of each turkey piece.

2. Broil turkey 4 to 5 inches from the heat for 5 minutes. Turn turkey; broil for 2 minutes more. Brush turkey with apple jelly. Broil for 2 to 3 minutes more or until turkey is tender and no longer pink (170°F).

Nutrition Facts per serving: 192 cal., 5 g total fat (1 g sat. fat), 68 mg chol., 247 mg sodium, 8 g carbo., 0 g fiber, 27 g pro.

PREP:
10 minutes
BROIL:
9 minutes
MAKES:
4 servings

15 minutes

5 net grams carbs

SERVE-ALONG SUGGESTIONS

Summer Squash with Cheese and Sage (see p.265)

Low-carb chocolate-flavored ice cream

Peppered Strawberries (see p.337)

GRILLED TURKEY STEAKS

WITH SWEET PEPPER-CITRUS SALSA

4	turkey breast tenderloins (about 2 pounds total)
⅓	cup olive oil
¼	cup lemon juice
1	teaspoon finely shredded orange peel
¼	cup orange juice
2	teaspoons bottled minced garlic (4 cloves)
¼	teaspoon salt
¼	teaspoon black pepper
1	recipe Sweet Pepper-Citrus Salsa (see recipe, below)

PREP:
15 minutes
MARINATE:
2 to 4 hours
GRILL:
12 minutes
MAKES:
8 servings

1. Split each turkey breast tenderloin in half horizontally. Place turkey in a resealable plastic bag set in a shallow dish. For marinade, in a small bowl combine oil, lemon juice, orange peel, orange juice, garlic, salt, and pepper. Pour over turkey. Seal bag; turn to coat turkey. Marinate in the refrigerator for at least 2 hours or up to 4 hours, turning bag occasionally.

2. Drain turkey, reserving marinade. Place turkey on the rack of an uncovered grill directly over medium coals. Grill for 12 to 15 minutes or until turkey is tender and no longer pink (170°F), turning once halfway through grilling and brushing with reserved marinade the first 6 minutes of grilling. Discard any remaining marinade. Serve turkey with Sweet Pepper-Citrus Salsa.

> **Sweet Pepper-Citrus Salsa:** In a small bowl combine one 7-ounce jar roasted red sweet peppers, drained and chopped; 1 orange, peeled, seeded, and cut up; 2 green onions, sliced; 2 tablespoons balsamic vinegar; and 1 tablespoon snipped fresh basil or 1 teaspoon dried basil, crushed. Cover and chill until ready to serve. Makes 1½ cups salsa.

Nutrition Facts per serving: 228 cal., 10 g total fat (1 g sat. fat), 70 mg chol., 117 mg sodium, 6 g carbo., 1 g fiber, 28 g pro.

15 minutes

1

net gram carbs

SERVE-ALONG SUGGESTIONS

Low-carb tortilla chips and bottled red or green salsa

Garlicky Mushrooms (see p.273)

Mixture of sliced fresh strawberries, nectarines, and/or kiwi fruit

TURKEY TENDERLOINS

WITH CILANTRO PESTO

1½ cups lightly packed fresh cilantro sprigs or basil leaves
⅓ cup walnuts
3 tablespoons olive oil
3 tablespoons lime juice
1 teaspoon bottled minced garlic (2 cloves)
¼ teaspoon salt
4 turkey breast tenderloins (about 2 pounds total)
Lime or lemon wedges (optional)

PREP:
15 minutes
GRILL:
12 minutes
MAKES:
8 servings

1. For pesto, in blender container or food processor bowl combine cilantro, walnuts, oil, lime juice, garlic, and salt. Cover and blend or process until nearly smooth. Set aside.

2. Split cach turkey tenderloin in half horizontally. Sprinkle lightly with salt and black pepper.

3. Place turkey on the rack of an uncovered grill directly over medium coals. Grill for 7 minutes. Turn turkey; brush lightly with pesto. Grill for 5 to 8 minutes more or until turkey is tender and no longer pink (170°F). Serve turkey with remaining pesto. If desired, serve with lime wedges to squeeze over turkey.

Nutrition Facts per serving: 213 cal., 10 g total fat (2 g sat. fat), 68 mg chol., 134 mg sodium, 2 g carbo., 1 g fiber, 28 g pro.

15 minutes

2 net grams carbs

SERVE-ALONG SUGGESTIONS

Italian-Style Chips
(see p.309)

Broiled Asparagus and
Fresh Mozzarella
(see p.283)

Low-calorie lemonade-
flavored drink mix served
with lemon wedges,
if desired

GRILLED TURKEY PICCATA

PREP:
15 minutes
GRILL:
15 minutes
MAKES:
4 servings

2   turkey breast tenderloins (about 1 pound total)
2   lemons
4   teaspoons olive oil
2   teaspoons snipped fresh rosemary or ½ teaspoon dried rosemary, crushed
¼   teaspoon salt
¼   teaspoon freshly ground black pepper
1   tablespoon drained capers
1   tablespoon snipped fresh flat-leaf parsley

1. Split each turkey tenderloin in half horizontally. Finely shred enough peel from 1 of the lemons to make 1 teaspoon. Cut that lemon in half; squeeze enough juice to make 3 tablespoons. Cut the other lemon into very thin slices.

2. For rub, in a small bowl combine the 1 teaspoon lemon peel, 2 teaspoons of the oil, the rosemary, salt, and pepper. Sprinkle lemon mixture evenly over both sides of each turkey piece; rub in with your fingers.

3. In a grill with a cover, arrange medium-hot coals around a drip pan. Test for medium heat above the pan. Place turkey on grill rack over drip pan. Cover and grill for 8 minutes. Turn turkey; arrange lemon slices on top of turkey, overlapping if necessary. Cover and grill for 7 to 10 minutes more or until turkey is tender and no longer pink (170°F). Transfer turkey to a serving platter. Cover turkey; keep warm.

4. In a small saucepan combine the 3 tablespoons lemon juice, the remaining 2 teaspoons oil, and capers; heat through. Drizzle over turkey. Sprinkle with parsley.

Nutrition Facts per serving: 176 cal., 5 g total fat (1 g sat. fat), 70 mg chol., 252 mg sodium, 4 g carbo., 2 g fiber, 28 g pro.

STUFFED TURKEY TENDERLOINS

PREP:

15 minutes

GRILL:

16 minutes

MAKES:

4 servings

2 turkey breast tenderloins (about 1 pound total)

2 cups chopped fresh spinach leaves

3 ounces semisoft goat cheese (chèvre) or feta cheese, crumbled (¾ cup)

½ teaspoon black pepper

1 tablespoon olive oil

1 teaspoon paprika

½ teaspoon salt

⅛ to ¼ teaspoon cayenne pepper

1. To cut a pocket in each turkey tenderloin, use a sharp knife to make a lengthwise cut from one side almost to the other side; set aside. For stuffing, in a medium bowl combine spinach, goat cheese, and black pepper. Divide stuffing evenly between pockets in turkey. Tie each tenderloin in 3 or 4 places with 100 percent cotton string.

2. In a small bowl combine oil, paprika, salt, and cayenne pepper; brush evenly over turkey. Place on the greased rack of an uncovered grill directly over medium coals. Grill for 16 to 20 minutes or until turkey is tender and no longer pink (170°F), turning once halfway through grilling. Remove and discard strings; slice turkey.

Nutrition Facts per serving: 220 cal., 12 g total fat (4 g sat. fat), 68 mg chol., 458 mg sodium, 1 g carbo., 1 g fiber, 26 g pro.

0
net grams carbs

SERVE-ALONG SUGGESTIONS

Deviled Eggs with Spicy Crab (see p.54)

Cranberry Coleslaw (see p.391)

Orange and/or grapefruit sections sprinkled with sugar substitute, if desired

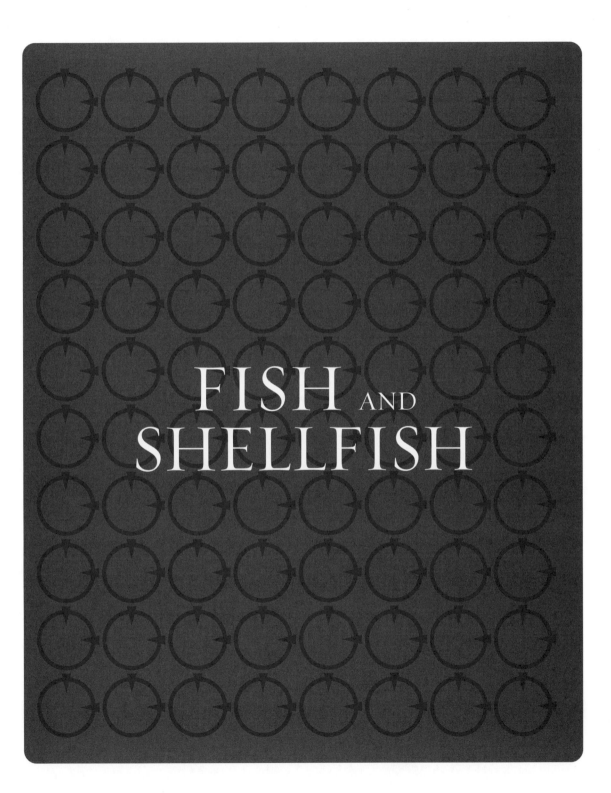

FISH AND SHELLFISH

10 minutes

0 net grams carbs

SERVE-ALONG SUGGESTIONS

Teeny Zucchini with Onions (see p.285)

Cottage cheese sprinkled with snipped fresh chives and/or freshly ground black pepper

Sugar-free orange-flavored gelatin made with mandarin oranges and chopped peaches

HERB-BUTTERED FISH STEAKS

4   4-ounce fresh or frozen halibut, salmon, shark, or swordfish steaks, cut 1 inch thick

2   tablespoons butter or margarine, softened

1   teaspoon snipped fresh tarragon or rosemary or ¼ teaspoon dried tarragon or rosemary, crushed

1   teaspoon finely shredded lime peel or lemon peel

1   teaspoon lime juice or lemon juice

1   teaspoon butter or margarine, melted

PREP:
10 minutes
BROIL:
8 minutes
MAKES:
4 servings

1. Thaw fish, if frozen. Preheat broiler. For herb butter, in a small bowl stir together the 2 tablespoons softened butter, tarragon, lime peel, and lime juice. Set aside.

2. Rinse fish; pat dry with paper towels. Place fish on the greased unheated rack of a broiler pan. Brush with the 1 teaspoon melted butter. Broil about 4 inches from the heat for 8 to 12 minutes or until fish flakes easily when tested with a fork, turning once halfway through broiling. Serve fish with herb butter.

Nutrition Facts per serving: 184 cal., 9 g total fat (2 g sat. fat), 36 mg chol., 140 mg sodium, 0 g carbo., 0 g fiber, 24 g pro.

10 minutes

3
net grams
carbs

SERVE-ALONG SUGGESTIONS

Teeny Zucchini with
Onions (see p.285)

Strawberries with Orange
Cream Dip (see p.333)

Chai (see p.328)

BROILED FISH STEAKS

WITH TARRAGON CHEESE SAUCE

4 5-ounce fresh or frozen salmon, swordfish, or tuna steaks, cut ¾ inch thick

½ cup plain yogurt or light dairy sour cream

½ cup shredded mozzarella or Monterey Jack cheese (2 ounces)

2 teaspoons snipped fresh tarragon or ½ teaspoon dried tarragon, crushed

1. Thaw fish, if frozen. Preheat broiler. For sauce, in a small bowl stir together yogurt, mozzarella cheese, and tarragon. Set aside.

2. Rinse fish; pat dry with paper towels. Place fish on the greased unheated rack of a broiler pan. Sprinkle fish with salt and black pepper. Broil about 4 inches from the heat for 6 to 9 minutes or until fish flakes easily when tested with a fork.

3. Spoon sauce over fish. Broil for 30 to 60 seconds more or until sauce is heated through and cheese is starting to melt.

Nutrition Facts per serving: 188 cal., 8 g total fat (3 g sat. fat), 36 mg chol., 236 mg sodium, 3 g carbo., 0 g fiber, 25 g pro.

PREP:
10 minutes

BROIL:
6½ minutes

MAKES:
4 servings

15 minutes

2 net grams carbs

SERVE-ALONG SUGGESTIONS

Tomatillo Guacamole
(see p.296)

Orange-Cantaloupe Pops
(see p.341)

Low-calorie strawberry-
lemonade-flavored drink mix

GRILLED SALMON

WITH HERB CRUST

12	ounces fresh or frozen skinless salmon fillets, about ¾ inch thick
⅓	cup coarsely snipped fresh oregano
⅓	cup coarsely snipped fresh cilantro
¼	cup sliced green onions
1	tablespoon lemon juice
2	teaspoons olive oil
½	teaspoon bottled minced garlic (1 clove)
¼	teaspoon salt
⅛	teaspoon black pepper

1. Thaw fish, if frozen. Rinse fish; pat dry with paper towels. Cut into 4 serving-size pieces; set aside.

2. In a food processor bowl combine oregano, cilantro, green onions, lemon juice, oil, garlic, salt, and pepper. Cover and process until chopped. Transfer to a shallow dish. (Or use a sharp knife to finely chop oregano, cilantro, and green onions. Transfer to a shallow dish. Stir in lemon juice, oil, garlic, salt, and pepper.) Generously coat both sides of fish with herb mixture.

3. Place fish on the greased rack of an uncovered grill directly over medium coals. Grill for 6 to 9 minutes or until fish flakes easily when tested with a fork, turning once halfway through grilling.

Nutrition Facts per serving: 126 cal., 5 g total fat (1 g sat. fat), 44 mg chol., 207 mg sodium, 2 g carbo., 0 g fiber, 17 g pro.

PREP:
15 minutes
GRILL:
6 minutes
MAKES:
4 servings

15 minutes

3
net grams
carbs

SERVE-ALONG SUGGESTIONS

Roasted Pepper-Cheese
Mold (see p.25)

Zucchini alla Romana
(see p.281)

Double Berry Delight
(see p.361)

TROUT

WITH MUSHROOMS

4	8-ounce fresh or frozen boned pan-dressed trout
1	large lemon, halved
¼	cup olive oil
4	teaspoons snipped fresh thyme or 1 teaspoon dried thyme, crushed
¼	teaspoon salt
¼	teaspoon crushed red pepper
1½	cups sliced fresh mushrooms
1	bunch green onions (8 to 10)
4	fresh thyme sprigs

1. Thaw fish, if frozen. Squeeze juice from 1 of the lemon halves; strain into a small bowl. Thinly slice remaining lemon half; cut slices in half.

2. Preheat broiler. In a small bowl stir together lemon juice, oil, thyme, salt, and crushed red pepper. Reserve ¼ cup of the lemon juice mixture. Toss mushrooms with the remaining lemon juice mixture. Cover and set aside.

3. Trim the root ends plus the first inch of the green tops off the green onions. Cut green onions into 2½-inch pieces. Place green onion pieces in a single layer on the unheated rack of a broiler pan. Brush with some of the reserved lemon juice mixture.

4. Arrange trout on top of green onions. Tuck halved lemon slices and thyme sprigs inside cavities of trout. Brush skin and inside flesh of trout with remaining lemon juice mixture.

5. Broil about 4 inches from the heat for 8 to 12 minutes or until fish flakes easily when tested with a fork, turning once halfway through broiling.

6. Serve trout on green onions. Spoon mushrooms over trout.

PREP:
15 minutes
BROIL:
8 minutes
MAKES:
4 servings

Nutrition Facts per serving: 454 cal., 26 g total fat (5 g sat. fat), 133 mg chol., 231 mg sodium, 4 g carbo., 1 g fiber, 49 g pro.

10
minutes

3
net grams
carbs

SERVE-ALONG SUGGESTIONS

Tomatillo Guacamole
(see p. 296)

Broccoli and Peppers
(see p. 275)

Strawberry–Citrus Slush
(see p. 365)

FISH TACOS

1 pound fresh or frozen skinless cod, orange roughy, or other fish fillets, ½ to ¾ inch thick
2 teaspoons Mexican seasoning blend
¼ teaspoon salt
1 medium lime
½ cup dairy sour cream
8 romaine lettuce leaves or four 8-inch low-carb whole wheat tortillas

PREP:
10 minutes
BROIL:
4 to 6 minutes per ½-inch thickness
MAKES:
4 servings

1. Thaw fish, if frozen. Preheat broiler. In a small bowl combine Mexican seasoning and salt. Rinse fish; pat dry with paper towels. Measure thickness of fish. Sprinkle seasoning mixture over both sides of each fish fillet.

2. Place fish on the greased unheated rack of a broiler pan. Tuck under any thin edges. Broil about 4 inches from the heat for 4 to 6 minutes per ½-inch thickness or until fish flakes easily when tested with a fork.

3. Meanwhile, finely shred enough peel from lime to make ½ teaspoon. Cut lime in half; squeeze enough juice to make 1 tablespoon. In a small bowl stir together the ½ teaspoon lime peel, the 1 tablespoon lime juice, and sour cream. Set aside.

4. Using a fork, flake fish into bite-size pieces. Divide fish among romaine leaves; roll up. Serve with sour cream mixture.

Nutrition Facts per serving: 154 cal., 6 g total fat (3 g sat. fat), 59 mg chol., 315 mg sodium, 3 g carbo., 0 g fiber, 22 g pro.

15 minutes

4
net grams
carbs

SERVE-ALONG SUGGESTIONS

Fresh spinach leaves tossed with mandarin oranges, chopped hard-cooked egg, and low-carb bottled Italian salad dressing

Almond Cream with Berries (see p.351)

CITRUS BAKED HALIBUT

1   pound fresh or frozen halibut steaks, cut ¾ inch thick
1   tablespoon butter
⅓   cup finely chopped onion
½   teaspoon bottled minced garlic (1 clove)
2   tablespoons snipped fresh parsley
½   teaspoon finely shredded orange peel
¼   teaspoon salt
⅛   teaspoon black pepper
¼   cup orange juice
1   tablespoon lemon juice

PREP:
15 minutes
BAKE:
15 minutes
OVEN:
400°F
MAKES:
4 servings

1. Thaw fish, if frozen. Rinse fish; pat dry with paper towels. If necessary, cut fish into 4 serving-size pieces. Place in a 2-quart square baking dish.

2. In a small saucepan melt butter over medium heat. Add onion and garlic; cook until onion is tender. Remove from heat. Stir in parsley, orange peel, salt, and pepper; spoon over fish. Drizzle with orange juice and lemon juice.

3. Cover and bake in a 400° oven for 15 to 20 minutes or until fish flakes easily when tested with a fork. Serve pan juices over fish.

Nutrition Facts per serving: 166 cal., 6 g total fat (2 g sat. fat), 44 mg chol., 239 mg sodium, 4 g carbo., 0 g fiber, 24 g pro.

15 minutes

4
net grams
carbs

SERVE-ALONG SUGGESTIONS

Mixed baby greens tossed with oil and fruit-flavored vinegar

Lemon-Marinated Veggies (see p.277)

Coffee and Cream Dessert (see p.399)

SALMON
WITH FRUIT SALSA

14 to 16 ounces fresh or frozen salmon or halibut fillets, about 1 inch thick

¾ cup chopped strawberries or chopped peeled peaches or nectarines

⅓ cup chopped peeled kiwi fruit or apricots

1 tablespoon snipped fresh cilantro

1 tablespoon orange juice or apple juice

1 fresh jalapeño chile pepper, seeded and chopped*

1 teaspoon olive oil or cooking oil

¼ teaspoon lemon-pepper seasoning

PREP:
15 minutes
BROIL:
8 minutes
MAKES:
4 servings

1. Thaw fish, if frozen. Preheat broiler. For fruit salsa, in a medium bowl combine strawberries, kiwi fruit, cilantro, orange juice, and jalapeño pepper. Set aside.

2. Rinse fish; pat dry with paper towels. Cut into 4 serving-size pieces. Brush oil over both sides of each fish piece. Sprinkle with lemon-pepper seasoning.

3. Place fish on the greased unheated rack of a broiler pan. Broil about 4 inches from the heat for 8 to 12 minutes or until fish flakes easily when tested with a fork, turning once halfway through broiling. Serve fish with fruit salsa.

> **Note:* Because chile peppers contain volatile oils that can burn your skin and eyes, avoid direct contact with them as much as possible. When working with chile peppers, wear plastic or rubber gloves. If your bare hands do touch the peppers, wash your hands and nails well with soap and warm water.
>
> **Grill Method:** Place fish on the greased rack of an uncovered grill directly over medium coals. Grill for 8 to 12 minutes or until fish flakes easily when tested with a fork, turning once halfway through grilling.

Nutrition Facts per serving: 123 cal., 5 g total fat (1 g sat. fat), 18 mg chol., 95 mg sodium, 5 g carbo., 1 g fiber, 15 g pro.

15 minutes

3
net grams
carbs

SERVE-ALONG SUGGESTIONS

Asian-Spiced Pecans
(see p.53)

Mesclun with
Olives and Oranges
(see pg.84)

Hot herbal tea

GINGER-MARINATED SEA BASS

4 6- to 7-ounce fresh or frozen sea bass or halibut steaks, cut 1 inch thick
¼ cup teriyaki sauce
2 tablespoons lemon juice
1 tablespoon grated fresh ginger
1 teaspoon bottled minced garlic (2 cloves)
⅛ teaspoon cayenne pepper

PREP:
15 minutes
BROIL:
8 minutes
MARINATE:
1 to 2 hours
MAKES:
4 servings

1. Thaw fish, if frozen. Rinse fish; pat dry with paper towels. In a shallow dish combine teriyaki sauce, lemon juice, ginger, garlic, and cayenne pepper. Add fish; turn to coat. Cover and marinate in the refrigerator for 1 to 2 hours, turning fish occasionally.

2. Preheat broiler. Drain fish, reserving marinade. Place fish on the greased unheated rack of a broiler pan. Broil about 4 inches from the heat for 8 to 12 minutes or until fish flakes easily when tested with a fork, turning and brushing once with reserved marinade halfway through broiling. Discard any remaining marinade.

Nutrition Facts per serving: 179 cal., 3 g total fat (1 g sat. fat), 71 mg chol., 462 mg sodium, 3 g carbo., 0 g fiber, 32 g pro.

15 minutes

2
net grams
carbs

SERVE-ALONG SUGGESTIONS

Summer Squash with
Cheese and Sage
(see p.265)

Fresh pineapple

Whole milk yogurt topped
with toasted chopped nuts

GRILLED SWORDFISH

WITH TOMATO CHUTNEY

2	6- to 8-ounce fresh or frozen swordfish or halibut steaks, cut 1 inch thick
2	teaspoons olive oil
1	small leek or 2 green onions, chopped (¼ cup)
1	cup chopped seeded tomatoes
¼	cup snipped fresh basil
1	tablespoon drained capers
¼	teaspoon black pepper
⅛	teaspoon salt
2	teaspoons olive oil

PREP:
15 minutes
GRILL:
8 minutes
MAKES:
4 servings

1. Thaw fish, if frozen. For tomato chutney, in a medium saucepan heat 2 teaspoons oil over medium heat. Add leek; cook and stir just until tender. Remove from heat. Stir in tomatoes, basil, capers, pepper, and salt. Cover and keep warm.

2. Rinse fish; pat dry with paper towels. Brush 2 teaspoons oil over both sides of each fish steak. Place fish on the greased rack of an uncovered grill directly over medium coals. Grill for 8 to 12 minutes or until fish flakes easily when tested with a fork, turning once halfway through grilling.

3. Cut each fish steak in half. Serve fish with tomato chutney.

Nutrition Facts per serving: 155 cal., 8 g total fat (2 g sat. fat), 32 mg chol., 218 mg sodium, 3 g carbo., 1 g fiber, 17 g pro.

15 minutes

0 net grams carbs

SERVE-ALONG SUGGESTIONS

Grilled or sautéed sweet onion wedges

Vegetables in Spicy Sour Cream (see p.290)

Lemon Berry Fizz (see p.327)

RED SNAPPER

WITH FRESH HERB-PECAN CRUST

4	5- to 6-ounce fresh or frozen red snapper fillets with skin, ½ to 1 inch thick
⅓	cup finely chopped pecans
2	tablespoons fine dry bread crumbs
2	tablespoons butter or margarine, softened
1	tablespoon snipped fresh flat-leaf parsley
1	teaspoon finely shredded lemon peel
1	teaspoon bottled minced garlic (2 cloves)
¼	teaspoon salt
⅛	teaspoon black pepper
	Dash cayenne pepper
	Lemon wedges (optional)

PREP:
15 minutes
GRILL:
4 to 6 minutes per
½-inch thickness
MAKES:
4 servings

1. Thaw fish, if frozen. In a small bowl combine pecans, bread crumbs, butter, parsley, lemon peel, garlic, salt, black pepper, and cayenne pepper. Set aside.

2. Rinse fish; pat dry with paper towels. Measure thickness of fish. Place fish, skin sides down, on the greased rack of an uncovered grill directly over medium coals. Spoon pecan mixture on top of fish; spread slightly. Grill for 4 to 6 minutes per ½-inch thickness or until fish flakes easily when tested with a fork. If desired, serve with lemon wedges to squeeze over fish.

Nutrition Facts per serving: 268 cal., 14 g total fat (4 g sat. fat), 67 mg chol., 287 mg sodium, 7 g carbo., 8 g fiber, 30 g pro.

15 minutes

9
net grams
carbs

SERVE-ALONG SUGGESTIONS

Corn and Chicken Soup
(see p.59)

Fragrant Ginger Cashews
(see p.321)

Wedges of fresh pineapple

SESAME-SEARED TUNA

4 6-ounce fresh or frozen tuna fillets, about ¾ inch thick
1 tablespoon olive oil
⅓ cup bottled hoisin sauce
3 tablespoons orange juice
1 tablespoon sesame seeds, toasted

START TO FINISH:
15 minutes
MAKES:
4 servings

1. Thaw fish, if frozen. Rinse fish; pat dry with paper towels. In a large skillet heat oil over medium-high heat. Add fish; cook for 6 to 8 minutes or until fish flakes easily when tested with a fork (tuna can be slightly pink in the center), turning once.

2. Meanwhile, in a small saucepan stir together hoisin sauce and orange juice; heat through.

3. To serve, drizzle the hoisin mixture over fish. Sprinkle with sesame seeds.

Nutrition Facts per serving: 271 cal., 7 g total fat (1 g sat. fat), 76 mg chol., 297 mg sodium, 9 g carbo., 0 g fiber, 41 g pro.

15 minutes

3
net grams
carbs

SERVE-ALONG SUGGESTIONS

Sliced red and/or yellow tomatoes sprinkled with coarse salt and freshly ground pepper

Wedges of crenshaw, honeydew, and/or cantaloupe melon

Tiramisu Cream (see p.359)

WASABI-GLAZED WHITEFISH WITH VEGETABLE SLAW

4	4-ounce fresh or frozen white-fleshed fish fillets, ½ to ¾ inch thick
2	tablespoons reduced-sodium soy sauce
1	teaspoon toasted sesame oil
¼	teaspoon wasabi powder or 1 tablespoon prepared horseradish
1	medium zucchini, coarsely shredded (about 1⅓ cups)
1	cup sliced radishes
1	cup fresh pea pods, strings removed
3	tablespoons snipped fresh chives
3	tablespoons rice vinegar

PREP:
15 minutes
GRILL:
4 to 6 minutes per ½-inch thickness
MAKES:
4 servings

1. Thaw fish, if frozen. In a small bowl combine soy sauce, ½ teaspoon of the sesame oil, and the wasabi powder. Set aside.

2. Rinse fish; pat dry with paper towels. Measure thickness of fish. Brush soy mixture over both sides of each fish fillet. Place fish in a greased grill basket. Tuck under any thin edges.

3. Place fish on the rack of an uncovered grill directly over medium coals. Grill for 4 to 6 minutes per ½-inch thickness or until fish flakes easily when tested with a fork, turning basket once halfway through grilling.

4. Meanwhile, for vegetable slaw, in a medium bowl combine zucchini, radishes, pea pods, and 2 tablespoons of the chives. In a small bowl combine vinegar and the remaining sesame oil. Drizzle over zucchini mixture; toss gently to coat.

5. To serve, sprinkle fish with the remaining chives. Serve with vegetable slaw.

Nutrition Facts per serving: 136 cal., 2 g total fat (0 g sat. fat), 48 mg chol., 362 mg sodium, 5 g carbo., 2 g fiber, 22 g pro.

15 minutes

0

net grams
carbs

SERVE-ALONG SUGGESTIONS

Lemon-Marinated Veggies
(see p.277)

Watermelon slices

Strawberry-Citrus Slush
(see p.365)

MUSTARD JALAPEÑO SALMON

4   5-ounce fresh or frozen skinless salmon fillets, ½ to 1 inch thick
2   tablespoons Dijon-style mustard
1   tablespoon finely chopped, seeded fresh jalapeño chile pepper*
⅛   teaspoon onion powder
⅛   teaspoon garlic powder
1   tablespoon olive oil
¼   teaspoon salt

PREP:
15 minutes
GRILL:
4 to 6 minutes per ½-inch thickness
MAKES:
4 servings

1. Thaw fish, if frozen. For glaze, in a small bowl stir together mustard, jalapeño pepper, onion powder, and garlic powder. Set aside.

2. Rinse fish; pat dry with paper towels. Measure thickness of fish. Brush oil over both sides of each fish fillet. Sprinkle with salt.

3. Place fish on the greased rack of an uncovered grill directly over medium coals. Grill for 4 to 6 minutes per ½-inch thickness or until fish flakes easily when tested with a fork, turning once halfway through grilling and spreading with glaze the last 2 minutes.

> ***Note:** Because chile peppers contain volatile oils that can burn your skin and eyes, avoid direct contact with them as much as possible. When working with chile peppers, wear plastic or rubber gloves. If your bare hands do touch the peppers, wash your hands and nails well with soap and warm water.

> **Broiler Method:** Preheat broiler. Place fish on the greased unheated rack of a broiler pan. Broil about 4 inches from the heat for 4 to 6 minutes per ½-inch thickness or until fish flakes easily when tested with a fork, spreading with glaze the last 2 minutes of broiling. If fish is 1 inch thick, turn once halfway through broiling.

Nutrition Facts per serving: 240 cal., 13 g total fat (3 g sat. fat), 75 mg chol., 414 mg sodium, 0 g carbo., 0 g fiber, 29 g pro.

15 minutes

4
net grams
carbs

SERVE-ALONG SUGGESTIONS

Cooked Wild Rice

Chilled Avocado Soup
(see p.69)

Orange-Cantaloupe Pops
(see p.341)

SWORDFISH

WITH SPICY TOMATO SAUCE

4	5-ounce fresh or frozen swordfish steaks, cut 1 inch thick
4	teaspoons cooking oil
½	teaspoon salt
¼	teaspoon black pepper
¼	cup chopped onion
1	small fresh serrano or jalapeño chile pepper, seeded and finely chopped*
½	teaspoon ground turmeric
½	teaspoon bottled minced garlic (1 clove)
¼	teaspoon ground coriander
1½	cups chopped Roma tomatoes
1	tablespoon snipped fresh cilantro

PREP:
15 minutes
COOK:
4 minutes
GRILL:
8 minutes
MAKES:
4 servings

1. Thaw fish, if frozen. Rinse fish; pat dry with paper towels. Drizzle 2 teaspoons of the oil over fish. Sprinkle with ¼ teaspoon of the salt and the black pepper.

2. Place fish on the greased rack of an uncovered grill directly over medium coals. Grill for 8 to 12 minutes or until fish flakes easily when tested with a fork, turning once halfway through grilling. Transfer to a serving platter. Cover fish; keep warm.

3. For spicy tomato sauce, in a medium skillet heat the remaining 2 teaspoons oil over medium heat. Add onion, serrano pepper, turmeric, garlic, and coriander; cook about 2 minutes or until onion is tender. Stir in tomatoes and the remaining ¼ teaspoon salt; cook for 2 to 3 minutes or just until tomatoes are heated through. Remove from heat; stir in cilantro. Serve spicy tomato sauce over fish.

> ***Note:** Because chile peppers contain volatile oils that can burn your skin and eyes, avoid direct contact with them as much as possible. When working with chile peppers, wear plastic or rubber gloves. If your bare hands do touch the peppers, wash your hands and nails well with soap and warm water.

Nutrition Facts per serving: 237 cal., 11 g total fat (2 g sat. fat), 56 mg chol., 402 mg sodium, 5 g carbo., 1 g fiber, 29 g pro.

10 minutes

7

net grams
carbs

SERVE-ALONG SUGGESTIONS

Romaine lettuce with
sliced sweet peppers and
bottled low-carb red wine
vinaigrette salad dressing

Steamed cauliflower
topped with butter and
crushed red pepper,
if desired

Chocolate Mousse
(see p.397)

EASY CITRUS SALMON STEAKS

1   8-ounce fresh or frozen salmon fillet, about 1 inch thick
1   teaspoon finely shredded lemon peel or orange peel
1   tablespoon lemon juice or orange juice
½   teaspoon bottled minced garlic (1 clove)
⅛   teaspoon black pepper
1   tablespoon sliced green onion
1   medium orange, peeled and sliced crosswise

PREP:
10 minutes
BROIL:
8 minutes
MAKES:
2 servings

1. Thaw fish, if frozen. Preheat broiler. In a small bowl stir together lemon peel, lemon juice, garlic, and pepper.

2. Rinse fish; pat dry with paper towels. Place fish on the greased unheated rack of a broiler pan. Brush with half of the lemon juice mixture. Broil about 4 inches from the heat for 5 minutes. Turn fish; brush with the remaining lemon juice mixture. Broil for 3 to 7 minutes more or until fish flakes easily when tested with a fork.

3. Cut fish in half. Sprinkle with green onion. Serve with orange slices.

Nutrition Facts per serving: 226 cal., 10 g total fat (2 g sat. fat), 70 mg chol., 54 mg sodium, 9 g carbo., 2 g fiber, 25 g pro.

15 minutes

3
net grams carbs

SERVE-ALONG SUGGESTIONS

Assorted cheeses, such as cheddar, Swiss and or blue cheese, served with low-carb crackers

Asparagus with Sorrel Dressing (see p.259)

Fresh blueberries topped with whipped cream

GRILLED ROSEMARY TROUT
WITH LEMON BUTTER

2	8- to 10-ounce fresh or frozen boned pan-dressed trout
4	teaspoons butter, softened
1	tablespoon finely chopped shallot or onion
1	teaspoon finely shredded lemon peel
2	medium tomatoes, halved crosswise
1	tablespoon snipped fresh rosemary
1	tablespoon lemon juice
2	teaspoons olive oil
1	tablespoon snipped fresh parsley

PREP:
15 minutes
GRILL:
6 minutes
MAKES:
4 servings

1. Thaw fish, if frozen. For lemon butter, in a small bowl stir together butter, half of the shallot, and the lemon peel. Sprinkle with salt and black pepper. Dot each tomato half with ¼ teaspoon of the butter mixture; set aside.

2. Rinse fish; pat dry with paper towels. Spread each fish open, skin side down. Sprinkle the remaining shallot and the rosemary evenly over each fish; rub in with your fingers. Sprinkle with salt and black pepper. Drizzle with lemon juice and oil.

3. Place fish, skin sides down, on the greased rack of an uncovered grill directly over medium coals. Grill for 6 to 9 minutes or until fish flakes easily when tested with a fork. Place tomatoes, cut sides up, on grill rack next to fish. Grill about 5 minutes or until tomatoes are heated through.

4. To serve, in a small saucepan melt remaining lemon butter. Cut each fish in half lengthwise; sprinkle with parsley. Drizzle melted lemon butter over fish and tomatoes.

Nutrition Facts per serving: 210 cal., 12 g total fat (4 g sat. fat), 69 mg chol., 301 mg sodium, 4 g carbo., 1 g fiber, 21 g pro.

10 minutes

1
net gram
carbs

SERVE-ALONG SUGGESTIONS

Down-South Green Beans
(see p.253)

Fresh sliced strawberries

Your favorite flavor of
low-carb ice cream

SALMON FILLETS BATHED IN GARLIC

6 4-ounce fresh or frozen skinless salmon fillets, about 1 inch thick
¼ cup snipped fresh flat-leaf parsley
¼ cup reduced-sodium chicken broth
¼ cup dry white wine
1 tablespoon olive oil
2 teaspoons bottled minced garlic (4 cloves)
½ teaspoon crushed red pepper

1. Thaw fish, if frozen. In a small bowl combine parsley, chicken broth, wine, oil, garlic, and crushed red pepper. Set aside.

2. Rinse fish; pat dry with paper towels. Sprinkle fish with salt and black pepper. Place fish in a 2-quart rectangular baking dish. Tuck under any thin edges. Pour parsley mixture evenly over fish.

3. Bake in a 450° oven for 8 to 12 minutes or until fish flakes easily when tested with a fork.

Nutrition Facts per serving: 163 cal., 6 g total fat (1 g sat. fat), 59 mg chol., 201 mg sodium, 1 g carbo., 0 g fiber, 23 g pro.

PREP:
10 minutes
BAKE:
8 minutes
OVEN:
450°F
MAKES:
6 servings

10 minutes

0
net grams
carbs

SERVE-ALONG SUGGESTIONS

Ruby and Gold Grapefruit
(see p.313)

Braised Seasoned
Brussels Sprouts
(see p.269)

Sugar-free instant
butterscotch- or vanilla-
flavored pudding

PARMESAN BAKED FISH

4   4-ounce fresh or frozen skinless salmon or other firm fish
fillets, ¾ to 1 inch thick

¼   cup mayonnaise or salad dressing

2   tablespoons grated Parmesan cheese

1   tablespoon snipped fresh chives or sliced green onion

1   teaspoon white wine Worcestershire sauce

1. Thaw fish, if frozen. In a small bowl stir together mayonnaise,
Parmesan cheese, chives, and Worcestershire sauce. Set aside.

2. Rinse fish; pat dry with paper towels. Place fish in a greased
2-quart square or rectangular baking dish. Tuck under any thin
edges. Spread mayonnaise mixture evenly over fish.

3. Bake, uncovered, in a 450° oven for 12 to 15 minutes or until
fish flakes easily when tested with a fork.

Nutrition Facts per serving: 302 cal., 22 g total fat (4 g sat. fat), 77 mg chol., 185 mg sodium,
0 g carbo., 0 g fiber, 25 g pro.

PREP:

10 minutes

BAKE:

12 minutes

OVEN:

450°F

MAKES:

4 servings

15 minutes

4 net grams carbs

SERVE-ALONG SUGGESTIONS

Napa Cabbage Slaw
(see p.289)

Steamed snow peas

Orange-Ginger Rhubarb
(see p.353)

GRILLED TUNA

WITH PEANUT SAUCE

4	4-ounce fresh or frozen tuna steaks or fillets (albacore or yellow fin), cut 1 inch thick
½	cup lightly salted peanuts
¼	cup water
1	green onion, cut into 1-inch pieces
2	tablespoons toasted sesame oil
1	tablespoon soy sauce
1	tablespoon rice vinegar
1	teaspoon grated fresh ginger
½	teaspoon bottled minced garlic (1 clove)
2	tablespoons water
1	tablespoon teriyaki sauce
1	tablespoon water

PREP:
15 minutes
COOK:
5 minutes
GRILL:
8 minutes
MAKES:
4 servings

1. Thaw fish, if frozen. For peanut sauce, in a blender container or food processor bowl combine peanuts, the ¼ cup water, green onion, sesame oil, soy sauce, rice vinegar, ginger, and garlic. Cover and blend or process until nearly smooth. Transfer to a small saucepan. Stir in the 2 tablespoons water. Set aside.

2. In a small bowl combine teriyaki sauce and the 1 tablespoon water. Rinse fish; pat dry with paper towels. Brush teriyaki mixture over both sides of each fish steak.

3. Place fish on the greased rack of an uncovered grill directly over medium coals. Grill for 8 to 12 minutes or until fish flakes easily when tested with a fork (tuna can be slightly pink in the center), turning once halfway through grilling.

4. Slowly heat peanut sauce over medium-low heat until warm. (Sauce will thicken slightly as it is heated. If necessary, stir in additional water to reach desired consnstency.) Serve peanut sauce over fish.

Nutrition Facts per serving: 303 cal., 17 g total fat (3 g sat. fat), 51 mg chol., 446 mg sodium, 5 g carbo., 1 g fiber, 32 g pro.

10 minutes

0
net grams
carbs

SERVE-ALONG SUGGESTIONS

Feta-Stuffed Mushrooms
(see p.319)

Steamed sugar snap peas
with butter and finely
shredded lemon peel,
if desired

Spiced Cantaloupe
(see p.347)

BASIL-BUTTERED SALMON STEAKS

4   6-ounce fresh or frozen salmon, halibut, or sea bass steaks, cut 1 inch thick
3   tablespoons butter, softened
1   tablespoon snipped fresh basil, lemon basil, or savory or 1 teaspoon dried basil or savory, crushed
1   tablespoon snipped fresh parsley
2   teaspoons lemon juice

1. Thaw fish, if frozen. Preheat broiler. In a small bowl stir together butter, basil, parsley, and lemon juice. Set aside.

2. Rinse fish; pat dry with paper towels. Place fish on the greased unheated rack of a broiler pan. Brush fish with some of the butter mixture. Broil about 4 inches from the heat for 5 minutes. Turn fish; brush with the remaining butter mixture. Broil for 3 to 7 minutes more or until fish flakes easily when tested with a fork.

Nutrition Facts per serving: 231 cal., 14 g total fat (7 g sat. fat), 54 mg chol., 190 mg sodium, 0 g carbo., 0 g fiber, 24 g pro.

PREP:
10 minutes
BROIL:
8 minutes
MAKES:
4 servings

15 minutes

1
net gram
carbs

SERVE-ALONG SUGGESTIONS

Peppers Stuffed with Goat Cheese (see p.263)

Make-Believe Champagne (see p.394)

Raspberry and Chocolate Tulips (see p.343)

GRILLED LOBSTER

WITH ROSEMARY BUTTER

4	8-ounce frozen lobster tails, thawed
2	teaspoons olive oil
½	cup butter
4	teaspoons finely shredded orange peel
2	fresh rosemary sprigs

PREP:
15 minutes
GRILL:
12 minutes
MAKES:
4 servings

1. Rinse lobster; pat dry with paper towels. Place lobster, shell sides down, on a cutting board. To butterfly, use kitchen shears to cut each lobster tail in half lengthwise, cutting to but not through the back shell. Bend backward to crack back shell and expose the meat. Brush lobster meat with oil.

2. Place lobster, shell sides down, on the greased rack of an uncovered grill directly over medium coals. Grill for 12 to 15 minutes or until lobster meat is opaque and shells are bright red, turning once halfway through grilling.

3. While lobster is grilling, in a small saucepan heat butter, orange peel, and rosemary, without stirring, over low heat until butter is melted; cool slightly. Pour the clear butter layer through a fine sieve into a serving dish; discard milky bottom layer, orange peel, and rosemary. Serve butter with lobster.

Nutrition Facts per serving: 346 cal., 27 g total fat (16 g sat. fat), 147 mg chol., 434 mg sodium, 1 g carbo., 0 g fiber, 24 g pro.

15 minutes

2 net grams carbs

SERVE-ALONG SUGGESTIONS

Shredded green and/or red leaf lettuce tossed with oil and vinegar and cracked black pepper

Garlicky Mushrooms (see p.273)

Sliced fresh peaches

GRILLED SALMON
WITH CUCUMBER SALSA

4   6- to 8-ounce fresh or frozen salmon or halibut steaks, cut 1 inch thick
1   cup chopped seeded cucumber
2   tablespoons sliced green onion
2   tablespoons white wine vinegar
2   teaspoons snipped fresh mint or ¼ teaspoon dried mint, crushed
2   teaspoons olive oil or cooking oil
1   tablespoon olive oil or cooking oil
1   tablespoon lemon juice

PREP:
15 minutes
GRILL:
8 minutes
MAKES:
4 servings

1. Thaw fish, if frozen. For salsa, in a small bowl combine cucumber, green onion, vinegar, mint, and the 2 teaspoons oil. Cover and chill until ready to serve.

2. Rinse fish; pat dry with paper towels. In a small bowl combine the 1 tablespoon oil and lemon juice; brush over fish. Place fish on the greased rack of an uncovered grill directly over medium coals. Grill for 8 to 12 minutes or until fish flakes easily when tested with a fork, turning and brushing once with lemon mixture halfway through grilling. Serve salsa over fish.

Nutrition Facts per serving: 210 cal., 11 g total fat (2 g sat. fat), 31 mg chol., 103 mg sodium, 2 g carbo., 0 g fiber, 24 g pro.

LEMON-HERB SWORDFISH STEAKS

PREP:

15 minutes

MARINATE:

30 minutes

GRILL:

8 minutes

MAKES:

4 to 6 servings

2 net grams carbs

SERVE-ALONG SUGGESTIONS

Grilled Portobellos with Avocado Salsa (see p.279)

Mixed greens with thinly sliced cucumber, radish, and toasted sunflower seeds

Peppered Strawberries (see p.337)

1½	pounds fresh or frozen swordfish, tuna, or shark steaks, cut 1 inch thick
¼	cup snipped fresh parsley
¼	cup reduced-sodium chicken broth
1	teaspoon finely shredded lemon peel
2	tablespoons lemon juice
1	shallot, finely chopped
1	tablespoon snipped fresh rosemary
1	tablespoon olive oil
1½	teaspoons snipped fresh tarragon
1½	teaspoons bottled minced garlic (3 cloves)
¼	teaspoon salt

1. Thaw fish, if frozen. Rinse fish; pat dry with paper towels. Place fish in a resealable plastic bag set in a shallow dish. For marinade, in a small bowl combine parsley, chicken broth, lemon peel, lemon juice, shallot, rosemary, oil, tarragon, garlic, and salt. Pour over fish. Seal bag; turn to coat fish. Marinate in the refrigerator for 30 minutes, turning bag occasionally.

2. Drain fish, reserving marinade. Place fish on the greased rack of an uncovered grill directly over medium coals. Grill for 8 to 12 minutes or until fish flakes easily when tested with a fork, turning and brushing once with reserved marinade halfway through grilling. Discard any remaining marinade.

Nutrition Facts per serving: 248 cal., 10 g total fat (2 g sat. fat), 22 mg chol., 337 mg sodium, 2 g carbo., 0 g fiber, 34 g pro.

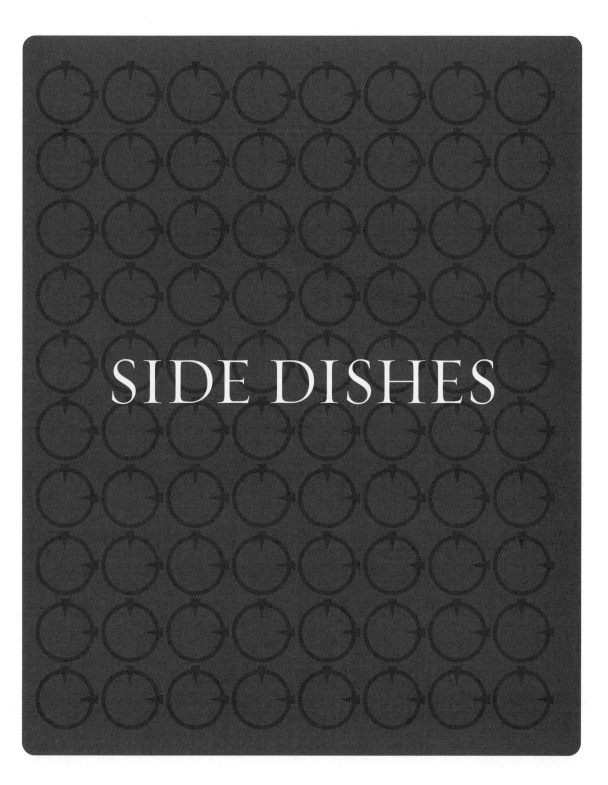

SIDE DISHES

15 minutes

5 net grams carbs

SERVE-ALONG SUGGESTIONS

Nut-Crusted Turkey Breast
(see p.377)

Spiced Cantaloupe
(see p.347)

Decaf fruit-flavored
iced tea

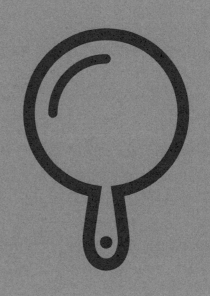

DOWN-SOUTH GREEN BEANS

2 pounds fresh green beans or two 16-ounce packages frozen whole green beans

½ to 1 teaspoon finely snipped dried chipotle chile pepper*

4 teaspoons garlic-flavored olive oil or olive oil

1 cup pecan halves, coarsely chopped

1. In a covered large saucepan cook fresh green beans and chipotle pepper in a small amount of boiling lightly salted water for 10 to 12 minutes or just until beans are crisp-tender. (Cook frozen beans and chipotle pepper for 5 minutes.) Drain.

2. Meanwhile, in a large skillet heat oil over medium heat. Add pecans; cook and stir for 30 seconds. Add drained beans; cook and stir for 1 to 2 minutes more or until beans are heated through and nuts are toasted.

> ***Note:** Because chile peppers contain volatile oils that can burn your skin and eyes, avoid direct contact with them as much as possible. When working with chile peppers, wear plastic or rubber gloves. If your bare hands do touch the peppers, wash your hands and nails well with soap and warm water.

Nutrition Facts per serving: 101 cal., 8 g total fat (1 g sat. fat), 0 mg chol., 15 mg sodium, 8 g carbo., 3 g fiber, 2 g pro.

START TO FINISH:
15 minutes
MAKES:
12 servings

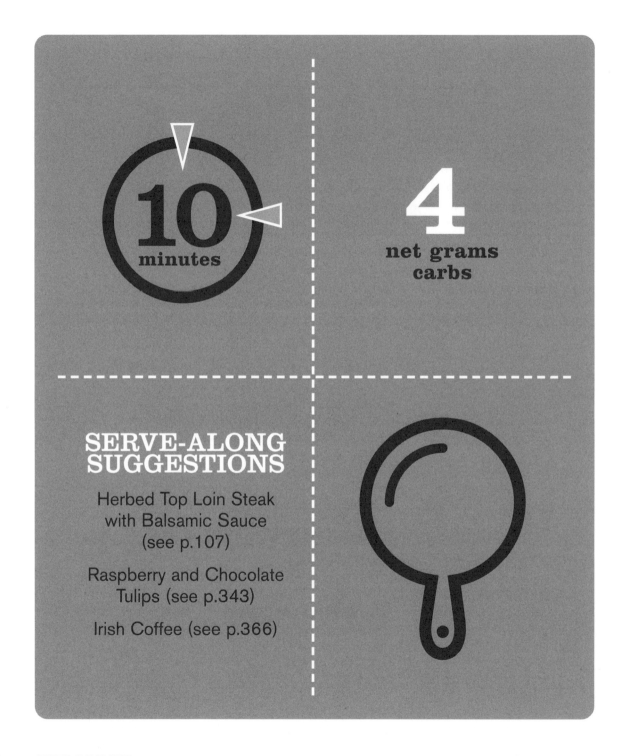

10 minutes

4 net grams carbs

SERVE-ALONG SUGGESTIONS

Herbed Top Loin Steak with Balsamic Sauce (see p.107)

Raspberry and Chocolate Tulips (see p.343)

Irish Coffee (see p.366)

SAUCY SKILLET MUSHROOMS

4 slices turkey bacon, chopped
1 tablespoon olive oil
1 pound large fresh button mushrooms (each 1½ to 2 inches in diameter)
2 tablespoons stone-ground mustard
2 tablespoons snipped fresh flat-leaf parsley

PREP:
10 minutes
COOK:
15 minutes
MAKES:
4 servings

1. In a large heavy skillet cook bacon over medium heat until crisp. Using a slotted spoon, remove bacon and drain on paper towels, reserving any drippings in skillet.

2. Add oil to skillet; heat over medium heat. Add mushrooms; cook and stir for 1 to 2 minutes or just until mushrooms start to brown. Cover and cook about 8 minutes more or until mushrooms are tender, stirring occasionally. Stir in cooked bacon and mustard; heat through. Sprinkle with parsley.

Nutrition Facts per serving: 101 cal., 7 g total fat (2 g sat. fat), 9 mg chol., 310 mg sodium, 6 g carbo., 2 g fiber, 6 g pro.

10 minutes

6 net grams carbs

SERVE-ALONG SUGGESTIONS

Herbed Steak (see p.89)

Broiled or steamed asparagus sprinkled with lemon-pepper seasoning

Almond Cream with Berries (see p.351)

BROILED EGGPLANT

WITH CHEESE

2	tablespoons finely chopped green onion
1	tablespoon olive oil or cooking oil
1	tablespoon balsamic vinegar
1	teaspoon bottled minced garlic (2 cloves)
	Dash crushed red pepper
1	medium eggplant (about 1 pound)
⅓	cup shredded reduced-fat mozzarella cheese
1	teaspoon dried oregano, crushed, or 1 tablespoon snipped fresh oregano

PREP:
10 minutes
BROIL:
8 minutes
MAKES:
4 servings

1. Preheat broiler. In a small bowl combine green onion, oil, balsamic vinegar, garlic, and crushed red pepper. Set aside.

2. Cut eggplant crosswise into 16 slices (about ½ inch thick). Place eggplant on the unheated rack of a broiler pan. Broil 4 to 5 inches from the heat for 8 to 10 minutes or until tender, turning and brushing once with green onion mixture halfway through broiling.

3. Sprinkle eggplant with mozzarella cheese and, if using, dried oregano. Broil for 1 minute more. If using, sprinkle with fresh oregano.

Nutrition Facts per serving: 92 cal., 5 g total fat (2 g sat. fat), 5 mg chol., 53 mg sodium, 9 g carbo., 3 g fiber, 4 g pro.

15
minutes

3
net grams
carbs

SERVE-ALONG SUGGESTIONS

Grilled Veal Chops with
Pesto Mushrooms
(see p.123)

Mixed fresh raspberries
and/or blackberries topped
with half-and-half and
grated fresh nutmeg,
if desired

Low-calorie lemonade-
flavored soft drink mix

ASPARAGUS

WITH SORREL DRESSING

¼	cup plain low-fat yogurt
¼	cup mayonnaise or salad dressing
¼	cup finely snipped sorrel or fresh spinach
1	green onion, thinly sliced
1	teaspoon lemon-pepper seasoning (optional)
1	pound asparagus spears, trimmed
2	tablespoons water

1. For dressing, in a small bowl combine yogurt, mayonnaise, sorrel, green onion, and, if desired, lemon-pepper seasoning. Cover and chill until ready to serve.

2. Fold a 36×18-inch piece of heavy foil in half to make a double thickness of foil that measures 18×18 inches. Place asparagus in center of foil. Fold up edges of foil slightly; drizzle asparagus with the water. Bring up 2 opposite edges of foil; seal with a double fold. Fold remaining ends to completely enclose asparagus, leaving space for steam to build.

3. Place asparagus on the rack of an uncovered grill directly over medium-hot coals. Grill about 15 minutes or until asparagus is crisp-tender, turning once halfway through grilling. Serve the asparagus with dressing.

Nutrition Facts per serving: 129 cal., 11 g total fat (2 g sat. fat), 9 mg chol., 95 mg sodium, 5 g carbo., 2 g fiber, 3 g pro.

PREP:
15 minutes
GRILL:
15 minutes
MAKES:
4 servings

15 minutes

3
net grams
carbs

SERVE-ALONG SUGGESTIONS

Thyme and Garlic Chicken
Breasts (see p.185)

Steamed green beans

Macadamia-White
Chocolate Dessert
(see p.363)

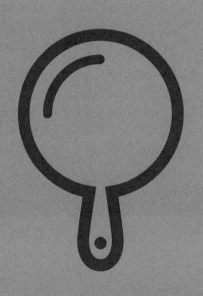

DANCING MUSHROOMS

2	tablespoons olive oil or cooking oil
3	shallots, cut into thin wedges
1½	teaspoons bottled minced garlic (3 cloves)
8	cups sliced fresh oyster, crimini, or button mushrooms
¼	cup snipped fresh mixed herbs (such as tarragon, rosemary, basil, oregano, and/or parsley)
¼	teaspoon salt
¼	teaspoon cracked black pepper

1. In a large skillet heat oil over medium-high heat. Add shallots and garlic; cook and stir for 2 minutes.

2. Add mushrooms; cook for 6 to 8 minutes or until mushrooms are tender, stirring occasionally. Stir in herbs, salt, and pepper.

Nutrition Facts per serving: 81 cal., 5 g total fat (1 g sat. fat), 0 mg chol., 118 mg sodium, 5 g carbo., 2 g fiber, 5 g pro.

PREP:
15 minutes
COOK:
6 minutes
MAKES:
6 to 8 servings

15 minutes

3 net grams carbs

SERVE-ALONG SUGGESTIONS

Grilled ribeye steaks

Purchased vinaigrette coleslaw

Warm Spiced Peaches (see p.357)

PEPPERS STUFFED

WITH GOAT CHEESE

1   ounce soft goat cheese (chèvre)
¼   cup shredded Monterey Jack cheese (1 ounce)
1   tablespoon snipped fresh chives
1   tablespoon snipped fresh basil or 1 teaspoon dried
    basil, crushed
2   medium red, yellow, and/or green sweet peppers, quartered
    lengthwise and seeded

1. In a small bowl combine goat cheese, Monterey Jack cheese, chives, and basil. Set aside.

2. Place sweet peppers on the rack of an uncovered grill directly over medium-hot coals. Grill about 8 minutes or until peppers are crisp-tender and starting to brown, turning once halfway through grilling. Remove peppers from grill.

3. Spoon cheese mixture into sweet pepper pieces; return to grill. Grill for 2 to 3 minutes more or until cheese is melted.

Nutrition Facts per serving: 60 cal., 4 g total fat (2 g sat. fat), 13 mg chol., 80 mg sodium, 3 g carbo., 0 g fiber, 3 g pro.

PREP:
15 minutes
GRILL:
10 minutes
MAKES:
4 servings

10 minutes

4 net grams carbs

SERVE-ALONG SUGGESTIONS

Beef Steaks with Tomato-Garlic Butter (see p.101)

Grilled or sautéed snow peas

Decaf iced tea served with fresh mint leaves, if desired

SUMMER SQUASH

WITH CHEESE AND SAGE

1   pound small yellow summer squash or zucchini
1   teaspoon olive oil
¼   cup bottled mild picante sauce
2   tablespoons crumbled goat cheese (chèvre) or shredded
    Monterey Jack cheese
1   tablespoon snipped fresh sage, oregano, or cilantro

PREP:
10 minutes
GRILL:
6 minutes
MAKES:
4 servings

1. Trim ends from squash; cut squash in half lengthwise. In a medium bowl combine squash and oil; toss gently to coat.

2. Place squash, cut sides down, on the greased rack of an uncovered grill directly over medium coals. Grill for 6 to 8 minutes or until squash is crisp-tender, turning once and brushing occasionally with picante sauce. Transfer squash to a serving bowl. Sprinkle with goat cheese and sage.

Nutrition Facts per serving: 54 cal., 4 g total fat (1 g sat. fat), 7 mg chol., 156 mg sodium, 5 g carbo., 1 g fiber, 2 g pro.

10 minutes

2 net grams carbs

SERVE-ALONG SUGGESTIONS

Cumberland Pork Medallions (see p.135)

Cooked spaghetti squash

Low-carb vanilla- or chocolate-flavored ice cream with sliced fresh strawberries

ROASTED ASPARAGUS PARMESAN

2 pounds asparagus spears
2 tablespoons olive oil
  Salt
  Black pepper
½ cup grated Parmesan cheese (2 ounces)

1. Snap off and discard woody bases from asparagus. If desired, scrape off scales. Place asparagus in a 15×10×1-inch baking pan. Drizzle with oil. Sprinkle with salt and black pepper; toss gently to coat.

2. Roast in a 400° oven about 15 minutes or until asparagus is crisp-tender. Transfer to a serving platter; sprinkle with Parmesan cheese.

Nutrition Facts per serving: 95 cal., 7 g total fat (2 g sat. fat), 8 mg chol., 102 mg sodium, 4 g carbo., 2 g fiber, 5 g pro.

PREP:
10 minutes
ROAST:
15 minutes
OVEN:
400°F
MAKES:
6 servings

15 minutes

4 net grams carbs

SERVE-ALONG SUGGESTIONS

Portobello Pizzas
(see p.35)

Trout with Mushrooms
(see p.213)

Fresh apricot halves

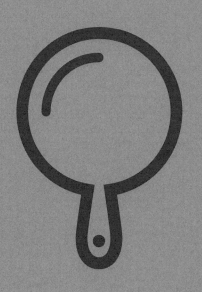

BRAISED SEASONED BRUSSELS SPROUTS

Nonstick cooking spray
½ teaspoon mustard seeds
½ teaspoon cumin seeds
½ teaspoon fennel seeds
8 ounces Brussels sprouts, halved (2 cups)
⅓ cup chicken broth or vegetable broth
2 teaspoons grated fresh ginger
¼ teaspoon salt
¼ teaspoon crushed red pepper
1 tablespoon coarsely chopped cashews or peanuts
2 teaspoons sherry vinegar or red wine vinegar

PREP:
15 minutes
COOK:
10 minutes
MAKES:
4 servings

1. Lightly coat a medium saucepan with cooking spray; heat saucepan over medium-high heat. Add mustard seeds, cumin seeds, and fennel seeds; cook and stir for 30 seconds. Add Brussels sprouts, chicken broth, ginger, salt, and crushed red pepper.

2. Bring to boiling; reduce heat. Simmer, covered, for 10 to 12 minutes or until Brussels sprouts are tender, stirring occasionally. Stir in nuts and vinegar.

Nutrition Facts per serving: 51 cal., 3 g total fat (0 g sat. fat), 0 mg chol., 225 mg sodium, 6 g carbo., 2 g fiber, 2 g pro.

15 minutes

6 net grams carbs

SERVE-ALONG SUGGESTIONS

Ginger-Marinated Sea Bass (see p.221)

Sugar-free pineapple- or orange-flavored gelatin

Strawberry-Citrus Slush (see p.365)

LEMON-TARRAGON VEGETABLES

8	ounces large fresh mushrooms, halved or quartered
2	small yellow summer squash or zucchini, halved lengthwise and cut into ½-inch slices
¾	cup bias-sliced celery
1	medium onion, cut into wedges
2	tablespoons chopped bottled roasted red sweet pepper or pimiento
½	teaspoon finely shredded lemon peel
1	tablespoon lemon juice
2	teaspoons snipped fresh tarragon or ¼ teaspoon dried tarragon, crushed
⅛	teaspoon salt

1. In a covered large saucepan cook mushrooms, squash, celery, and onion in a small amount of boiling water about 7 minutes or until vegetables are tender. Drain. Return vegetables to saucepan.

2. Stir in roasted red pepper, lemon peel, lemon juice, tarragon, and salt. Cook and stir about 1 minute or until heated through.

Nutrition Facts per serving: 38 cal., 0 g total fat (0 g sat. fat), 0 mg chol., 91 mg sodium, 8 g carbo., 2 g fiber, 2 g pro.

PREP:
15 minutes
COOK:
8 minutes
MAKES:
4 servings

15 minutes

4 net grams carbs

SERVE-ALONG SUGGESTIONS

Salsa-Topped Rosemary T-Bones (see p.93)

Grilled or sautéed zucchini and/or summer squash

Mint Julep Melon (see p.339)

GARLICKY MUSHROOMS

1   pound fresh portobello mushrooms
¼   cup butter, melted
1½ teaspoons bottled minced garlic (3 cloves)
¼   teaspoon salt
⅛   teaspoon black pepper
1   tablespoon snipped fresh chives

PREP:
15 minutes
GRILL:
6 minutes
MAKES:
4 servings

1. Cut off mushroom stems even with caps; discard stems. Lightly rinse mushroom caps; gently pat dry with paper towels. In a small bowl stir together melted butter, garlic, salt, and pepper; brush over mushrooms.

2. Place mushrooms on the rack of an uncovered grill directly over medium coals. Grill for 6 to 8 minutes or just until mushrooms are tender, turning once halfway through grilling. Sprinkle mushrooms with chives.

Nutrition Facts per serving: 133 cal., 12 g total fat (7 g sat. fat), 31 mg chol., 252 mg sodium, 6 g carbo., 2 g fiber, 3 g pro.

15 minutes

2 net grams carbs

SERVE-ALONG SUGGESTIONS

Asian-Spiced Pecans
(see p.53)

Plum-Sauced Chicken
(see p.179)

Hot herbal tea

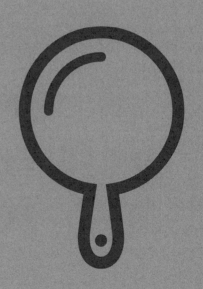

BROCCOLI AND PEPPERS

3 tablespoons soy sauce
1 tablespoon lemon juice
1 teaspoon toasted sesame oil
8 cups broccoli florets
2 medium red and/or yellow sweet peppers, cut into strips

PREP:
15 minutes
COOK:
7 minutes
MAKES:
12 servings

1. For sauce, in a small bowl stir together soy sauce, lemon juice, and sesame oil. Set aside.

2. Place a steamer basket in a 12-inch skillet. Add enough water to come just below bottom of basket. Bring to boiling. Place broccoli in steamer basket. Reduce heat to medium low. Cover and steam for 4 minutes. Add sweet peppers. Cover and steam for 3 to 4 minutes more or until vegetables are crisp-tender.

3. Transfer vegetables to a serving bowl. Drizzle sauce over vegetables; toss gently to coat.

Nutrition Facts per serving: 28 cal., 1 g total fat (0 g sat. fat), 0 mg chol., 246 mg sodium, 4 g carbo., 2 g fiber, 2 g pro.

15 minutes

6 net grams carbs

SERVE-ALONG SUGGESTIONS

Grilled meaty chicken pieces

Wedges of fresh pineapple

Chocolate Mousse (see p.397)

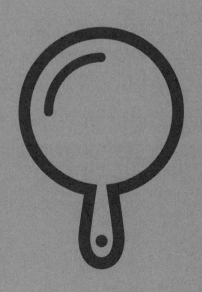

LEMON-MARINATED VEGGIES

⅓ cup olive oil or cooking oil
⅓ cup lemon juice
2 tablespoons snipped fresh basil
1 tablespoon Dijon-style mustard
½ teaspoon bottled minced garlic (1 clove)
⅛ teaspoon salt
⅛ teaspoon black pepper
8 ounces fresh green beans, trimmed
12 ounces baby carrots with tops, peeled and trimmed
8 ounces fresh mushrooms, stems removed
2 medium red and/or yellow sweet peppers, cut into 1-inch pieces
1 cup cherry tomatoes

PREP:
15 minutes
COOK:
10 minutes
MARINATE:
4 to 24 hours
MAKES:
8 to 10 servings

1. For vinaigrette, in a screw-top jar combine oil, lemon juice, basil, mustard, garlic, salt, and black pepper. Cover and shake well. Set aside.

2. In a covered large saucepan cook green beans in a small amount of boiling water for 2 minutes. Add carrots; cook, covered, about 8 minutes more or until vegetables are crisp-tender. Drain. Rinse with cold water; drain again.

3. Place beans, carrots, mushrooms, sweet peppers, and cherry tomatoes in a resealable plastic bag set in a large bowl. Pour vinaigrette over vegetables. Seal bag; turn to coat vegetables. Marinate in the refrigerator for at least 4 hours or up to 24 hours, turning bag occasionally.

4. To serve, bring vegetables to room temperature. Drain vegetables; arrange on a serving platter.

Nutrition Facts per serving: 78 cal., 5 g total fat (1 g sat. fat), 0 mg chol., 53 mg sodium, 9 g carbo., 3 g fiber, 2 g pro.

15 minutes

3
net grams
carbs

SERVE-ALONG SUGGESTIONS

Mesclun with Olives and Oranges (see p.84)

Turkey Tenderloins with Cilantro Pesto (see p.201)

Blueberries topped with heavy cream, if desired

GRILLED PORTOBELLOS

WITH AVOCADO SALSA

4	6- to 8-ounce fresh portobello mushrooms
3	tablespoons balsamic vinegar
2	tablespoons red wine vinegar
2	tablespoons olive oil
¼	teaspoon crushed red pepper
1	medium avocado, seeded, peeled, and chopped
6	cherry tomatoes, quartered
4	green onions, sliced
¼	cup crumbled, crisp-cooked bacon (about 4 slices)
2	tablespoons snipped fresh cilantro

PREP:
15 minutes
GRILL:
8 minutes
MAKES:
8 servings

1. Cut off mushroom stems even with caps; discard stems. Lightly rinse mushroom caps; gently pat dry with paper towels. In a small bowl combine balsamic vinegar, red wine vinegar, oil, and crushed red pepper. Reserve ¼ cup of the vinegar mixture for salsa.

2. Place mushrooms on the rack of an uncovered grill directly over medium coals. Grill for 8 to 10 minutes or just until mushrooms are tender, turning and brushing once with the remaining vinegar mixture halfway through grilling.

3. For salsa, in a medium bowl combine the ¼ cup reserved vinegar mixture, the avocado, cherry tomatoes, green onions, bacon, and fresh cilantro.

4. Cut the mushrooms into ½-inch slices. Spoon the salsa over mushroom slices.

Nutrition Facts per serving: 124 cal., 9 g total fat (2 g sat. fat), 3 mg chol., 65 mg sodium, 7 g carbo., 4 g fiber, 5 g pro.

15 minutes

2
net grams
carbs

SERVE-ALONG SUGGESTIONS

Sautéed fresh spinach leaves with sliced portobello mushrooms and olive oil

Chicken with Creamy Chive Sauce (see p.183)

Spicy Baked Oranges (see p.355)

ZUCCHINI ALLA ROMANA

2   cloves garlic
2   teaspoons olive oil
4   cups sliced zucchini (4 to 5 small)
1   tablespoon snipped fresh mint or basil, or 1 teaspoon dried
    mint or basil, crushed
¼   teaspoon salt
    Dash black pepper
2   tablespoons finely shredded Parmesan or Romano cheese

1. In a large skillet cook whole garlic cloves in hot oil until light brown; discard garlic. Add zucchini, fresh mint, salt, and pepper to oil in skillet.

2. Cook, uncovered, over medium heat about 5 minutes or until zucchini is crisp-tender, stirring occasionally. To serve, sprinkle with Parmesan cheese, and fresh mint.

Nutrition Facts per serving: 35 cal., 2 g total fat (1 g sat. fat), 2 mg chol., 125 mg sodium, 3 g carbo., 1 g fiber, 2 g pro.

START TO FINISH:
15 minutes
MAKES:
6 servings

15 minutes

1
net gram
carbs

SERVE-ALONG SUGGESTIONS

Beef Tenderloins with
Wine Sauce (see p.87)

Sliced fresh mango,
papaya and/or strawberries
served with whipped
cream and sprinkled with
ground ginger, if desired

Hazelnut-flavored
decaf coffee

BROILED ASPARAGUS AND FRESH MOZZARELLA

1   pound asparagus spears
2   ounces fresh mozzarella cheese, cut or torn into pieces
1   teaspoon snipped fresh lemon verbena or ¼ teaspoon finely shredded lemon peel

START TO FINISH:
15 minutes
MAKES:
4 to 6 servings

1. Preheat broiler. Snap off and discard woody bases from asparagus. Using a sharp knife, carefully cut thick asparagus spears in half lengthwise.

2. Place a steamer basket in a large skillet. Add enough water to come just below bottom of basket. Bring to boiling. Place asparagus in steamer basket. Reduce heat to medium low. Cover and steam for 1 to 2 minutes or until asparagus is crisp-tender. Arrange asparagus on an ovenproof serving platter. Top with mozzarella cheese. Sprinkle with salt and freshly ground black pepper.

3. Broil asparagus about 4 inches from the heat about 2 minutes or until cheese bubbles slightly. Sprinkle with lemon verbena.

Nutrition Facts per serving: 56 cal., 3 g total fat (2 g sat. fat), 11 mg chol., 134 mg sodium, 2 g carbo., 1 g fiber, 5 g pro.

15 minutes

5
net grams
carbs

SERVE-ALONG SUGGESTIONS

Fragrant Ginger Cashews
(see p.321)

Sesame-Seared Tuna
(see p.227)

Peach and/or nectarine
halves filled with
whipped cream

TEENY ZUCCHINI
WITH ONIONS

1 pound baby zucchini or 3 medium zucchini
1 tablespoon olive oil
1 small onion, cut into thin wedges
¼ cup chopped walnuts
½ teaspoon dried oregano, crushed
¼ teaspoon salt
¼ teaspoon black pepper

START TO FINISH:
15 minutes
MAKES:
4 to 6 servings

1. Trim ends from zucchini. If using medium zucchini, cut in half lengthwise; cut into ½-inch slices.

2. In a large nonstick skillet heat oil over medium heat. Add zucchini and onion; cook for 6 to 8 minutes or just until vegetables are tender, stirring occasionally.

3. Add walnuts, oregano, salt, and pepper. Cook and stir for 1 minute more.

Nutrition Facts per serving: 106 cal., 9 g total fat (1 g sat. fat), 0 mg chol., 146 mg sodium, 6 g carbo., 1 g fiber, 4 g pro.

15 minutes

8
net grams
carbs

SERVE-ALONG SUGGESTIONS

Keys-Style Citrus Chicken
(see p.181)

Steamed sugar snap peas

Chopped watermelon
and/or honeydew melon
tossed with lime juice and
finely shredded lime peel,
if desired

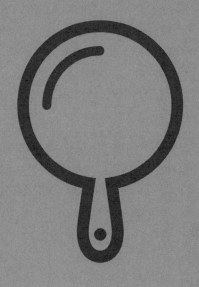

GO-WITH-ANYTHING TOMATO SAUTÉ

2½ cups red grape tomatoes, yellow pear-shape tomatoes, and/or cherry tomatoes
Nonstick olive oil cooking spray
¼ cup finely chopped shallots
1 teaspoon snipped fresh lemon thyme or thyme
½ teaspoon bottled minced garlic (1 clove)
¼ teaspoon salt
¼ teaspoon black pepper
4 ounces fresh mozzarella cheese, cut into ½-inch cubes (1 cup)

1. Halve about 1½ cups of the tomatoes; set aside. Lightly coat a large nonstick skillet with olive oil cooking spray; heat skillet over medium heat. Add shallots, lemon thyme, and garlic; cook and stir for 2 to 3 minutes or until shallots are tender.

2. Add all of the tomatoes, the salt, and pepper. Cook and stir for 1 to 2 minutes more or just until tomatoes are warmed. Remove from heat. Stir in mozzarella cheese.

Nutrition Facts per serving: 107 cal., 5 g total fat (3 g sat. fat), 16 mg chol., 289 mg sodium, 9 g carbo., 1 g fiber, 8 g pro.

START TO FINISH:
15 minutes
MAKES:
4 servings

15 minutes

0 net grams carbs

SERVE-ALONG SUGGESTIONS

Pineapple-Glazed Pork (see p.145)

Skewers of sliced kiwi fruit

Low-calorie citrus carbonated beverage

NAPA CABBAGE SLAW

3   cups finely shredded Chinese (napa) cabbage
1   cup finely shredded bok choy
¼   of a small red sweet pepper, cut into very thin strips
    (about ¼ cup)
¼   cup rice vinegar or white vinegar
1   tablespoon salad oil
½   teaspoon toasted sesame oil

1. In a large bowl combine cabbage, bok choy, and sweet pepper.

2. For dressing, in a small bowl stir together vinegar, salad oil, and sesame oil. Pour over cabbage mixture; toss gently to coat. If desired, cover and chill for up to 2 hours.

Nutrition Facts per serving: 40 cal., 3 g total fat (0 g sat. fat), 0 mg chol., 81 mg sodium, 2 g carbo., 2 g fiber, 1 g pro.

START TO FINISH:
15 minutes
MAKES:
6 servings

VEGETABLES IN SPICY SOUR CREAM

PREP:

15 minutes

CHILL:

1 to 6 hours

MAKES:

6 servings

3

net grams carbs

SERVE-ALONG SUGGESTIONS

Mixed baby greens tossed with mandarin oranges, chopped hard-cooked egg, diced ham and bottled low-carb Italian salad dresing

Grilled or pan-fried boneless, skinless chicken breast halves

Orange-Cantaloupe Pops (see p.341)

½   cup dairy sour cream
1   tablespoon white wine vinegar or lemon juice
½   teaspoon salt
⅛   teaspoon cayenne pepper
1   medium cucumber, halved lengthwise and thinly sliced (about 1½ cups)
1   medium yellow summer squash or zucchini, sliced (about 1 ¼ cup)
½   of a medium onion, halved lengthwise and thinly sliced
¼   cup chopped red sweet pepper

1. In a large bowl stir together sour cream, vinegar, salt, and cayenne pepper.

2. Add cucumber, squash, onion, and sweet pepper; toss gently to coat. Cover and chill for at least 1 hour or up to 6 hours. Stir before serving.

Nutrition Facts per serving: 48 cal., 3 g total fat (2 g sat. fat), 7 mg chol., 204 mg sodium, 4 g carbo., 1 g fiber, 1 g pro.

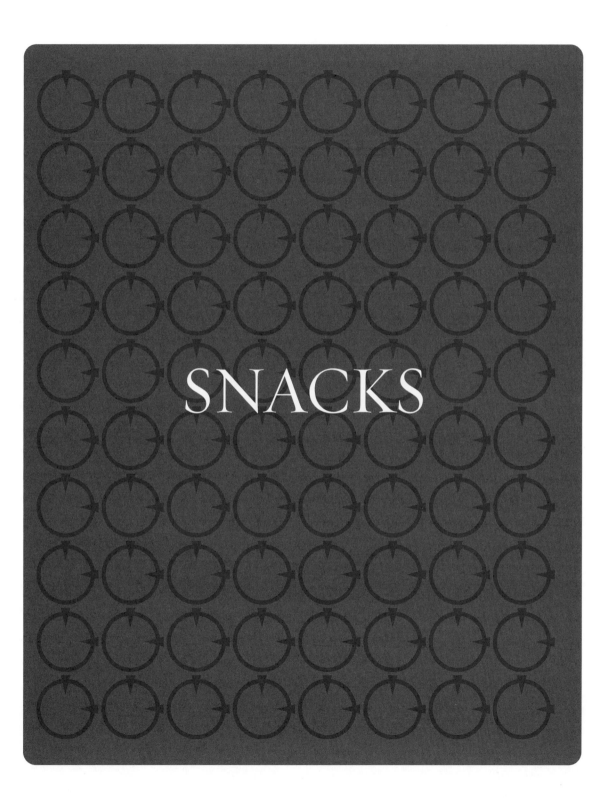

SNACKS

15 minutes

5 net grams carbs

SERVE-ALONG SUGGESTIONS

Mixed greens tossed with oil and vinegar and topped with assorted chopped sweet peppers

Chicken with New Mexican-Style Rub (see p.173)

Low-carb ice cream topped with mango and/or papaya

ARTICHOKE-FETA TORTILLA WRAPS

1	14-ounce can artichoke hearts, drained and finely chopped
½	of an 8-ounce tub cream cheese
3	green onions, thinly sliced
⅓	cup grated Parmesan or Romano cheese
¼	cup crumbled feta cheese (1 ounce)
3	tablespoons purchased pesto
8	8-inch low-carb flour tortillas
1	7-ounce jar roasted red sweet peppers, drained and cut into strips
	Nonstick cooking spray
1	recipe Yogurt-Chive Sauce (see recipe, below)

PREP:
15 minutes
BAKE:
15 minutes
OVEN:
350°F
MAKES:
24 servings

1. For filling, in a large bowl stir together artichoke hearts, cream cheese, green onions, Parmesan cheese, feta cheese, and pesto.

2. Place about ¼ cup filling on each tortilla. Top with roasted pepper strips; roll up. Arrange tortilla rolls in a greased 3-quart rectangular baking dish. Lightly coat tortilla rolls with cooking spray. Bake in a 350° oven about 15 minutes or until heated through.

3. Cut each tortilla roll into thirds; arrange on a serving platter. Serve with Yogurt-Chive Sauce.

> **Yogurt-Chive Sauce:** In a small bowl stir together one 8-ounce carton plain low-fat yogurt and 1 tablespoon snipped fresh chives.

Nutrition Facts per serving: 88 cal., 4 g total fat (2 g sat. fat), 8 mg chol., 238 mg sodium, 9 g carbo., 4 g fiber, 4 g pro.

15 minutes

4
net grams
carbs

SERVE-ALONG SUGGESTIONS

Balsamic Chicken over
Greens (see p.191)

Grilled or broiled baby
zucchini, summer and/or
pattypan squash

Mixed fresh berries served
with half-and-half

CHEESY PECAN QUESADILLAS

2	8- to 9-inch low-carb whole wheat flour tortillas
¼	cup chopped Brie cheese (1 ounce)
2	tablespoons chopped pecans or walnuts, toasted
2	tablespoons snipped fresh flat-leaf parsley
	Nonstick cooking spray
¼	cup dairy sour cream

1. Sprinkle half of each tortilla with Brie cheese. Top with nuts and parsley. Fold tortillas in half, pressing gently.

2. Lightly coat a large skillet or griddle with cooking spray; heat skillet or griddle over medium heat. Add quesadillas; cook for 2 to 3 minutes or until lightly browned, turning once. Cut quesadillas into wedges. Serve with sour cream.

Nutrition Facts per serving: 128 cal., 8 g total fat (3 g sat. fat), 12 mg chol., 217 mg sodium, 10 g carbo., 6 g fiber, 5 g pro.

START TO FINISH:
15 minutes
MAKES:
4 servings

TOMATILLO GUACAMOLE

1	small avocado, seeded, peeled, and chopped (about 1 cup)
4	canned tomatillos, rinsed, drained, and finely chopped
2	roma tomatoes, chopped
2	tablespoons canned diced green chile peppers
4	teaspoons lemon juice
¼	teaspoon garlic salt
	Low-carb tortilla chips (optional)

1. In a small bowl stir together avocado, tomatillos, roma tomatoes, chile peppers, lemon juice, and garlic salt. If desired, cover and chill for up to 24 hours.

2. If desired, serve guacamole with tortilla chips.

Nutrition Facts per serving: 40 cal., 3 g total fat (0 g sat. fat), 0 mg chol., 159 mg sodium, 4 g carbo., 1 g fiber, 1 g pro.

3
net grams carbs

SERVE-ALONG SUGGESTIONS

Skewered grilled shrimp

Grilled asparagus spears tossed with butter and bottled minced garlic

Spiced Cantaloupe (see p.347)

GARLIC-FETA CHEESE SPREAD

1 cup crumbled feta cheese (4 ounces)
½ of an 8-ounce package cream cheese or reduced-fat cream cheese (Neufchâtel), softened
⅓ cup mayonnaise or salad dressing or light mayonnaise or salad dressing
½ teaspoon bottled minced garlic (1 clove)
¼ teaspoon dried basil, crushed
¼ teaspoon dried oregano, crushed
⅛ teaspoon dried thyme, crushed
⅛ teaspoon dried dill
 Vegetable slices and/or assorted low-carb crackers (optional)

1. In a food processor bowl or small mixing bowl combine feta cheese, cream cheese, mayonnaise, garlic, basil, oregano, thyme, and dill. Cover and process or beat with an electric mixer on medium speed until combined.

2. Serve with vegetables.

> **Make-Ahead Directions:** Prepare as directed through step 1. Cover and chill for up to 48 hours. Let stand at room temperature for 30 minutes before serving.

Nutrition Facts per 1 tablespoon spread: 51 cal., 5 g total fat (2 g sat. fat), 10 mg chol., 83 mg sodium, 0 g carbo., 0 g fiber, 1 g pro.

START TO FINISH:
15 minutes
MAKES:
1½ cups spread
(24 servings)

0
net grams carbs

SERVE-ALONG SUGGESTIONS

Salmon with Fruit Salsa (see p.219)

Teeny Zucchini with Onions (see p.285)

Sugar-free triple berry-flavored gelatin topped with whipped cream, if desired

15 minutes

3
net grams
carbs

SERVE-ALONG SUGGESTIONS

Pesto Chicken Breasts
with Summer Squash
(see p.187)

Cooked green beans with
slivered toasted almonds
and crisp-cooked bacon,
if desired

Double Berry Delight
(see p.361)

CARROT HUMMUS

1   cup chopped carrots
1   15-ounce can garbanzo beans (chickpeas), rinsed and drained
¼   cup tahini (sesame seed paste)
2   tablespoons lemon juice
1   teaspoon bottled minced garlic (2 cloves)
½   teaspoon ground cumin
¼   teaspoon salt
2   tablespoons snipped fresh parsley
    Vegetable dippers and/or assorted low-carb
    crackers (optional)

1. In a covered small saucepan cook carrots in a small amount of boiling water for 6 to 8 minutes or until tender; drain.

2. In a food processor bowl combine cooked carrots, garbanzo beans, tahini, lemon juice, garlic, cumin, and salt. Cover and process until smooth. Transfer to a small serving bowl. Stir in parsley.

3. Cover and chill for at least 1 hour. If necessary, stir in enough water, 1 tablespoon at a time, to reach dipping consistency. Serve with vegetable dippers.

Nutrition Facts per serving dip: 30 cal., 1 g total fat (0 g sat. fat), 0 mg chol., 62 mg sodium, 4 g carbo., 1 g fiber, 1 g pro.

PREP:
15 minutes
CHILL:
1 hour
MAKES:
2 cups dip
(32 servings)

10 minutes

4 net grams carbs

SERVE-ALONG SUGGESTIONS

Bell-Ringer Salsa Cheesecake (see p.369)

Hot and Sweet Cocktail Wieners (see p.50)

Strawberry-Citrus Slush (see p.365)

CHILI POPCORN

8	cups popped popcorn
2	tablespoons butter or margarine, melted
1	teaspoon chili powder
⅛	teaspoon garlic powder
2	tablespoons grated Parmesan cheese

1. Place popped popcorn in a large bowl. In a small bowl combine melted butter, chili powder, and garlic powder.

2. Drizzle butter mixture evenly over popcorn. Sprinkle with Parmesan cheese; toss gently to coat.

Nutrition Facts per serving: 51 cal., 3 g total fat (2 g sat. fat), 7 mg chol., 46 mg sodium, 5 g carbo., 1 g fiber, 1 g pro.

START TO FINISH:
10 minutes
MAKES:
10 servings

SPICED POPCORN

START TO FINISH:

10 minutes

MAKES:

4 servings

8

net grams carbs

6 cups popped popcorn
Nonstick cooking spray
¼ teaspoon ground cumin
¼ teaspoon chili powder
⅛ teaspoon salt
Dash cayenne pepper
Dash ground cinnamon

1. Spread popped popcorn in an even layer in a large shallow baking pan. Lightly coat popcorn with cooking spray.

2. In a small bowl stir together cumin, chili powder, salt, cayenne pepper, and cinnamon. Sprinkle cumin mixture evenly over popcorn; toss gently to coat.

Nutrition Facts per serving: 47 cal., 1 g total fat (0 g sat. fat), 0 mg chol., 72 mg sodium, 10 g carbo., 2 g fiber, 1 g pro.

SERVE-ALONG SUGGESTIONS

Chili Chicken Appeteasers (see p.33)

Cheesy Spinach Quesadillas (see p.41)

Make-Believe Champagne (see p.394)

LEMONY HERBED OLIVES

1   pound kalamata olives and/or green olives (about 3½ cups)
1   tablespoon olive oil
½   teaspoon finely shredded lemon peel
1   tablespoon lemon juice
2   teaspoons snipped fresh oregano or ½ teaspoon dried oregano, crushed
½   to 1 teaspoon crushed red pepper

1. Place olives in a resealable plastic bag set in a shallow dish. For marinade, in a small bowl combine oil, lemon peel, lemon juice, oregano, and crushed red pepper. Pour over olives. Seal bag; turn to coat olives. Marinate in the refrigerator for at least 4 hours or up to 24 hours, turning bag occasionally.

2. To serve, let olives stand at room temperature for 30 minutes. Drain olives, discarding marinade.

Nutrition Facts per serving: 15 cal., 1 g total fat (0 g sat. fat), 0 mg chol., 94 mg sodium, 1 g carbo., 0 g fiber, 0 g pro.

PREP:
10 minutes
MARINATE:
4 to 24 hours
STAND:
30 minutes
MAKES:
56 servings

1
net gram carbs

SERVE-ALONG SUGGESTIONS

Dijon-Rosemary Roast Leg of Lamb
(see p.375)

Cooked spaghetti squash tossed with melted butter, grated Parmesan cheese and snipped fresh chives

Macadamia-White Chocolate Dessert
(see p.363)

HERBED SOY NUTS AND SEEDS

PREP:
10 minutes

BAKE:
15 minutes

OVEN:
350°F

MAKES:
10 servings

6
net grams carbs

SERVE-ALONG SUGGESTIONS

Spicy Broccoli Spread (see p.315)

Italian Cocktail Meatballs (see p.51)

Assorted fresh fruit tray with fresh strawberries; sliced peaches, kiwi fruit, and pears; and chunks of fresh melon

1	tablespoon olive oil or cooking oil
1	teaspoon chili powder
1	teaspoon dried basil, crushed
½	teaspoon dried oregano, crushed
¼	teaspoon garlic powder
1½	cups lightly salted dry roasted soy nuts* (6 ounces)
½	cup raw pumpkin seeds
½	cup dried vegetables (such as carrots, corn, and/or peas)

1. In a medium bowl stir together oil, chili powder, basil, oregano, and garlic powder. Add soy nuts and pumpkin seeds; toss gently to coat. Spread the mixture in a 13×9×2-inch baking pan.

2. Bake in a 350° oven for 15 to 20 minutes or until soy nuts are toasted, stirring after 10 minutes. Stir in dried vegetables.

*Note: If using unsalted roasted soy nuts, add ⅛ teaspoon salt to the chili powder mixture.

Nutrition Facts per serving: 126 cal., 8 g total fat (2 g sat. fat), 0 mg chol., 48 mg sodium, 8 g carbo., 2 g fiber, 7 g pro.

SPANISH OLIVE SPREAD

1½ cups finely shredded Swiss cheese (6 ounces)
1 3-ounce jar pimiento-stuffed green olives, drained and chopped
½ cup mayonnaise or salad dressing
Assorted low-carb crackers (optional)

1. In a medium bowl stir together Swiss cheese and olives. Stir in mayonnaise. Cover and chill for at least 4 hours or up to 24 hours.

2. Before serving, gently stir mixture. Serve with crackers.

Nutrition Facts per 1 tablespoon spread: 76 cal., 7 g total fat (2 g sat. fat), 10 mg chol., 140 mg sodium, 0 g carbo., 0 g fiber, 2 g pro.

PREP:
15 minutes
CHILL:
4 to 24 hours
MAKES:
about 1¼ cups spread
(20 servings)

0
net grams carbs

SERVE-ALONG SUGGESTIONS

Peppery Pork Chops (see p.151)

Orange, tangerine, and/or grapefruit sections

Broiled Eggplant with Cheese (see p.257)

TEXAS CAVIAR

PREP:
15 minutes
CHILL:
1 to 24 hours
MAKES:
4½ cups dip
(18 servings)

6
net grams
carbs

**SERVE-ALONG
SUGGESTIONS**

Garlicky Steak and
Asparagus (see p.91)

Strawberries with
Orange Cream Dip
(see p.333)

Decaf fruit-flavored iced
tea sweetened with
sugar substitute

2	15-ounce cans black-eyed peas with jalapeño chile peppers, rinsed and drained
1	cup chopped red sweet pepper
½	cup chopped onion
½	cup snipped fresh parsley
½	to 1 teaspoon bottled minced garlic (1 to 2 cloves)
½	teaspoon salt
⅛	teaspoon black pepper
¼	cup olive oil
¼	cup rice vinegar or white vinegar
	Low-carb tortilla chips (optional)

1. In a large bowl combine black-eyed peas, sweet pepper, onion, parsley, garlic, salt, and black pepper. Add oil and vinegar; toss gently to coat.

2. Cover and chill for at least 1 hour or up to 24 hours. Serve with tortilla chips.

Nutrition Facts per serving dip: 80 cal., 3 g total fat (0 g sat. fat), 0 mg chol., 202 mg sodium, 9 g carbo., 3 g fiber, 3 g pro.

ARTICHOKE HUMMUS DIP

1 15-ounce can garbanzo beans (chickpeas), drained
¼ cup mayonnaise or salad dressing
2 tablespoons lemon juice
½ teaspoon bottled minced garlic (1 clove)
⅛ teaspoon salt
1 14-ounce can artichoke hearts, drained
¼ cup grated Parmesan cheese (1 ounce)
   Assorted low-carb crackers and/or vegetable
   dippers (optional)

1. In a food processor* combine garbanzo beans, mayonnaise, lemon juice, garlic, and salt. Cover and process until smooth. Add artichokes and Parmesan cheese. Cover and process with several on/off turns until artichokes are coarsely chopped.

2. Transfer the mixture to a 1-quart soufflé dish. Bake in a 350° oven for 20 to 25 minutes or until heated through. Serve with crackers.

*Note: If you don't have a food processor, mash the garbanzo beans well with a potato masher; chop the artichokes. In a medium bowl stir together mashed beans, mayonnaise, lemon juice, garlic, and salt. Stir in chopped artichokes and Parmesan cheese. Continue as directed in step 2.

Nutrition Facts per 2 tablespoons dip: 62 cal., 3 g total fat (1 g sat. fat), 3 mg chol., 195 mg sodium, 7 g carbo., 2 g fiber, 2 g pro.

PREP:
10 minutes
BAKE:
20 minutes
OVEN:
350°F
MAKES:
about 2⅓ cups dip
(18 servings)

5
net grams carbs

SERVE-ALONG SUGGESTIONS

Sweet-Pepper Steak (see p.113)

Wedges of fresh melon, such as, watermelon, cantaloupe and/or crenshaw

Whole milk yogurt topped with wheat germ and toasted nuts

15 minutes

4 net grams carbs

SERVE-ALONG SUGGESTIONS

Fast Italian-Style Chicken Soup (see p.57)

Fresh baby spinach leaves tossed with bottled low-carb balsamic vinaigrette salad dressing and snipped fresh oregano

Crème Fraîche Fool with Berries (see p.400)

ITALIAN-STYLE CHIPS

<table>
<tr><td>2</td><td>tablespoons butter or margarine</td></tr>
<tr><td>⅔</td><td>cup finely chopped onion</td></tr>
<tr><td>1</td><td>teaspoon dried Italian seasoning, crushed</td></tr>
<tr><td>4</td><td>8-inch low-carb flour tortillas</td></tr>
<tr><td></td><td>Bottled salsa (optional)</td></tr>
</table>

1. In a small skillet melt butter over medium heat. Add onion; cook for 3 to 5 minutes or until tender. Stir in Italian seasoning. Carefully brush onion mixture evenly over tortillas. Cut each tortilla into 8 wedges. Spread in a single layer in a 15×10×1-inch baking pan.

2. Bake in a 350° oven for 8 to 10 minutes or until tortilla wedges are crisp and edges are lightly browned. If desired, serve with salsa.

Nutrition Facts per serving: 87 cal., 4 g total fat (2 g sat. fat), 8 mg chol., 196 mg sodium, 10 g carbo., 6 g fiber, 3 g pro.

PREP:
15 minutes
BAKE:
8 minutes
OVEN:
350°F
MAKES:
8 servings

15 minutes

2 net grams carbs

SERVE-ALONG SUGGESTIONS

Effortless Shrimp Chowder
(see p.65)

Mixed greens topped with sliced cucumber, shredded fresh basil leaves, and bottled low-carb vinaigrette salad dressing

Double Berry Delight
(see p.361)

TOASTED CHEESE TORTILLA CHIPS

6 6-inch low-carb whole wheat flour tortillas
2 tablespoons butter or margarine, melted
3 tablespoons grated Parmesan or Romano cheese
¼ teaspoon dried basil, Italian seasoning, or oregano, crushed

1. Brush one side of each tortilla with melted butter. In a small bowl combine Parmesan cheese and basil. Sprinkle evenly over tortillas. Cut each tortilla into 6 wedges. Spread in a single layer on a large baking sheet.

2. Bake in a 350° oven for 12 to 15 minutes or until tortilla wedges are crisp and lightly browned. Cool.

Nutrition Facts per serving: 64 cal., 3 g total fat (2 g sat. fat), 6 mg chol., 164 mg sodium, 6 g carbo., 4 g fiber, 2 g pro.

PREP:
15 minutes
BAKE:
12 minutes
OVEN:
350°F
MAKES:
12 servings

15 minutes

7
net grams
carbs

SERVE-ALONG SUGGESTIONS

Portobello Pizzas
(see p.35)

Herbed Steak (see p.89)

Chocolate Mousse
(see p.397)

RUBY AND GOLD GRAPEFRUIT

2   cups red and/or white grapefruit sections
2   teaspoons rosemary-flavored olive oil or olive oil
½   teaspoon cracked black pepper
     Snipped fresh rosemary

1. In a medium bowl combine grapefruit sections, oil, and pepper; toss gently to coat.

2. Spoon the grapefruit mixture into small serving bowls. Sprinkle with rosemary.

Nutrition Facts per serving: 55 cal., 2 g total fat (0 g sat. fat), 0 mg chol., 0 mg sodium, 9 g carbo., 2 g fiber, 1 g pro.

START TO FINISH:
15 minutes
MAKES:
4 servings

10
minutes

1
net gram
carbs

SERVE-ALONG SUGGESTIONS

Peppered Pork with Chive
Sauce (see p.129)

Mint Julep Melon
(see p.339)

Decaf iced tea with lemon
and/or lime wedges

SPICY BROCCOLI SPREAD

2 cups broccoli florets
1 tablespoon olive oil
½ cup chopped onion
2 tablespoons grated Parmesan cheese
¼ to ½ teaspoon crushed red pepper
  Vegetable slices (optional)

1. In a covered medium saucepan cook broccoli in a small amount of boiling salted water about 8 minutes or until tender. Drain, reserving cooking liquid.

2. Meanwhile, in a small skillet heat oil over medium heat. Add onion; cook about 10 minutes or until onion is soft. In a food processor bowl or blender container combine broccoli, onion, Parmesan cheese, and crushed red pepper. Cover and process or blend until nearly smooth. If mixture seems dry and thick, add reserved cooking liquid, 1 tablespoon at a time, to reach desired consistency.

3. Cover and chill for at least 3 hours or up to 24 hours. Serve with vegetables.

Nutrition Facts per 1 tablespoon spread: 15 cal., 1 g total fat (0 g sat. fat), 0 mg chol., 15 mg sodium, 1 g carbo., 0 g fiber, 1 g pro.

PREP:
10 minutes
COOK:
18 minutes
CHILL:
3 to 24 hours
MAKES:
1 cup spread
(16 servings)

15 minutes

1
net gram
carbs

SERVE-ALONG SUGGESTIONS

Lime-Cilantro Flank Steak
(see p.117)

Fresh sliced kiwi fruit,
mango, and/or papaya

Low-calorie carbonated
beverage served with lime
and/or lemon wedges

ZUCCHINI BITES

1   medium to large zucchini, cut into ¼-inch slices
½   of an 8-ounce tub cream cheese with salmon or ⅓ cup semisoft cheese with garlic and herb
1   tablespoon sliced or chopped pitted ripe olives
1   tablespoon snipped fresh chives

1. Pat zucchini slices dry with paper towels. Spread cream cheese over zucchini slices. Sprinkle with olives and chives.

Nutrition Facts per serving: 12 cal., 1 g total fat (1 g sat. fat), 3 mg chol., 27 mg sodium, 1 g carbo., 0 g fiber, 0 g pro.

PREP:
15 minutes
MAKES:
about 36 servings

15 minutes

1
net gram
carbs

SERVE-ALONG SUGGESTIONS

Steak with Creamy Onion
Sauce (see p.97)

Steamed green beans

Warm Spiced Peaches
(see p.357)

FETA-STUFFED MUSHROOMS

4   5- to 6-ounce fresh portobello mushrooms
1   tablespoon olive oil
1   4-ounce package crumbled feta cheese with garlic and herb or crumbled feta cheese
¼   cup chopped pitted ripe olives
2   tablespoons snipped oil-packed dried tomatoes

1. Cut off mushroom stems even with caps; discard stems. Lightly rinse mushroom caps; gently pat dry with paper towels. Place mushrooms, stemmed sides up, on a baking sheet. Brush with olive oil (or substitute 1 tablespoon oil from dried tomatoes); set aside.

2. In a small bowl stir together feta cheese, olives, and dried tomatoes. Spoon cheese mixture into mushroom caps.

3. Bake in a 425° oven about 10 minutes or until heated through. Cut each mushroom cap into 4 wedges.

Nutrition Facts per serving: 40 cal., 3 g total fat (1 g sat. fat), 6 mg chol., 102 mg sodium, 2 g carbo., 1 g fiber, 2 g pro.

PREP:
15 minutes
BAKE:
10 minutes
OVEN:
425°F
MAKES:
16 servings

HERBED SOY SNACKS

PREP:

10 minutes

BAKE:

5 minutes

OVEN:

350°F

MAKES:

2 cups (16 servings)

5
net grams carbs

SERVE-ALONG SUGGESTIONS

Cabbage and Chicken with Sesame Dressing (see p.75)

Vanilla Cream-Topped Raspberries (see p.335)

Iced decaf flavored coffee

2 cups lightly salted dry roasted soy nuts (8 ounces)
1½ teaspoons dried thyme, crushed
¼ teaspoon garlic salt
⅛ to ¼ teaspoon cayenne pepper
1 tablespoon olive oil

1. Place soy nuts in a 15×10×1-inch baking pan. In a small bowl combine thyme, garlic salt, and cayenne pepper. Sprinkle evenly over soy nuts. Drizzle with olive oil; toss gently to coat. Spread nuts in a single layer.

2. Bake in a 350° oven about 5 minutes or just until heated through, shaking pan once. Cool.

Nutrition Facts per serving: 106 cal., 5 g total fat (1 g sat. fat), 0 mg chol., 15 mg sodium, 7 g carbo., 2 g fiber, 9 g pro.

FRAGRANT GINGER CASHEWS

1 tablespoon butter or margarine, melted
1 tablespoon minced or grated fresh ginger
2 teaspoons garam masala
2 cups lightly salted cashews

1. Line a shallow baking pan with foil or parchment paper. In a medium bowl combine melted butter, ginger, and garam masala. Add cashews; toss gently to coat. Spread nuts in the prepared baking pan.

2. Bake in a 300° oven about 20 minutes or until nuts are golden and very fragrant, stirring occasionally. Serve warm or at room temperature.

Make-Ahead Directions: Prepare as directed. Store in a tightly covered container at room temperature for up to 24 hours or in the refrigerator for up to 2 days. If desired, reheat nuts on a baking sheet in a 300° oven about 5 minutes or until warm.

Nutrition Facts per serving: 114 cal., 10 g total fat (2 g sat. fat), 2 mg chol., 42 mg sodium, 5 g carbo., 1 g fiber, 4 g pro.

PREP:
10 minutes
BAKE:
20 minutes
OVEN:
300°F
MAKES:
2 cups (16 servings)

4
net grams carbs

SERVE-ALONG SUGGESTIONS

Asian Grilled Salmon Salad (see p.81)

Napa Cabbage Slaw (see p.289)

Iced herbal tea

10 minutes

3 net grams carbs

SERVE-ALONG SUGGESTIONS

Cooked beef ribeye roast

Mesclun with Olives and Oranges (see p.84)

Whole fresh strawberries topped with whipped cream

TOASTED ALMONDS WITH ROSEMARY

8 ounces whole almonds or pecan halves (about 2 cups)
1 tablespoon olive oil or cooking oil
1 tablespoon snipped fresh rosemary or 1 teaspoon dried rosemary, crushed
¼ to ½ teaspoon salt

1. Place nuts in a shallow baking pan. Drizzle with oil; toss gently to coat. Sprinkle with rosemary and salt; toss gently to coat. Spread nuts in a single layer.

2. Bake in a 350° oven for 10 to 15 minutes or until nuts are toasted, stirring every 5 minutes. Spread in a single layer of a large piece of foil to cool.

Nutrition Facts per serving: 179 cal., 16 g total fat (1 g sat. fat), 0 mg chol., 73 mg sodium, 6 g carbo., 3 g fiber, 6 g pro.

PREP:
10 minutes
BAKE:
10 minutes
OVEN:
350°F
MAKES:
2 cups (8 servings)

MEDITERRANEAN WALNUT SPREAD

1
net gram carbs

1   cup canned garbanzo beans (about ½ of a
     15-ounce can), undrained
½   cup chopped walnuts
½   cup lightly packed fresh basil leaves
2   tablespoons olive oil
2   to 3 teaspoons lemon juice
⅛   teaspoon salt
⅛   teaspoon black pepper
     Assorted low-carb crackers (optional)

1. Drain garbanzo beans, reserving liquid. In a blender container or food processor bowl combine beans and 2 tablespoons of the reserved liquid. Add walnuts, basil, oil, lemon juice, salt, and pepper. Cover and blend or process until nearly smooth. (If mixture seems stiff, add additional reserved liquid to reach desired consistency.)

2. Serve the spread with crackers.

Nutrition Facts per 1 tablespoon spread: 34 cal., 3 g total fat (0 g sat. fat), 0 mg chol., 25 mg sodium, 1 g carbo., 0 g fiber, 1 g pro.

BLUE CHEESE-WALNUT DIP

8   ounces blue cheese
½   cup unsalted butter, softened
½   cup finely chopped walnuts, toasted
     Assorted fruit dippers (optional)

1. In a food processor container combine blue cheese and butter. Cover and process until smooth. (When necessary, stop food processor and use a rubber spatula to scrape sides of bowl.) Stir in walnuts.

2. To serve, transfer the dip to a serving bowl. If desired, sprinkle with additional walnuts. Serve with fruit dippers.

> **Make-Ahead Tip:** Prepare as directed through step 1. Cover and chill for up to 24 hours. Before serving, let stand at room temperature about 1 hour to soften.

Nutrition Facts per serving dip: 73 cal., 7 g total fat (4 g sat. fat), 15 mg chol., 114 mg sodium, 0 g carbo., 0 g fiber, 2 g pro.

START TO FINISH:
15 minutes
MAKES:
1¾ cups dip
(28 servings)

0
net grams carbs

SERVE-ALONG SUGGESTIONS

Grilled beef loin strip steaks

Down-South Green Beans (see p.253)

Coffee and Cream Dessert (see p.399)

PISTACHIOS WITH A KICK

PREP:

10 minutes

BAKE:

20 minutes

OVEN:

350°F

MAKES:

1½ cups (6 servings)

6

net grams carbs

SERVE-ALONG SUGGESTIONS

Purchased beef and/or chicken kabobs; grilled or broiled

Skewered button mushrooms, sweet pepper chunks, and red onion wedges; grilled or broiled

Strawberry-Citrus Slush (see p.365) (double recipe)

2	tablespoons margarine or butter, melted
1	teaspoon ground coriander
½	teaspoon salt
¼	teaspoon ground cloves
¼	teaspoon cayenne pepper
1½	cups pistachio nuts

1. In a 9×9×2-inch baking pan combine melted margarine, coriander, salt, cloves, and cayenne pepper. Add pistachio nuts; toss gently to coat.

2. Bake in a 350° oven for 20 to 25 minutes or until toasted, stirring occasionally. Spread nuts on a large piece of foil to cool.

Nutrition Facts per serving: 212 cal., 18 g total fat (2 g sat. fat), 0 mg chol., 239 mg sodium, 9 g carbo., 3 g fiber, 7 g pro.

LEMON BERRY FIZZ

6	small whole strawberries
8	fresh mint leaves
1½	cups club soda or seltzer water, chilled
1	teaspoon sugar-free lemonade mix
	Ice cubes

1. Thread strawberries onto 2 wooden skewers. Set aside.

2. Place mint leaves in a small pitcher. Using a spoon, slightly crush mint leaves. Gently stir in club soda and lemonade mix.

3. Serve in ice-filled glasses. Add a strawberry skewer to each glass.

Nutrition Facts per serving: 14 cal., 0 g total fat (0 g sat. fat), 0 mg chol., 38 mg sodium, 3 g carbo., 1 g fiber, 0 g pro.

START TO FINISH: 15 minutes

MAKES: 2 servings

2
net grams carbs

SERVE-ALONG SUGGESTIONS

Grilled or pan-fried boneless, skinless chicken breast halves brushed with bottled low-carb raspberry vinaigrette salad dressing

Sautéed sweet onion wedges and red sweet pepper strips

Broiled Asparagus and Fresh Mozzarella (see p.283)

CHAI

START TO FINISH:

15 minutes

MAKES:

8 servings

1¼ cups nonfat dry milk powder
¼ cup loose black tea
12 cardamom pods
4 2-inch pieces stick cinnamon
2 teaspoons finely shredded lemon peel
8 cups water

1. In a large saucepan combine milk powder, tea, cardamom pods, stick cinnamon, and lemon peel. Stir in the water. Bring to boiling; remove from heat.

2. Cover and let stand for 5 minutes. Strain through a sieve lined with 100-percent cotton cheesecloth or a clean paper coffee filter.

Nutrition Facts per serving: 40 cal., 0 g total fat (0 g sat. fat), 2 mg chol., 62 mg sodium, 6 g carbo., 0 g fiber, 4 g pro.

6
net grams carbs

SERVE-ALONG SUGGESTIONS

Savory Nuts (see p.52)

Grilled Chicken and Raspberry Salad (see p.73)

Chocolate Mousse (see p.397)

REALLY HOT
ICED COFFEE

⅓ cup ground coffee

1 2-inch piece stick cinnamon

¼ to ½ teaspoon crushed red pepper

6 cardamom pods, crushed, or ¼ teaspoon ground cardamom

8 to 10 cups cold water
    Ice cubes

½ cup whipped cream or vanilla ice cream (optional)

½ teaspoon ground nutmeg (optional)

1. Measure coffee into the filter-lined basket of a 10-cup coffeemaker. Add cinnamon, crushed red pepper, and cardamom. Pour cold water into water compartment. Prepare coffee according to manufacturer's directions. Cover and chill for at least 1 hour.

2. Serve coffee over ice. If desired, top with whipped cream and sprinkle with nutmeg.

Nutrition Facts per serving: 4 cal., 0 g total fat (0 g sat. fat), 0 mg chol., 4 mg sodium, 1 g carbo., 0 g fiber, 0 g pro.

PREP:
15 minutes

CHILL:
1 hour

MAKES:
10 servings

1
net gram carbs

SERVE-ALONG SUGGESTIONS

Grilled Beef, Red Onion, and Blue Cheese Salad (see p.71)

Fresh sliced strawberries with whipped cream and toasted whole almonds

Steamed asparagus drizzled with olive oil and black pepper

CURRIED APPLE SPREAD

START TO FINISH:

10 minutes

MAKES:

¾ cup spread

(12 servings)

1

net gram carbs

½   of an 8-ounce package cream cheese, softened
1   teaspoon finely shredded orange peel
1   tablespoon orange juice
½   teaspoon curry powder
¼   of a medium apple (such as Delicious, Gala, or Braeburn), finely chopped
Low-carb bread, toasted and cut into quarters (optional)

1. In a small bowl combine cream cheese, orange peel, orange juice, and curry powder. Gently stir in apple.

2. Serve the spread with toasted bread.

Nutrition Facts per serving spread: 36 cal., 3 g total fat (2 g sat. fat), 10 mg chol., 28 mg sodium, 1 g carbo., 0 g fiber, 1 g pro.

SERVE-ALONG SUGGESTIONS

Chili-Rubbed Steaks (see p.109)

Grilled sweet onion slices

Low-carb fruit-flavored ice cream topped with toasted nuts

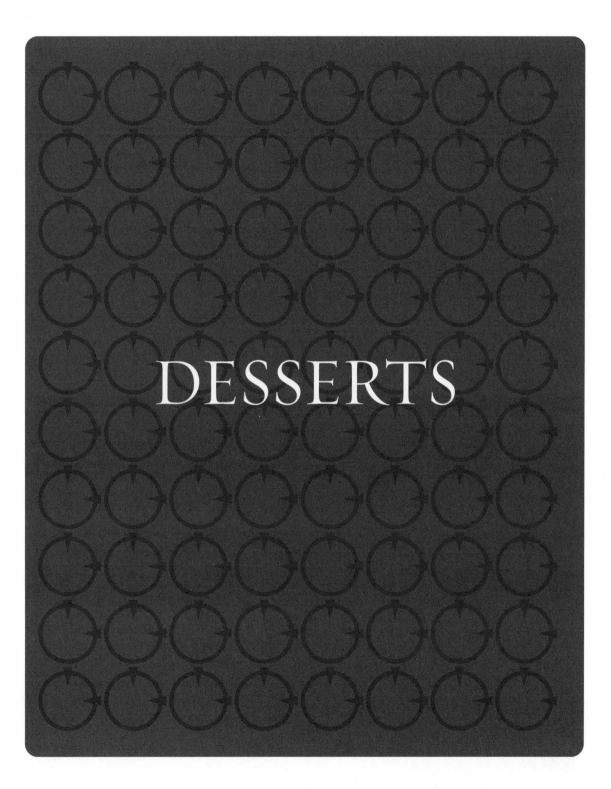

DESSERTS

10 minutes

5
net grams
carbs

SERVE-ALONG SUGGESTIONS

Pepper-Marinated Flank Steak (see p.119)

Grilled sliced red and/or sweet onion

Low-calorie lemonade-flavored drink mix

ATRAWBERRIES

WITH ORANGE CREAM DIP

1   8-ounce carton dairy sour cream
2   tablespoons heat-stable granular sugar substitute (Splenda)
2   teaspoons finely shredded orange peel
1   tablespoon orange juice
3   cups small strawberries

PREP:
10 minutes
MAKES:
8 servings

1. For dip, in a small bowl stir together sour cream, sugar substitute, orange peel, and orange juice. Set aside.

2. Rinse strawberries, but do not remove stems. Drain on several layers of paper towels. Serve the strawberries with dip.

Nutrition Facts per serving: 80 cal., 6 g total fat (4 g sat. fat), 12 mg chol., 16 mg sodium, 6 g carbo., 1 g fiber, 1 g pro.

10 minutes

3
net grams
carbs

SERVE-ALONG SUGGESTIONS

Balsamic Chicken over Greens (see p.191)

Summer Squash with Cheese and Sage (see p.265)

Assorted mixed salted nuts

VANILLA CREAM-TOPPED RASPBERRIES

1 cup whipping cream
½ teaspoon vanilla
1 6-ounce carton raspberry, blueberry, or strawberry fat-free
   yogurt with sweetener
2 cups raspberries, blueberries, or sliced strawberries*
   Finely shredded orange peel (optional)

1. In a chilled medium mixing bowl beat whipping cream and vanilla with the chilled beaters of an electric mixer on medium speed until soft peaks form (tips curl). Fold in yogurt.

2. Divide whipped cream mixture among dessert dishes. Top with berries. If desired, sprinkle with orange peel.

> ***Note:*** When choosing fresh berries, look for berries with healthy color for the particular variety. Once you have them home, spread them in a single layer, loosely cover, and store in the refrigerator until you're ready to use them. Because berries are highly perishable, they need to be used within 1 to 2 days. Just before you're ready to eat them, wash them.

Nutrition Facts per serving: 166 cal., 15 g total fat (9 g sat. fat), 55 mg chol., 32 mg sodium, 6 g carbo., 3 g fiber, 3 g pro.

START TO FINISH:
10 minutes
MAKES:
6 servings

10 minutes

4 net grams carbs

SERVE-ALONG SUGGESTIONS

Corn and Chicken Soup (see p.59)

Mixed greens tossed with toasted sesame seeds and bottled low-carb red wine vinaigrette salad dressing

Garlicky Steak and Asparagus (see p.91)

PEPPERED STRAWBERRIES

3 cups sliced strawberries

2 tablespoons heat-stable granular sugar substitute (Splenda)

4 teaspoons sherry vinegar or balsamic vinegar

¼ teaspoon freshly ground black pepper

1. In a medium bowl combine strawberries, sugar substitute, vinegar, and pepper; toss gently to combine. Spoon into dessert dishes.

Nutrition Facts per serving: 25 cal., 0 g total fat (0 g sat. fat), 0 mg chol., 1 mg sodium, 6 g carbo., 2 g fiber, 0 g pro.

START TO FINISH:
10 minutes

MAKES:
6 servings

10 minutes

8
net grams
carbs

SERVE-ALONG SUGGESTIONS

Portobello Pizzas
(see p.35)

Chili-Rubbed Steaks
(see p.109)

Vegetables in Spicy Sour
Cream (see p.290)

MINT JULEP MELON

2 tablespoons snipped fresh mint
2 tablespoons heat-stable granular sugar substitute (Splenda)
2 tablespoons bourbon
2 cups cubed honeydew melon

1. In a medium bowl crush mint with the back of a spoon. Stir in sugar substitute and bourbon. Add melon; toss gently to combine.

2. Spoon into dessert dishes or martini glasses.

Nutrition Facts per serving: 52 cal., 0 g total fat (0 g sat. fat), 0 mg chol., 10 mg sodium, 9 g carbo., 1 g fiber, 0 g pro.

10 minutes

4
net grams
carbs

SERVE-ALONG SUGGESTIONS

Sesame-Ginger
Barbecued Chicken
(see p.169)

Sliced red tomato drizzled
with olive oil and snipped
fresh chives

Iced decaf tea

ORANGE-CANTALOUPE POPS

1   4-serving-size package sugar-free orange-flavored gelatin
½   cup boiling water
2   cups cubed ripe cantaloupe
1   8-ounce carton plain low-fat yogurt

1. In a small bowl stir together gelatin and boiling water until gelatin is dissolved.

2. In a blender container combine gelatin mixture, cantaloupe, and yogurt. Cover and blend until smooth. Pour into ten 3-ounce ice-pop molds or paper cups. If using paper cups, cover each cup with foil. Cut a small slit in the center of each foil cover; insert a rounded wooden stick into each pop. Freeze pops for 4 to 6 hours or until firm.

3. To serve, remove pops from ice-pop molds or remove foil from paper cups; tear paper away from pops.

Nutrition Facts per serving: 29 cal., 0 g total fat (0 g sat. fat), 1 mg chol., 45 mg sodium, 4 g carbo., 0 g fiber, 2 g pro.

PREP:
10 minutes
FREEZE:
4 to 6 hours
MAKES:
10 servings

15 minutes

3
net grams carbs

SERVE-ALONG SUGGESTIONS

Nut-Crusted Turkey Breast
(see p.377)

Pear-Chutney Salsa
(see p.383)

Steamed asparagus with butter and finely shredded orange or lemon peel

RASPBERRY AND CHOCOLATE TULIPS

1	cup raspberries
¼	cup heat-stable granular sugar substitute (Splenda)
¼	cup whipping cream
1	tablespoon heat-stable granular sugar substitute
¼	teaspoon vanilla
1	2.1-ounce package (15) baked miniature phyllo dough shells
1	tablespoon grated unsweetened chocolate

START TO FINISH: 15 minutes

MAKES: 15 servings

1. In a small saucepan combine raspberries and the ¼ cup sugar substitute. Cook and stir over medium heat for 3 to 5 minutes or until slightly thickened. Cool completely.

2. In a chilled small mixing bowl combine whipping cream, the 1 tablespoon sugar substitute, and vanilla. Beat with the chilled beaters of an electric mixer on medium speed until soft peaks form (tips curl).

3. To serve, place the phyllo shells on a serving platter. Spoon about 1 teaspoon of the raspberry mixture into the bottom of each shell. Top with whipped cream. Sprinkle with grated chocolate.

Nutrition Facts per serving: 46 cal., 3 g total fat (1 g sat. fat), 5 mg chol., 12 mg sodium, 4 g carbo., 1 g fiber, 1 g pro.

15 minutes

4
net grams
carbs

SERVE-ALONG SUGGESTIONS

Assorted olives, pickles and pepperoncini relish tray

Peppers Stuffed with Goat Cheese (see p. 263)

Garlic-Studded Veal Chops and Asparagus (see p.121)

FRUIT-TOPPED PHYLLO CUPS

2 tablespoons low-sugar apricot or strawberry preserves
½ of an 8-ounce package cream cheese, softened
1 2.1-ounce package (15) baked miniature phyllo dough shells
15 red or green seedless grape halves, strawberry halves, and/or small mango pieces

1. In a small saucepan heat and stir preserves over medium-low heat until melted. Cut up any large pieces of preserves. Stir in cream cheese until smooth.

2. Divide cream cheese mixture among phyllo shells. Place a piece of fruit on top of each tart. If desired, cover and chill for up to 4 hours before serving.

Nutrition Facts per serving: 55 cal., 4 g total fat (2 g sat. fat), 8 mg chol., 32 mg sodium, 4 g carbo., 0 g fiber, 1 g pro.

START TO FINISH:
15 minutes
MAKES:
15 servings

10 minutes

7

net grams
carbs

SERVE-ALONG SUGGESTIONS

Asian-Spiced Pecans
(see p.53)

Cabbage and Chicken
with Sesame Dressing
(see p.75)

Chai (see p.328)

SPICED CANTALOUPE

2 cups cubed cantaloupe
2 tablespoons lime juice
1 tablespoon heat-stable granular sugar substitute (Splenda)
¼ teaspoon ground nutmeg

1. In a medium bowl combine cantaloupe, lime juice, sugar substitute, and nutmeg; toss gently to combine. Spoon into dessert dishes.

Nutrition Facts per serving: 32 cal., 0 g total fat (0 g sat. fat), 0 mg chol., 8 mg sodium, 8 g carbo., 1 g fiber, 1 g pro.

START TO FINISH:
10 minutes
MAKES:
4 servings

10 minutes

6 net grams carbs

SERVE-ALONG SUGGESTIONS

Curried Apple Spread
(see p.330)

Pot Roast with Dill
(see p.115)

Cooked green beans

ALMOND-SAUCED BERRIES

2	cups blackberries
1	cup raspberries
¾	cup dairy sour cream
1½	teaspoons heat-stable granular sugar substitute (Splenda)
½	to ¾ teaspoon almond extract

1. Divide blackberries and raspberries among dessert dishes. Set aside.

2. In a small bowl stir together sour cream, sugar substitute, and almond extract. Spoon over berries.

Nutrition Facts per serving: 90 cal., 5 g total fat (3 g sat. fat), 11 mg chol., 13 mg sodium, 10 g carbo., 4 g fiber, 1 g pro.

START TO FINISH:

10 minutes

MAKES:

6 servings

15 minutes

5
net grams carbs

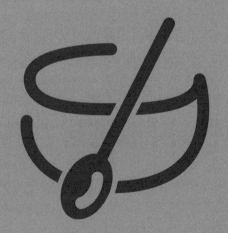

SERVE-ALONG SUGGESTIONS

Red Snapper with Fresh Herb-Pecan Crust (see p.225)

Garlicky Mushrooms (see p.273)

Grilled or steamed asparagus

ALMOND CREAM
WITH BERRIES

½   of an 8-ounce package cream cheese, softened
3   tablespoons heat-stable granular sugar substitute (Splenda)
½   cup dairy sour cream
¼   teaspoon almond extract
¼   teaspoon vanilla
1   cup sliced strawberries

1. In a small mixing bowl beat cream cheese and sugar substitute with an electric mixer on medium speed until fluffy. Beat in sour cream, almond extract, and vanilla until combined.

2. Spoon into dessert dishes. Top with strawberries.

Nutrition Facts per serving: 168 cal., 15 g total fat (9 g sat. fat), 42 mg chol., 98 mg sodium, 6 g carbo., 1 g fiber, 3 g pro.

START TO FINISH:
15 minutes
MAKES:
4 servings

15 minutes

5
net grams
carbs

SERVE-ALONG SUGGESTIONS

Fresh spinach leaves tossed with bottled low-carb Italian salad dressing

Basil-Buttered Salmon Steaks (see p.245)

Broiled Asparagus and Fresh Mozzarella (see p.283)

ORANGE-GINGER RHUBARB

2 tablespoons butter or margarine
3 cups fresh or frozen rhubarb cut into ½-inch pieces
1 teaspoon finely shredded orange peel
¼ cup orange juice
3 tablespoons heat-stable granular sugar substitute (Splenda)
2 teaspoons grated fresh ginger
 Whipping cream (optional)

PREP:
15 minutes
COOK:
7 minutes
MAKES:
4 servings

1. In a medium heavy saucepan melt butter over medium heat. Add fresh or frozen rhubarb; cook and stir for 2 minutes for fresh rhubarb or 4 minutes for frozen rhubarb. Stir in orange peel, orange juice, sugar substitute, and ginger.

2. Bring to boiling; reduce heat. Simmer, covered, for 5 to 10 minutes or until rhubarb is tender. Spoon into dessert dishes. Serve warm. If desired, serve with cream.

Nutrition Facts per serving: 85 cal., 6 g total fat (4 g sat. fat), 16 mg chol., 67 mg sodium, 7 g carbo., 2 g fiber, 1 g pro.

10 minutes

6 net grams carbs

SERVE-ALONG SUGGESTIONS

Stuffed Turkey Tenderloins (see p.204)

Sautéed bottled marinated artichoke hearts

Red and/or green leaf lettuce tossed with sliced mushrooms, diced ham and bottled blue cheese salad dressing

SPICY BAKED ORANGES

3 medium oranges
3 tablespoons chopped pecans
½ teaspoon pumpkin pie spice

1. Peel oranges; slice about ¼ inch thick. If present, remove any seeds.

2. Place orange slices in a 2-quart square baking dish. In a small bowl combine pecans and pumpkin pie spice. Sprinkle over orange slices.

3. Bake in a 400° oven for 8 to 10 minutes or until heated through.

Nutrition Facts per serving: 55 cal., 3 g total fat (0 g sat. fat), 0 mg chol., 0 mg sodium, 8 g carbo., 2 g fiber, 1 g pro.

PREP:
10 minutes
BAKE:
8 minutes
OVEN:
400°F
F **MAKES:**
6 servings

15 minutes

7

net grams
carbs

SERVE-ALONG SUGGESTIONS

Pecan-Glazed Pork Chops
(see p.143)

Steamed broccoli with
melted cheese, if desired

Low-carb vanilla or butter-
pecan-flavored
ice cream

WARM SPICED PEACHES

3 medium ripe peaches, peeled and sliced

2 teaspoons heat-stable granular sugar substitute (Splenda)

½ teaspoon ground cinnamon

½ teaspoon finely shredded orange peel

½ teaspoon vanilla

¼ teaspoon ground nutmeg

2 teaspoons snipped fresh basil or 1 teaspoon snipped fresh mint

1. In a medium bowl combine peaches, sugar substitute, cinnamon, orange peel, vanilla, and nutmeg; toss gently to combine. Divide among four 5-inch quiche dishes or 10-ounce custard cups.

2. Cover and bake in a 350° oven for 5 to 10 minutes or just until warm. (Or loosely cover and microwave on 100% power [high] for 1 to 1½ minutes or just until warm.) Sprinkle with basil.

Nutrition Facts per serving: 36 cal., 0 g total fat (0 g sat. fat), 0 mg chol., 0 mg sodium, 9 g carbo., 2 g fiber, 1 g pro.

PREP:
15 minutes

BAKE:
5 minutes

OVEN:
350°F

MAKES:
4 servings

15 minutes

8
net grams
carbs

SERVE-ALONG SUGGESTIONS

Grilled Lobster with
Rosemary Butter
(see p.247)

Cooked sugar snap peas
with lemon-pepper seasoning

Hazelnut-flavored decaf
iced coffee

TIRAMISU CREAM

1	8-ounce carton mascarpone cheese
¼	cup heat-stable granular sugar substitute (Splenda)
2	tablespoons dairy sour cream
2	tablespoons coffee liqueur
1	cup frozen whipped extra creamy dessert topping, thawed
½	ounce unsweetened chocolate, grated

1. In a small mixing bowl beat mascarpone cheese, sugar substitute, sour cream, and coffee liqueur with an electric mixer on low to medium speed until fluffy. Fold in whipped topping.

2. Spoon into martini glasses or dessert dishes. Sprinkle with grated chocolate.

Nutrition Facts per serving: 237 cal., 22 g total fat (14 g sat. fat), 50 mg chol., 31 mg sodium, 8 g carbo., 0 g fiber, 8 g pro.

START TO FINISH:
15 minutes
MAKES:
6 servings

10 minutes

7 net grams carbs

SERVE-ALONG SUGGESTIONS

Garlic-Feta Cheese Spread (see p.297)

Grilled Pork Chops with Mushroom Stuffing (see p.127)

Sautéed apple wedges and sliced sweet onion

DOUBLE BERRY DELIGHT

¼ cup sugar-free raspberry preserves
1 tablespoon water
1 tablespoon brandy
1⅓ cups quartered strawberries

START TO FINISH:
10 minutes
MAKES:
4 servings

1. In a small saucepan combine preserves and water. Cook and stir over medium-low heat until preserves are melted. Remove from heat. Stir in brandy.

2. Divide strawberries among dessert dishes. Drizzle with raspberry mixture.

Nutrition Facts per serving: 33 cal., 0 g total fat (0 g sat. fat), 0 mg chol., 1 mg sodium, 8 g carbo., 1 g fiber, 0 g pro.

15 minutes

6 net grams carbs

SERVE-ALONG SUGGESTIONS

Savory Baked Brie
(see p.45)

Pork au Poivre with
Mustard and Sage
(see p.133)

Cooked spaghetti squash

MACADAMIA-WHITE CHOCOLATE DESSERT

1¼ cups ricotta cheese
1 cup water
1 4-serving-size package fat-free, sugar-free instant white chocolate pudding mix
¼ cup macadamia nuts, chopped
½ ounce unsweetened chocolate, grated
6 strawberries (optional)

START TO FINISH:
15 minutes
MAKES:
6 servings

1. Place ricotta cheese in a food processor bowl. Cover and process until smooth. With processor running, gradually add water through tube, continuing to process until combined.

2. Add pudding mix. Cover and process until mixture thickens. Fold in macadamia nuts and chocolate. Spoon into dessert dishes. If desired, garnish with strawberries. If desired, cover and chill for up to 6 hours.

Nutrition Facts per serving: 158 cal., 12 g total fat (6 g sat. fat), 26 mg chol., 273 mg sodium, 7 g carbo., 1 g fiber, 6 g pro.

10
minutes

5
net grams
carbs

SERVE-ALONG SUGGESTIONS

Mixed baby greens tossed with shredded basil, shaved Parmesan cheese, and oil and vinegar

Easy Citrus Salmon Steaks (see p.235)

Sugar-free pistachio-flavored instant pudding

STRAWBERRY-CITRUS SLUSH

6 ounces frozen unsweetened whole strawberries (about 1⅓ cups)

1 12-ounce can low-calorie grapefruit carbonated beverage

1 cup ice cubes

2 teaspoons heat-stable granular sugar substitute (Splenda)

¼ teaspoon orange extract or lime extract (optional)

START TO FINISH:

10 minutes

MAKES:

3 servings

1. In a blender container combine strawberries, carbonated beverage, ice cubes, sugar substitute, and, if desired, orange extract. Cover and blend until smooth. Serve in wine glasses.

Nutrition Facts per serving: 22 cal., 0 g total fat (0 g sat. fat), 0 mg chol., 24 mg sodium, 6 g carbo., 1 g fiber, 0 g pro.

IRISH COFFEE

START TO FINISH:

10 minutes

MAKES:

4 servings

2

net grams carbs

SERVE-ALONG SUGGESTIONS

Filet Mignon with Portobello Sauce (see p.105)

Braised Seasoned Brussels Sprouts (see p.269)

Mixed fresh blackberries, raspberries and/or blueberries

½ cup whipping cream
2 cups hot strong coffee
¼ cup Irish whiskey
3 tablespoons heat-stable granular sugar substitute (Splenda)
   Ground cinnamon

1. In a chilled small mixing bowl beat whipping cream with the chilled beaters of an electric mixer on medium speed until soft peaks form (tips curl).

2. In a 4-cup glass measure stir together coffee and whiskey. Stir in sugar substitute. Pour into coffee mugs or other heat-proof glasses. Top with whipped cream; sprinkle with cinnamon.

Nutrition Facts per serving: 145 cal., 11 g total fat (7 g sat. fat), 41 mg chol., 15 mg sodium, 2 g carbo., 0 g fiber, 1 g pro.

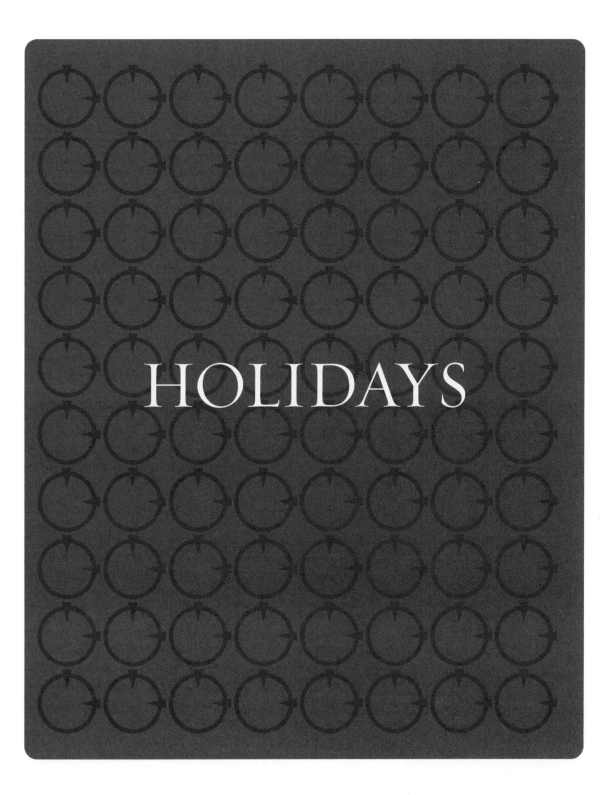

HOLIDAYS

15 minutes

3
net grams
carbs

SERVE-ALONG SUGGESTIONS

Grilled Salmon with Herb Crust (see p.210)

Steamed green beans

Really Hot Iced Coffee (see p.329)

BELL-RINGER SALSA CHEESECAKE

2	8-ounce packages cream cheese
2	cups shredded Monterey Jack or Colby Jack cheese (8 ounces)
2	8-ounce cartons dairy sour cream
3	eggs
1	cup bottled salsa
1	4-ounce can diced green chile peppers, drained
1	6-ounce container frozen avocado dip (guacamole), thawed
1	medium tomato, peeled, seeded, and chopped Low-carb tortilla chips and/or assorted low-carb crackers (optional)

PREP:
15 minutes
BAKE:
35 minutes
STAND:
30 minutes
COOL:
2 hours
CHILL:
4 to 24 hours
OVEN:
350°F
MAKES:
20 appetizer servings

1. For filling, let cream cheese stand at room temperature for 30 minutes to soften. In a large mixing bowl beat cream cheese with an electric mixer on low to medium speed until smooth. Add Monterey Jack cheese and 1 carton of the sour cream; beat until combined. Add eggs all at once; beat on low speed just until combined. Stir in salsa and chile peppers.

2. Pour filling into a 9-inch springform pan. Place pan in a shallow baking pan. Bake in a 350° oven for 35 to 40 minutes or until center appears nearly set when shaken. Place pan on a wire rack.

3. Spoon remaining carton of sour cream onto top of the hot cheesecake. Let stand about 1 minute to soften; carefully spread over top. Cool thoroughly. Cover and chill for at least 4 hours or up to 24 hours.

4. To serve, remove sides of pan. Spoon avocado dip around top outside edge of cheesecake. Sprinkle cheesecake with tomato. Serve with chips.

Nutrition Facts per serving cheesecake only: 203 cal., 19 g total fat (10 g sat. fat), 77 mg chol., 224 mg sodium, 3 g carbo., 0 g fiber, 7 g pro.

10 minutes

2 net grams carbs

SERVE-ALONG SUGGESTIONS

Purchased rotisserie cooked whole chicken

Roasted Asparagus Parmesan (see p.267)

Cranberry Coleslaw (see p.391)

PUMPKIN CREAM CHEESE SPREAD

1   8-ounce package cream cheese, softened
½   cup canned pumpkin
¼   cup heat-stable granular sugar substitute
1   teaspoon pumpkin pie spice
1   teaspoon vanilla
      Low-carb crackers, bagels, or breads (optional)

1. In a medium mixing bowl beat cream cheese with an electric mixer on medium speed for 30 seconds. Add pumpkin, sugar substitute, pumpkin pie spice, and vanilla. Beat until smooth.

2. Transfer mixture to a small serving bowl. Cover and chill for at least 1 hour or up to 24 hours. Serve with crackers.

Nutrition Facts per 1 tablespoon spread: 73 cal., 7 g total fat (4 g sat. fat), 21 mg chol., 57 mg sodium, 2 g carbo., 0 g fiber, 2 g pro.

PREP:
10 minutes
CHILL:
1 to 24 hours
MAKES:
about 1½ cups spread
(12 servings)

15
minutes

6
net grams
carbs

SERVE-ALONG SUGGESTIONS

Assorted breakfast meats,
such as crisp-cooked
bacon, sausage links,
cooked ham slices, etc.

Vanilla Cream-Topped
Raspberries (see p.335)

Make-Believe Champagne
(see p.394)

MUSHROOM-TOPPED EGG CUPS

12	wonton wrappers
2	eggs
1	cup half-and-half or light cream
¼	teaspoon salt
	Dash black pepper
½	cup sliced fresh mushrooms
½	cup diced cooked ham
½	cup finely shredded cheddar cheese (2 ounces)
½	cup finely shredded mozzarella cheese (2 ounces)
1	2-ounce jar sliced pimiento, drained
2	tablespoons snipped fresh parsley

1. Press wonton wrappers into 12 greased 2½-inch muffin cups. Set aside.

2. In a small bowl beat eggs with a fork; stir in half-and-half, salt, and pepper. Pour into muffin cups. Sprinkle with mushrooms, ham, cheddar cheese, and mozzarella cheese. Top with pimiento and parsley.

3. Bake in a 375° oven about 15 minutes or until a knife inserted near the centers comes out clean.

Nutrition Facts per serving: 105 cal., 6 g total fat (3 g sat. fat), 54 mg chol., 239 mg sodium, 6 g carbo., 0 g fiber, 6 g pro.

PREP:
15 minutes
BAKE:
15 minutes
OVEN:
375°F
MAKES:
12 side-dish servings

15 minutes

1
net gram
carbs

SERVE-ALONG SUGGESTIONS

Asparagus with Citrus
Mock Hollandaise
(see p.387)

Macadamia-White
Chocolate Dessert
(see p.363)

Cranberry Vodka
(see p.395)

DIJON-ROSEMARY ROAST LEG OF LAMB

3 tablespoons Dijon-style mustard

1 tablespoon finely chopped shallot

1 tablespoon lemon juice

1 tablespoon olive oil

1 tablespoon snipped fresh rosemary or ½ teaspoon dried rosemary, crushed

1 to 1½ teaspoons bottled minced garlic (2 to 3 cloves)

½ teaspoon salt

½ teaspoon freshly ground black pepper

1 6-pound whole leg of lamb with bone

1. In a small bowl whisk together mustard, shallot, lemon juice, oil, rosemary, garlic, salt, and pepper. Trim fat from meat. Spread mustard mixture evenly over all sides of meat.

2. Place meat, fat side up, on a rack in a shallow roasting pan. Roast in a 325° oven until desired doneness. Allow 1¾ to 2¼ hours for medium-rare doneness (140°F) or 2¼ to 2¾ hours for medium doneness (155°F). Transfer meat to a serving platter.

3. Cover with foil; let stand for 15 minutes before carving. Temperature of the meat after standing should be 145°F for medium-rare or 160°F for medium.

Nutrition Facts per serving: 425 cal., 17 g total fat (6 g sat. fat), 197 mg chol., 268 mg sodium, 1 g carbo., 0 g fiber, 64 g pro.

PREP:
15 minutes
ROAST:
1¾ hours
STAND:
15 minutes
OVEN:
325°F
MAKES:
12 to 16 main-dish servings

15 minutes

5
net grams
carbs

SERVE-ALONG SUGGESTIONS

Pear-Chutney Salsa
(see p.383)

Fresh spinach leaves
topped with crisp-cooked
bacon, crumbled blue
cheese and low-carb
bottled balsamic vinaigrette
salad dressing

Tiramisu Cream
(see p.359)

NUT-CRUSTED TURKEY BREAST

1   4- to 4½-pound turkey breast with bone
1   tablespoon olive oil or cooking oil
½   teaspoon bottled minced garlic (1 clove)
¼   teaspoon salt
⅓   cup slivered almonds
⅓   cup pine nuts
1   teaspoon ground coriander
1   teaspoon dried thyme, crushed
¼   teaspoon coarsely ground black pepper
¼   cup low-sugar orange marmalade

PREP:
15 minutes
ROAST:
1½ hours
STAND:
15 minutes
OVEN:
325°F
MAKES:
10 to 12 main-
dish servings

1. Remove skin from turkey. Place turkey on a greased rack in a shallow roasting pan. In a small bowl combine oil, garlic, and salt; brush over turkey. Roast in a 325° oven for 45 minutes.

2. Meanwhile, in a blender container or food processor bowl combine almonds and pine nuts. Cover and blend or process until finely chopped. In a small bowl combine the finely chopped nuts, coriander, thyme, and pepper.

3. Remove turkey from oven. Brush surface with orange marmalade. Sprinkle with nut mixture; press gently so nuts adhere. Roast for 45 to 60 minutes more or until turkey is tender and no longer pink (170°F). Remove from oven. Cover loosely with foil; let stand for 15 minutes before slicing.

Nutrition Facts per serving: 327 cal., 17 g total fat (4 g sat. fat), 105 mg chol., 131 mg sodium, 5 g carbo., 1 g fiber, 38 g pro.

15 minutes

6
net grams
carbs

SERVE-ALONG SUGGESTIONS

Corn and Chicken Soup
(see p.59)

Lemon-Tarragon
Vegetables (see p.271)

Double Berry Delight
(see p.361)

HOISIN-SAUCED CORNISH HENS

2 1- to 1½-pound Cornish game hens
½ cup bottled hoisin sauce
¼ cup raspberry vinegar or red wine vinegar
¼ cup orange juice
1 to 2 teaspoons chile paste

1. Rinse insides of hens; pat dry with paper towels. Using a sharp knife or kitchen shears, cut hens in half lengthwise. Sprinkle body cavities with salt. Place hens, breast sides up, on a rack in a shallow roasting pan. Cover loosely with foil. Bake in a 375° oven for 30 minutes.

2. Meanwhile, for glaze, in a small bowl stir together hoisin sauce, vinegar, orange juice, and chile paste.

3. Remove hens from oven. Brush some of the glaze over hens. Bake, uncovered, for 45 to 60 minutes more or until hens are tender and no longer pink (180°F), brushing occasionally with the remaining glaze.

Nutrition Facts per serving: 371 cal., 23 g total fat (5 g sat. fat), 120 mg chol., 2,223 mg sodium, 6 g carbo., 0 g fiber, 38 g pro.

PREP:
15 minutes
BAKE:
1¼ hours
OVEN:
375°F
MAKES:
4 main-dish servings

10 minutes

1
net gram
carbs

SERVE-ALONG SUGGESTIONS

Broiled Asparagus and
Fresh Mozzarella
(see p.283)

Strawberries with Orange
Cream Dip (see p.333)

Low-calorie lemonade-
flavored carbonated
beverage served with
lemon wedges, if desired

CORIANDER TURKEY BREAST

1   2- to 3-pound fresh or frozen turkey breast half with bone
1   tablespoon butter or margarine
2   teaspoons ground coriander
½   teaspoon onion powder
¼   teaspoon chili powder
    Dash cayenne pepper
1   tablespoon lemon juice

PREP:
10 minutes
GRILL:
1¼ hours
MAKES:
8 main-dish servings

1. Thaw turkey, if frozen. Remove skin and fat from turkey. In a small saucepan melt butter over medium heat. Stir in coriander, onion powder, chili powder, and cayenne pepper; cook for 1 minute. Remove from heat. Stir in lemon juice. Spread spice mixture evenly over all sides of turkey.

2. In a grill with a cover, arrange medium-hot coals around a drip pan. Test for medium heat above the pan. Place turkey on the grill rack over drip pan. Cover and grill for 1¼ to 2 hours or until turkey is tender and no longer pink (170°F). Add more coals as needed to maintain heat.

Nutrition Facts per serving: 189 cal., 9 g total fat (3 g sat. fat), 77 mg chol., 67 mg sodium, 1 g carbo., 0 g fiber, 25 g pro.

10 minutes

2 net grams carbs

SERVE-ALONG SUGGESTIONS

Chopped romaine lettuce tossed with snow pea pods, sliced mushrooms, sliced radish, and shredded cheese

Grilled or pan-fried 1½- inch-thick pork top loin chops

Almond-Sauced Berries (see p.349)

PEAR-CHUTNEY SALSA

3 tablespoons chutney
1 medium pear, peeled, cored, and chopped
½ cup peeled, seeded, and chopped cucumber
½ cup bottled chunky salsa
2 tablespoons slivered almonds, toasted

1. Cut up any large pieces of chutney. In a small bowl stir together chutney, pear, cucumber, and salsa. If desired, cover and chill until ready to serve.

2. Before serving, stir in almonds.

Nutrition Facts per serving: 12 cal., 0 g total fat (0 g sat. fat), 0 mg chol., 10 mg sodium, 2 g carbo., 0 g fiber, 0 g pro.

START TO FINISH:
10 minutes
MAKES:
2 cups (32 servings)

15 minutes

5 net grams carbs

SERVE-ALONG SUGGESTIONS

Pork au Poivre with
Mustard and Sage
(see p.133)

Steamed sugar snap peas

Orange-Ginger Rhubarb
(see p.353)

OYSTERS BROILED IN BLUE CHEESE BUTTER

1   cup crumbled blue cheese (4 ounces)
¼   cup unsalted butter, softened
¼   teaspoon black pepper
24   oysters on the half shell*

1. Preheat broiler. In a small bowl stir together blue cheese, butter, and pepper.

2. Dot each oyster with a rounded teaspoon of the blue cheese mixture. Place oyster shells, about half at a time, on the unheated rack of a broiler pan. Broil 4 to 5 inches from the heat for 3 to 5 minutes or until edges of the oysters start to curl. Serve immediately.

> ***Note:** For oysters in shells, thoroughly wash oysters. Using an oyster knife or other blunt-tipped knife, open the shells. Remove oysters; pat dry with paper towels. Discard the flat top shells; wash deep bottom shells. Place each oyster in a shell.

Nutrition Facts per serving: 149 cal., 9 g total fat (5 g sat. fat), 17 mg chol., 238 mg sodium, 5 g carbo., 0 g fiber, 12 g pro.

PREP:
15 minutes
BROIL:
3 minutes
MAKES:
12 appetizer servings

15 minutes

4
net grams
carbs

SERVE-ALONG SUGGESTIONS

Coriander-Studded
Tenderloin Steaks
(see p.103)

Warm Spiced Peaches
(see p.357)

Decaf coffee, hot or iced

ASPARAGUS

WITH CITRUS MOCK HOLLANDAISE

2	pounds asparagus spears
¼	cup dairy sour cream
¼	cup mayonnaise or salad dressing
½	teaspoon finely shredded lemon peel
1	teaspoon lemon juice
	Water

1. Snap off and discard woody bases from asparagus. If desired, scrape off scales. Place a steamer basket in a large skillet. Add enough water to come just below bottom of basket. Bring to boiling. Place asparagus in steamer basket. Reduce heat to medium low. Cover and steam for 3 to 5 minutes or until asparagus is crisp-tender.

2. Meanwhile, for sauce, in a small saucepan combine sour cream, mayonnaise, lemon peel, and lemon juice. Stir in enough water (1 to 2 teaspoons) to reach desired consistency. Cook and stir over low heat until heated through, but do not boil. Serve sauce over asparagus.

Nutrition Facts per serving: 105 cal., 10 g total fat (2 g sat. fat), 10 mg chol., 61 mg sodium, 4 g carbo., 4 g fiber, 2 g pro.

PREP:
15 minutes
COOK:
5 minutes
MAKES:
6 to 8 side-dish
servings

15 minutes

3
net grams
carbs

SERVE-ALONG SUGGESTIONS

Mixed greens tossed with bottled low-carb Italian salad dressing and shaved Parmesan cheese

Broiled boneless, skinless chicken breast halves

Peppered Strawberries (see p.337)

YAM AND PEANUT SOUP

2 tablespoons unsalted butter
3 cups sliced peeled yams or sweet potatoes (about 1 pound)
¼ cup chopped onion
¼ cup chopped celery
4 cups reduced-sodium chicken broth
⅓ cup natural creamy peanut butter
¼ teaspoon black pepper
  Chopped peanuts (optional)

PREP:
15 minutes
COOK:
35 minutes
MAKES:
6 side-dish servings

1. In a large saucepan melt butter over medium heat. Add yams, onion, and celery; cook for 5 minutes, stirring occasionally. Add chicken broth. Bring to boiling; reduce heat. Simmer, covered, about 30 minutes or until vegetables are tender. Cool slightly. Transfer half of the mixture to a food processor bowl or blender container. Cover and process or blend until smooth. Repeat with the remaining mixture. Return all of the mixture to saucepan.

2. Add peanut butter and pepper to yam mixture. Cook and stir over medium-low heat until combined and heated through. If desired, sprinkle each serving with peanuts and additional pepper.

Nutrition Facts per serving: 133 cal., 11 g total fat (4 g sat. fat), 11 mg chol., 483 mg sodium, 4 g carbo., 1 g fiber, 6 g pro.

15 minutes

2
net grams carbs

SERVE-ALONG SUGGESTIONS

Oven-Fried Coconut Chicken (see p.193)

Down-South Green Beans (see p.253)

Fruit-Topped Phyllo Cups (see p.345)

CRANBERRY COLESLAW

¼   cup mayonnaise or salad dressing
2   tablespoons heat-stable granular sugar substitute
1   tablespoon vinegar
¼   cup chopped fresh cranberries or snipped dried cranberries
5   cups shredded cabbage (1 small head)

1. For dressing, in a small bowl stir together mayonnaise, sugar substitute, and vinegar. Stir in cranberries.

2. Place shredded cabbage in a large bowl. Pour dressing over cabbage; toss gently to coat. Cover and chill for at least 45 minutes or up to 4 hours.

Nutrition Facts per serving: 86 cal., 8 g total fat (1 g sat. fat), 3 mg chol., 61 mg sodium, 4 g carbo., 2 g fiber, 1 g pro.

PREP:
15 minutes
CHILL:
45 minutes to 4 hours
MAKES:
6 side-dish servings

10 minutes

9 net grams carbs

SERVE-ALONG SUGGESTIONS

Apple-Glazed Turkey (see p.197)

Zucchini alla Romana (see p.281)

Fresh apricot halves and cranberries sprinkled with sugar substitute

CINNAMON-SPICED PUMPKIN SOUP

1	15-ounce can pumpkin
1	14-ounce can chicken broth
1	cup half-and-half or light cream
½	teaspoon ground cinnamon
⅛	to ¼ teaspoon ground nutmeg
⅛	teaspoon salt
	Dairy sour cream (optional)
	Snipped fresh chives or green onion tops (optional)

1. In a medium saucepan combine pumpkin, chicken broth, half-and-half, cinnamon, nutmeg, and salt. Bring just to boiling.

2. Ladle into soup bowls or mugs. If desired, top with sour cream and sprinkle with chives.

Nutrition Facts per serving: 128 cal., 8 g total fat (5 g sat. fat), 22 mg chol., 516 mg sodium, 12 g carbo., 3 g fiber, 4 g pro.

START TO FINISH: 10 minutes
MAKES: 4 to 6 side-dish servings

MAKE-BELIEVE CHAMPAGNE

START TO FINISH:

10 minutes

MAKES:

20 servings

1 1-liter bottle carbonated water, chilled
1 1-liter bottle ginger ale, chilled
1 24-ounce bottle unsweetened white grape juice, chilled
Ice cubes

1. In a large pitcher combine carbonated water, ginger ale, and white grape juice.

2. Pour over ice cubes in chilled champagne or wine glasses.

Nutrition Facts per serving: 37 cal., 0 g total fat (0 g sat. fat), 0 mg chol., 14 mg sodium, 9 g carbo., 0 g fiber, 0 g pro.

9
net grams carbs

SERVE-ALONG SUGGESTIONS

Feta-Stuffed Mushrooms (see p.319)

Oven-roasted beef tenderloin

Fresh strawberries topped with whipped cream and toasted pecans

CRANBERRY VODKA

2 cups fresh cranberries

2 cups vodka

1. Place cranberries in a clean 1-quart jar. Pour vodka over cranberries. Cover jar tightly with a nonmetallic lid (or cover jar with plastic wrap and tightly seal with a metal lid). Let stand in a cool dark place for at least 2 weeks or up to 2 months.

2. To serve, pour vodka and some of the cranberries into small vodka or schnapps glasses.

Nutrition Facts per serving: 80 cal., 0 g total fat (0 g sat. fat), 0 mg chol., 0 mg sodium, 2 g carbo., 1 g fiber, 0 g pro.

PREP:
10 minutes
STAND:
2 weeks to 2 months
MAKES:
16 servings

1
net gram carbs

SERVE-ALONG SUGGESTIONS

Toasted Almonds with Rosemary (see p.323)

Cheesy Spinach Quesadillas (see p.41)

Hot Ribeye Bites (see p.31)

15 minutes

6 net grams carbs

SERVE-ALONG SUGGESTIONS

Oysters Broiled in Blue Cheese Butter (see p.385)

Mixed greens tossed with sliced celery, thinly sliced green onions, and olive oil and white wine vinegar

Herbed Top Loin Steak with Balsamic Sauce (see p.107)

CHOCOLATE MOUSSE

3	tablespoons heat-stable granular sugar substitute (Splenda)
3	tablespoons unsweetened cocoa powder
1½	cups whipping cream
1	teaspoon vanilla

START TO FINISH:
15 minutes
MAKES:
4 servings

1. In a small bowl stir together sugar substitute and cocoa powder. Set aside.

2. In a chilled medium mixing bowl combine whipping cream and vanilla. Beat with the chilled beaters of an electric mixer on medium speed just until mixture starts to thicken.

3. Stir in cocoa mixture. Beat just until stiff peaks form (tips stand straight). Spoon into dessert dishes.

Nutrition Facts per serving: 335 cal., 34 g total fat (21 g sat. fat), 123 mg chol., 35 mg sodium, 6 g carbo., 0 g fiber, 3 g pro.

15 minutes

3
net grams
carbs

SERVE-ALONG SUGGESTIONS

Beef Tenderloins with
Wine Sauce (see p.87)

Lemon-Tarragon
Vegetables (see p.271)

Long-stemmed
fresh strawberries

COFFEE AND CREAM DESSERT

1   tablespoon hot water
2   teaspoons instant espresso coffee powder or 1 tablespoon
    instant coffee crystals
1½ cups whipping cream
2   tablespoons heat-stable granular sugar substitute (Splenda)
2   teaspoons vanilla
2   tablespoons sliced almonds, toasted

1. In a large mixing bowl stir hot water into coffee powder until dissolved. Place bowl in the freezer for 5 minutes.

2. Add whipping cream, sugar substitute, and vanilla to coffee mixture. Beat with the chilled beaters of an electric mixer on medium speed until stiff peaks form (tips stand straight).

3. Spoon into dessert dishes. Sprinkle with almonds.

Nutrition Facts per serving: 231 cal., 24 g total fat (14 g sat. fat), 82 mg chol., 24 mg sodium, 3 g carbo., 0 g fiber, 2 g pro.

START TO FINISH:
15 minutes
MAKES:
6 servings

CRÈME FRAÎCHE FOOL WITH BERRIES

START TO FINISH:

10 minutes

MAKES:

2 servings

10
net grams carbs

SERVE-ALONG SUGGESTIONS

Assorted cheese and vegetable tray, such as: red or orange sweet pepper strips, bite-size strips of jicama, celery sticks, cucumber slices; pepper jack, cheddar, and/or Swiss cheese cubes

Salmon Caesar Salad (see p.79)

Fruit-flavored decaf iced tea served with orange wedges, if desired

⅔ cup purchased crème fraîche
1 tablespoon heat-stable granular sugar substitute (Splenda)
1 tablespoon raspberry liqueur (optional)
¾ cup blackberries

1. In a small mixing bowl combine crème fraîche, sugar substitute, and, if desired, raspberry liqueur. Beat with an electric mixer on medium speed about 2 minutes or until thickened and fluffy.

2. Fold blackberries into crème fraîche mixture. Spoon into dessert dishes.

Nutrition Facts per serving: 456 cal., 44 g total fat (27 g sat. fat), 138 mg chol., 69 mg sodium, 13 g carbo., 3 g fiber, 4 g pro.

Carb Counts of Breads and Cereals

Breads	serving size	calories	carb(g)	net carb(g)
Bagels				
Cinnamon-raisin	One 3½-inch bagel	195	39	37
Egg	One 3½-inch bagel	197	38	36
Oat-bran	One 3½-inch bagel	181	38	35
Plain	One 3½-inch bagel	195	38	36
Banana bread	1 slice	196	33	32
Biscuits				
Baking powder from recipe	1 medium	212	27	26
Low fat from refrigerated dough	1 medium	63	12	12
Regular from refrigerated dough	1 medium	93	13	13
Bread crumbs, plain	1 cup	427	78	75
Bread crumbs, seasoned	1 cup	440	84	79
Bun, frankfurter	1 medium	123	22	21
Bun, hamburger	1 medium	123	22	21
Cinnamon roll with raisins	1 medium	223	31	30
Corn bread	One 2½-inch square	173	28	26
Cracked wheat bread	1 slice	65	12	11
Croissant	1 croissant	231	26	24
Croutons, seasoned	1 cup	186	25	23
Dinner roll	1 medium	84	14	13
Egg bread	1 slice	115	19	18
French bread	1 slice	69	13	12
French toast	1 slice	149	16	15
Hard rolls	1 medium	167	30	29
Italian bread	1 slice	54	10	10
Matzo, plain	1 medium	112	24	23
Mixed grain bread	1 slice	65	12	10
Muffins				
Blueberry	1 medium	158	27	26
Bran-raisin	1 medium	106	19	16
Corn	1 medium	174	29	27
English	1 medium	134	26	24
Oat-bran	1 medium	154	28	25
Oatmeal bread	1 slice	73	13	12
Pancakes, plain	One 4-inch	82	16	15
Pita bread	1 large	165	33	32
Pumpernickel bread	1 slice	80	15	13
Raisin bread, unfrosted	1 slice	71	14	13
Rye bread, reduced calorie	1 slice	47	9	6
Rye bread, regular	1 slice	83	15	13
Stuffing, made from mix	½ cup	178	22	19
Taco shell	1 medium	62	8	7
Tortilla, corn	1 medium	58	12	11
Tortilla, flour	1 medium	104	18	17
Waffle, low-fat	One 4-inch	83	15	15
Waffle, plain	One 4-inch	87	13	12
White bread, reduced calorie	1 slice	48	10	8
White bread, regular	1 slice	67	12	11
Whole wheat bread	1 slice	69	13	11

Cereals	serving size	calories	carb(g)	net carb(g)
Bite-size square corn cereal	1 cup	113	26	26
Bite-size square rice cereal	1¼ cups	117	27	27
Bite-size square wheat cereal	1 cup	104	24	21
Corn flakes	1 cup	102	24	23
Crisp rice cereal	1¼ cups	124	29	29
Crisp rice cereal, chocolate-flavored	¾ cup	120	27	27
Farina, cooked	1 cup	112	24	23
Granola with raisins, low-fat	½ cup	195	40	37
Granola, plain	¾ cup	248	36	32
Hominy grits, cooked	1 cup	145	31	30
Honey-graham cereal	¾ cup	116	26	25
Oat bran, cooked	1 cup	88	25	19
Oat square cereal, sweetened	¾ cup	121	25	23
Oatmeal				
Apple and cinnamon, instant	1 pkg.	125	26	24
Maple and brown sugar, instant	1 pkg.	153	31	28
Old-fashioned, cooked	1 cup	145	25	21
Peanut butter cereal	¾ cup	112	22	21
Puffed corn cereal	1 cup	118	28	28
Puffed rice cereal	1 cup	56	13	13
Puffed wheat cereal	1 cup	44	10	10
Raisin bran cereal	1 cup	178	43	38
Rice and wheat flakes	1 cup	115	22	21
Shredded wheat biscuits	2 biscuits	156	38	33
Toasted oat cereal	1 cup	110	23	20
Wheat cereal, cooked	1 cup	133	28	26
Wheat flakes cereal	¾ cup	95	23	18

Pasta	serving size	calories	carb(g)	net carb(g)
Couscous, cooked	1 cup	176	36	34
Macaroni, elbow, cooked	1 cup	197	40	38
Noodles, egg, cooked	1 cup	213	40	38
Noodles, rice, cooked	1 cup	192	44	42
Noodles, spinach, cooked	1 cup	211	39	35
Spaghetti, cooked	1 cup	197	40	38
Spaghetti, whole wheat, cooked	1 cup	174	37	31

Rice and Grains	serving size	calories	carb(g)	net carb(g)
Barley, cooked	1 cup	193	44	38
Buckwheat groats, cooked	1 cup	155	33	28
Bulgar, cooked	1 cup	151	34	26
Millet, cooked	1 cup	207	41	39
Rice, instant, cooked	1 cup	162	35	34
Rice, long-grain brown, cooked	1 cup	216	45	42
Rice, long-grain white, cooked	1 cup	205	45	44
Rice, wild, cooked	1 cup	166	35	32
Wheat germ, toasted	1 tbsp.	27	3	2

Carb Counts of Desserts

	serving size	calories	carb (g)	net carb (g)
Baked				
Brownies, unfrosted	One 2¾-inch square	227	36	35
Cakes				
Angel food	One 1-oz. slice	72	16	16
Chocolate, frosted	⅛ of 18-oz. cake	235	35	33
Pineapple upside down	One 2½-inch square	367	58	57
Pound, fat free	One 1-oz. slice	80	17	17
Pound, regular	One 1-oz. slice	109	14	14
Cheesecake	⅛ of 17-oz. cake	257	20	20
Cheese-filled Danish	1 medium	266	26	25
Cookies				
Butter	1 medium	23	3	3
Chocolate chip, reduced fat	1 medium	45	7	7
Chocolate chip, regular	1 medium	48	7	7
Chocolate chip, sugar free	1 medium	108	16	16
Chocolate, fat free	1 medium	49	12	12
Chocolate-filled sandwich	1 medium	47	7	7
Fig bar	1 medium	56	11	10
Molasses	1 medium	65	11	11
Oatmeal, soft, regular	1 medium	61	10	10
Oatmeal, sugar free	1 medium	106	16	16
Peanut butter	1 medium	72	9	9
Shortbread, plain	1 medium	40	5	5
Shortbread, pecan	1 medium	76	8	8
Sugar	1 medium	72	10	10
Vanilla wafer	1 medium	18	3	3
Vanilla-filled sandwich	1 medium	48	7	7
Éclair, filled	1 medium	262	24	23

	serving size	calories	carb (g)	net carb (g)
Gingerbread	One 2½-inch square	263	36	35
Glazed doughnut	1 medium	242	27	26
Pies				
Apple	⅛ pie	277	40	38
Blueberry	⅛ pie	271	41	40
Boston cream	⅛ pie	232	39	38
Cherry	⅛ pie	304	47	46
Chocolate cream	⅛ pie	344	38	36
Coconut custard	⅛ pie	270	31	29
Lemon meringue	⅛ pie	303	53	52
Pecan	⅛ pie	452	65	61
Pumpkin	⅛ pie	229	30	27
Shortcake, biscuit type	1 medium	225	32	31
Shortcake, sponge type	1 medium	87	18	18
Frozen				
Ice cream, chocolate	½ cup	143	19	18
Ice cream, strawberry	½ cup	127	18	17
Ice cream, vanilla	½ cup	133	16	16
Ice cream, vanilla, no sugar added	½ cup	99	12	11
Italian ices	½ cup	61	16	16
Sherbet, orange	½ cup	102	22	22
Others				
Gelatin dessert, reduced calorie	½ cup	8	1	1
Gelatin dessert, regular	½ cup	80	19	19
Pudding, chocolate, instant	½ cup	150	28	27
Pudding, tapioca	½ cup	134	22	22
Pudding, vanilla, instant	½ cup	148	28	28

Carb Counts of Fruits and Vegetables

Fruits	serving size	calories	carb (g)	net carb (g)
Apple juice	1 cup	117	29	29
Apples, dried	5 rings	78	21	18
Apples, unpeeled	1 small	81	21	17
Applesauce, unsweetened	1 cup	105	28	25
Apricot nectar	1 cup	141	36	34
Apricots, dried	10 halves	83	22	19
Apricots, unpeeled	1 medium	17	4	3
Bananas	1 medium	109	28	25
Blackberries	1 cup	75	18	10
Blueberries	1 cup	81	20	16
Cantaloupe, cubed	1 cup	56	13	12
Cherries, sour, canned	1 cup	88	22	19
Cherries, sweet	1 cup	91	23	20
Cranberries, dried	¼ cup	92	24	22
Dates, whole	5 dates	116	31	28
Figs, dried	2 figs	97	25	20
Grape juice	1 cup	154	38	38
Grapefruit	½ grapefruit	37	9	8
Grapefruit juice	1 cup	96	23	23
Grapes, seedless	10 grapes	36	9	8
Honeydew melon, cubed	1 cup	60	16	15
Kiwi fruit	1 medium	46	11	8
Mangoes, sliced	1 cup	107	28	25
Nectarines	1 medium	67	16	14
Orange juice	1 cup	112	26	26
Oranges	1 small	62	15	12
Papayas, cubed	1 cup	55	14	12
Peaches	1 medium	42	11	9
Peaches, canned (juice pack)	1 cup	109	29	26
Peaches, dried	3 halves	93	24	21
Pear juice	1 cup	124	32	28
Pears	1 medium	98	25	21
Pineapple chunks, canned (juice pack)	1 cup	149	39	37
Pineapple juice, unsweetened	1 cup	140	34	34
Pineapple, cubed	1 cup	76	19	17
Plums	1 medium	36	9	8
Plums, canned (juice pack)	1 cup	146	38	36
Raisins, seedless	1 cup	435	115	109
Raspberries	1 cup	60	14	6
Strawberries	1 cup	50	12	8
Tangerines	1 medium	37	9	7
Watermelon, cubed	1 cup	49	11	10

Vegetables	serving size	calories	carb (g)	net carb (g)
Artichokes, cooked	1 cup	84	19	10
Asparagus, cooked	1 cup	43	8	5
Bamboo shoots, canned	1 cup	25	4	2
Bean sprouts, cooked	1 cup	26	5	4
Beans				
Baked with pork and tomato sauce	1 cup	248	49	37
Baked, vegetarian	1 cup	236	52	39
Black, cooked	1 cup	227	41	26
Garbanzo, cooked	1 cup	269	45	32
Great northern, cooked	1 cup	209	37	25
Green, cooked	1 cup	44	10	6
Pinto, cooked	1 cup	234	44	29
Red kidney, cooked	1 cup	225	40	27
Beets, cooked	1 cup	75	17	14
Black-eyed peas, cooked	1 cup	200	36	25
Broccoli, cooked	1 cup	44	8	4
Broccoli, raw	1 cup	25	5	2

	serving size	calories	carb (g)	net carb (g)
Brussels sprouts, cooked	1 cup	61	14	10
Cabbage, cooked	1 cup	33	7	4
Cabbage, raw	1 cup	18	4	2
Carrots, cooked	1 cup	70	16	11
Carrots, raw	1 medium	31	7	5
Cauliflower, cooked	1 cup	29	5	2
Cauliflower, raw	1 cup	25	5	2
Celery, cooked	1 cup	27	6	4
Celery, raw	1 stalk	6	1	0
Corn, cooked	1 cup	131	32	28
Corn, cream style, cooked	1 cup	184	46	43
Cucumber, unpeeled	1 cup	14	3	2
Eggplant, cooked	1 cup	28	7	4
Green onion, raw	1 medium	5	1	1
Green or red sweet peppers, cooked	1 cup	38	9	7
Green or red sweet peppers, raw	1 cup	40	10	7
Green soybeans, cooked	1 cup	254	20	12
Greens				
Beet, cooked	1 cup	39	8	4
Collard, cooked	1 cup	49	9	4
Dandelion, cooked	1 cup	35	7	4
Mustard, cooked	1 cup	21	3	0
Kale, cooked	1 cup	36	7	4
Kohlrabi, cooked	1 cup	48	11	9
Leeks, cooked	1 cup	32	8	7
Lentils, cooked	1 cup	230	40	24
Lettuces				
Butterhead	1 cup	7	1	0
Iceberg	1 cup	6	1	0
Leaf	1 cup	10	2	1
Romaine	1 cup	8	1	0
Mushrooms, cooked	1 cup	42	8	5
Mushrooms, raw	1 cup	18	3	2
Okra, cooked	1 cup	51	12	8
Onions, cooked	1 cup	92	21	18
Onions, raw	1 cup	61	14	11
Parsnips, cooked	1 cup	126	30	24
Peas, cooked	1 cup	67	11	6
Potatoes				
Baked with skin	1 medium	220	51	46
Boiled	1 cup	134	31	28
Sweet, baked with skin	1 medium	150	35	31
Pumpkin, canned	1 cup	83	20	13
Radishes	1 medium	1	0	0
Rutabagas, cooked	1 cup	66	15	12
Sauerkraut, canned	1 cup	45	10	4
Spinach, cooked	1 cup	41	7	3
Spinach, raw	1 cup	7	1	0
Split peas, cooked	1 cup	231	41	25
Summer squash, cooked	1 cup	36	8	6
Summer squash, raw	1 cup	23	5	3
Tomatillos, raw	1 medium	11	2	1
Tomato juice	1 cup	41	10	9
Tomato paste	1 cup	215	51	40
Tomato sauce	1 cup	74	18	15
Tomatoes, canned	1 cup	46	10	8
Tomatoes, dried	1 piece	5	1	1
Tomatoes, raw	1 cup	38	8	6
Turnips, cooked	1 cup	33	8	5
Vegetable juice cocktail	1 cup	46	11	9
Water chestnuts, canned	1 cup	70	17	14
Winter squash, cooked and cubed	1 cup	80	18	12

Carb Counts of Dairy, Fish, Meats, and Poultry

	serving size	calories	carb (g)	net carb (g)
Dairy				
Cheese				
Cheddar	1 oz.	114	0	0
Cottage (2% fat)	1 cup	203	8	8
Cottage (4% fat)	1 cup	233	6	6
Cream (regular)	1 tbsp.	51	0	0
Cream (fat-free)	1 tbsp.	15	1	1
Feta	1 oz.	75	1	1
Mozzarella (part skim)	1 oz.	79	1	1
Muenster	1 oz.	104	0	0
Parmesan, grated	1 tbsp.	23	0	0
Process American	1 oz.	106	0	0
Provolone	1 oz.	100	1	1
Swiss	1 oz.	107	1	1
Milk and Cream				
Light cream	1 tbsp.	29	1	1
Nonfat milk	1 cup	86	12	12
Pressurized whipped topping	1 tbsp.	8	0	0
Reduced-fat milk (2% fat)	1 cup	121	12	12
Whipping cream	1 tbsp.	52	0	0
Whole milk (3.3% fat)	1 cup	150	11	11
Yogurt				
Fruit-flavored	8 oz.	231	43	43
Plain	8 oz.	144	16	16
Fruit-flavored with low-cal sweetener	8 oz.	98	17	17
Fish and Seafood				
Flounder, cooked	3 oz.	99	0	0
Orange roughy, cooked	3 oz.	76	0	0
Lobster, cooked	3 oz.	83	0	0
Salmon, cooked	3 oz.	184	0	0
Shrimp, unbreaded, cooked	3 oz.	84	0	0
Sardines, canned	3 oz.	177	0	0
Swordfish, cooked	3 oz.	132	0	0
Tuna, cooked	3 oz.	118	0	0
Beef				
83% lean ground beef, cooked	3 oz.	218	0	0
73% lean ground beef, cooked	3 oz.	246	0	0
Bottom round, cooked	3 oz.	178	0	0
Chuck blade, cooked	3 oz.	213	0	0
Eye of round, cooked	3 oz.	143	0	0

	serving size	calories	carb (g)	net carb (g)
Loin, top loin, cooked	3 oz.	176	0	0
Ribs, cooked	3 oz.	195	0	0
Sirloin, cooked	3 oz.	166	0	0
Tenderloin, cooked	3 oz.	189	0	0
Lamb				
Arm chop, cooked	3 oz.	237	0	0
Leg, cooked	3 oz.	162	0	0
Loin, cooked	3 oz.	184	0	0
Rib, cooked	3 oz.	197	0	0
Pork				
Baby back ribs, cooked	3 oz.	315	0	0
Bacon, cooked	3 slices	109	0	0
Canadian-style bacon, cooked	2 oz.	86	1	1
Country-style ribs, cooked	3 oz.	252	0	0
Lean ham	3 oz.	133	0	0
Loin chop, cooked	3 oz.	172	0	0
Rib chop, cooked	3 oz.	190	0	0
Shoulder cut, cooked	3 oz.	211	0	0
Spareribs, cooked	3 oz.	337	0	0
Tenderloin, cooked	3 oz.	159	0	0
Sausages				
Bologna	2 oz.	180	2	2
Brown and serve links, cooked	2 links	103	1	1
Frankfurters, cooked	1 medium	144	1	1
Pork sausage, cooked	1 patty	100	0	0
Salami	2 oz.	143	1	1
Veal				
Cutlet, cooked	3 oz.	179	0	0
Rib, cooked	3 oz.	194	0	0
Poultry				
Chicken				
Batter-dipped fried breast	½ breast	364	13	13
Batter-dipped fried drumstick	1 drumstick	193	6	6
Breast, cooked	½ breast	142	0	0
Drumstick, cooked	1 drumstick	76	0	0
Turkey				
Dark meat, cooked	3 oz.	159	0	0
Light meat, cooked	3 oz.	133	0	0

Carb Counts of Snack Foods

	serving size	calories	carb (g)	net carb (g)
Almonds, whole	1 oz.	164	6	3
Brown rice cake, plain	1 medium	35	7	7
Candy-coated chocolate pieces	10 pieces	34	5	5
Candy-coated chocolate pieces with peanuts	10 pieces	103	12	11
Caramel	1 piece	39	8	8
Caramel corn with peanuts	1 cup	168	34	32
Caramel corn without peanuts	1 cup	152	28	26
Cashews, dry-roasted	1 oz.	163	9	8
Cereal mix	1 oz.	120	18	16
Cheese crackers	10 crackers	50	6	6
Cheese puffs	1 oz.	157	15	15
Cheese-flavored popcorn	1 cup	58	6	5
Chocolate fudge, plain	1 piece	65	14	14
Chocolate fudge, with nuts	1 piece	81	14	14
Chocolate-covered peanut butter cups	1 miniature	38	4	4
Corn chips, barbecue flavor	1 oz.	148	16	14
Corn chips, plain	1 oz.	153	16	15
Fruit and juice bar	1 medium	63	16	16
Fruit leather pieces	1 oz.	97	22	21
Granola bar, chocolate chip	1 medium	119	20	19
Granola bar, plain	1 medium	134	18	16
Gumdrops	1 medium	16	4	4
Gummy Bears	10 pieces	85	22	22
Hard candy	1 piece	24	6	6
Hummus	1 tbsp.	23	2	1
Jelly beans	10 large	104	26	26

	serving size	calories	carb (g)	net carb (g)
Macadamia nuts, dry-roasted	1 oz.	203	4	2
Melba toast	4 pieces	78	15	14
Milk chocolate bar	1.55 oz.	226	26	24
Milk chocolate bar with crisp rice cereal	1.55 oz.	230	29	28
Milk chocolate bar wth almonds	1.45 oz.	216	22	20
Oyster crackers	1 cup	195	32	31
Peanut butter, chunky	1 tbsp.	94	3	2
Peanut butter, reduced fat	1 tbsp.	94	6	5
Peanut butter, smooth	1 tbsp.	95	3	2
Peanuts, dry-roasted	1 oz.	166	6	4
Popcorn, air popped	1 cup	31	6	5
Popcorn, oil popped	1 cup	55	6	5
Potato chips, barbecue flavor	1 oz.	139	15	14
Potato chips, fat free	1 oz.	75	17	16
Potato chips, plain	1 oz.	152	15	14
Potato chips, reduced fat	1 oz.	134	19	17
Potato chips, sour cream and onion flavor	1 oz.	151	15	14
Pretzel sticks (2¼ inches long)	10 pretzels	11	2	2
Pretzels, twisted	10 pretzels	229	48	46
Pumpkin seeds, dry-roasted	1 oz.	148	4	3
Saltine crackers	4 crackers	52	9	9
Sunflower seeds, dry-roasted	1 oz.	165	7	4
Thin square wheat crackers	4 crackers	38	5	5
Tortilla chips, nacho cheese flavor	1 oz.	141	18	16
Tortilla chips, plain	1 oz.	142	18	16
Trail mix, regular	1 cup	707	66	57
Trail mix, tropical	1 cup	570	92	81
Whole wheat crackers	4 crackers	71	11	9

A

Almonds
  Almond Cream with Berries, 351
  Almond-Sauced Berries, 349
  Nut-Crusted Turkey Breast, 377
  Savory Nuts, 52
  Toasted Almonds with Rosemary, 323
Appetizers. See also Snacks
  Asian-Spiced Pecans, 53
  Bell-Ringer Salsa Cheesecake, 369
  Cheesy Spinach Quesadillas, 41
  Chili Chicken Appeteasers, 33
  Classic Buffalo Wings, 43
  Deviled Eggs with Spicy Crab, 54
  Deviled Ham and Cheese Ball, 23
  Endive Leaves with Artichoke
    Caviar, 39
  Fennel and Onion Dip, 27
  Greek-Style Party Pizzettas, 47
  Hot and Sweet Cocktail Weiners, 50
  Hot Ribeye Bites, 31
  Italian Cocktail Meatballs, 51
  Oysters Broiled in Blue Cheese
    Butter, 385
  Pear-Chutney Salsa, 383
  Portobello Pizzas, 35
  Pumpkin Cream Cheese Spread, 371
  Roasted Pepper-heese Mold, 25
  Romas with Chèvre and Basil
    Pesto, 49
  Savory Baked Brie, 45
  Savory Nuts, 52
  Speedy Crab Dip, 29
  Warm Feta Cheese Dip, 37
Apples
  Apple-Glazed Turkey, 197
  Curried Apple Spread, 330
  Veal with Apple-Marsala
    Sauce, 124
Artichokes
  Artichoke-Feta Tortilla Wraps, 293
  Artichoke Hummus Dip, 307
  Endive Leaves with Artichoke
    Caviar, 39
Asian Dressing, 81
Asian Grilled Salmon Salad, 81
Asian-Spiced Pecans, 53

Asparagus
  Asian Grilled Salmon Salad, 81
  Asparagus with Citrus Mock
    Hollandaise, 387
  Asparagus with Sorrel Dressing, 259
  Broiled Asparagus and Fresh
    Mozzarella, 283
  Garlicky Steak and Asparagus, 91
  Garlic-Studded Veal Chops and
    Asparagus, 121
  Herbed Tenderloin Steaks and
    Vegetables, 99
  Roasted Asparagus Parmesan, 267
  Warm Asparagus, Fennel, and
    Spinach Salad, 83
Avocados
  Chilled Avocado Soup, 69
  Grilled Portobellos with Avocado
    Salsa, 279
  Tomatillo Guacamole, 296

B

Balsamic Chicken over Greens, 191
Basil-Buttered Salmon Steaks, 245
Beans
  Artichoke Hummus Dip, 307
  Carrot Hummus, 299
  Down-South Green Beans, 253
  Lemon-Marinated Veggies, 277
  Mediterranean Walnut Spread, 324
  Texas Caviar, 306
Beef
  Beef Steaks with Tomato-Garlic
    Butter, 101
  Beef Tenderloins with Wine
    Sauce, 87
  broiling, 12
  Chili-Rubbed Steaks, 109
  Coriander-Studded Tenderloin
    Steak, 103
  direct grilling, 13
  Filet Mignon with Portobello
    Sauce, 105
  Garlicky Steak and Asparagus, 91
  Grilled Beef, Red Onion, and Blue
    Cheese Salad, 71
  Herbed Steak, 89

Herbed Tenderloin Steaks and
    Vegetables, 99
  Herbed Top Loin Steak with
    Balsamic Sauce, 107
  Hot Ribeye Bites, 31
  Lime-Cilantro Flank Steak, 117
  Pepper-Marinated Flank Steak, 119
  Pot Roast with Dill, 115
  Round Steak with Herbs, 111
  Salsa-Topped Rosemary T-Bones, 93
  Sirloin with Mustard and Chives, 95
  skillet cooking, 11
  Steak with Creamy Onion Sauce, 97
  Sweet-Pepper Steak, 113
Bell-Ringer Salsa Cheesecake, 369
Berries
  Almond Cream with Berries, 351
  Almond-Sauced Berries, 349
  Cranberry Coleslaw, 391
  Cranberry Vodka, 395
  Crème Fraîche Fool with Berries, 400
  Double Berry Delight, 361
  Fruit-Topped Phyllo Cups, 345
  Grilled Chicken and Raspberry
    Salad, 73
  Lemon Berry Fizz, 327
  Peppered Strawberries, 337
  Raspberry and Chocolate Tulips, 343
  Salmon with Fruit Salsa, 219
  Strawberries with Orange Cream
    Dip, 333
  Strawberry-Citrus Slush, 365
  Vanilla Cream-Topped
    Raspberries, 335
Beverages
  Chai, 328
  Cranberry Vodka, 395
  Irish Coffee, 366
  Lemon Berry Fizz, 327
  Make-Believe Champagne, 394
  Really Hot Iced Coffee, 329
  Strawberry-Citrus Slush, 365
Blackberries
  Almond-Sauced Berries, 349
  Crème Fraîche Fool with Berries, 400
Black-eyed peas
  Texas Caviar, 306

Blue cheese
    Blue Cheese-Walnut Dip, 325
    Classic Buffalo Wings, 43
    Grilled Beef, Red Onion, and Blue
        Cheese Salad, 71
    Oysters Broiled in Blue Cheese
        Butter, 385
Braised Seasoned Brussels Sprouts, 269
Brie cheese
    Cheesy Pecan Quesadillas, 295
    Portobello Pizzas, 35
    Savory Baked Brie, 45
Broccoli
    Broccoli and Peppers, 275
    Spicy Broccoli Spread, 315
Broiled Asparagus and Fresh
    Mozzarella, 283
Broiled Chops with Italian
    Vegetables, 141
Broiled Eggplant with Cheese, 257
Broiled Fish Steaks with Tarragon
    Cheese Sauce, 209
Burgers
    Indian Pork Patties, 131
    internal cooking temperatures, 131

C

Cabbage
    Cabbage and Chicken with
        Sesame Dressing, 75
    Cranberry Coleslaw, 391
    Napa Cabbage Slaw, 289
Cantaloupe
    Orange-Cantaloupe Pops, 341
    Spiced Cantaloupe, 347
Carrots
    Carrot Hummus, 299
    Lemon-Marinated Veggies, 277
Cashews
    Fragrant Ginger Cashews, 321
Chai, 328
Cheddar cheese
    Cheesy Spinach Quesadillas, 41
    Deviled Ham and Cheese Ball, 23
    Mushroom-Topped Egg Cups, 373
Cheese
    Almond Cream with Berries, 351

Artichoke-Feta Tortilla Wraps, 293
Bell-Ringer Salsa Cheesecake, 369
Blue Cheese-Walnut Dip, 325
Broiled Asparagus and Fresh
    Mozzarella, 283
Broiled Eggplant with Cheese, 257
Broiled Fish Steaks with Tarragon
    Cheese Sauce, 209
Cheesy Pecan Quesadillas, 295
Cheesy Spinach Quesadillas, 41
Classic Buffalo Wings, 43
Deviled Ham and Cheese Ball, 23
Feta-Stuffed Mushrooms, 319
Fruit-Topped Phyllo Cups, 345
Garlic-Feta Cheese Spread, 297
Go-With-Anything Tomato Sauté, 287
Greek-Style Party Pizzettas, 47
Grilled Beef, Red Onion, and Blue
    Cheese Salad, 71
Macadamia-White Chocolate
    Dessert, 363
Mushroom-Topped Egg Cups, 373
Oysters Broiled in Blue Cheese
    Butter, 385
Parmesan Baked Fish, 241
Peppers Stuffed with Goat
    Cheese, 263
Portobello Pizzas, 35
Pumpkin Cream Cheese Spread, 371
Roasted Asparagus Parmesan, 267
Roasted Pepper-Cheese Mold, 25
Romas with Chèvre and Basil
    Pesto, 49
Savory Baked Brie, 45
Spanish Olive Spread, 305
Stuffed Turkey Tenderloins, 204
Summer Squash with Cheese and
    Sage, 265
Tiramisu Cream, 359
Toasted Cheese Tortilla Chips, 311
Warm Feta Cheese Dip, 37
Zucchini Bites, 317
Chicken
Balsamic Chicken over Greens, 191
broiling, 14
Cabbage and Chicken with
    Sesame Dressing, 75

Chicken Alfredo, 189
Chicken and Pea Pods, 167
Chicken with Creamy Chive
    Sauce, 183
Chicken with New Mexican-Style
    Rub, 173
Chili Chicken Appeteasers, 33
Chili Powder Nuggets with Cilantro
    Cream, 195
Classic Buffalo Wings, 43
Corn and Chicken Soup, 59
Fast Italian-Style Chicken Soup, 57
Grilled Chicken and Raspberry
    Salad, 73
Keys-Style Citrus Chicken, 181
Lemon-Mustard Chicken, 171
microwaving, 15
Middle-Eastern Grilled
    Chicken, 175
Mustard Baked Chicken, 165
Oven-Fried Coconut Chicken, 193
Papaya-Glazed Chicken, 163
Pepper-Lime Chicken, 177
Pesto Chicken Breasts with
    Summer Squash, 187
Plum-Sauced Chicken, 179
Sesame-Ginger Barbecued
    Chicken, 169
Thyme and Garlic Chicken
    Breasts, 185
Chickpeas
    Artichoke Hummus Dip, 307
    Carrot Hummus, 299
    Mediterranean Walnut
        Spread, 324
Chiles
    Bell-Ringer Salsa Cheesecake, 369
    handling, 131
    Hot Ribeye Bites, 31
    Indian Pork Patties, 131
    Mustard Jalapeño Salmon, 231
    Salmon with Fruit Salsa, 219
    Swordfish with Spicy Tomato
        Sauce, 233
    Tomatillo Guacamole, 296
Chili Chicken Appeteasers, 33
Chili Popcorn, 301

Chili Powder Nuggets with Cilantro
Cream, 195
Chili-Rubbed Steaks, 109
Chilled Avocado Soup, 69
Chips
Homemade Low-Carb Tortilla
Chips, 37
Italian-Style Chips, 309
Toasted Cheese Tortilla Chips, 311
Chocolate
Chocolate Mousse, 397
Macadamia-White Chocolate
Dessert, 363
Raspberry and Chocolate Tulips, 343
Chowders
Effortless Shrimp Chowder, 65
North Sea Chowder, 63
Cilantro
Chili Powder Nuggets with Cilantro
Cream, 195
Lime-Cilantro Flank Steak, 117
Turkey Tenderloins with Cilantro
Pesto, 201
Cinnamon-Spiced Pumpkin Soup, 393
Citrus Baked Halibut, 217
Classic Buffalo Wings, 43
Coconut
Oven-Fried Coconut Chicken, 193
Coffee
Coffee and Cream Dessert, 399
Irish Coffee, 366
Really Hot Iced Coffee, 329
Coriander-Studded Tenderloin
Steak, 103
Coriander Turkey Breast, 381
Corn and Chicken Soup, 59
Cornish game hens
broiling, 14
Hoisin-auced Cornish Hens, 379
microwaving, 15
Country Chops and Peppers, 153
Crab
cooking methods, 17
Deviled Eggs with Spicy Crab, 54
Speedy Crab Dip, 29
Cranberries
Cranberry Coleslaw, 391

Cranberry Vodka, 395
Cream cheese
Almond Cream with Berries, 351
Artichoke-Feta Tortilla Wraps, 293
Bell-Ringer Salsa Cheesecake, 369
Deviled Ham and Cheese Ball, 23
Fruit-Topped Phyllo Cups, 345
Garlic-Feta Cheese Spread, 297
Pumpkin Cream Cheese Spread, 371
Roasted Pepper–Cheese Mold, 25
Warm Feta Cheese Dip, 37
Zucchini Bites, 317
Crème Fraîche Fool with Berries, 400
Cucumbers
Grilled Salmon with Cucumber
Salsa, 249
Middle-Eastern Grilled Chicken, 175
Pear-Chutney Salsa, 383
Salmon Caesar Salad, 79
Vegetables in Spicy Sour Cream, 290
Cumberland Pork Medallions, 135
Curried Apple Spread, 330

D
Dancing Mushrooms, 261
Desserts
Almond Cream with Berries, 351
Almond-Sauced Berries, 349
Chocolate Mousse, 397
Coffee and Cream Dessert, 399
Crème Fraîche Fool with Berries, 400
Double Berry Delight, 361
Fruit-Topped Phyllo Cups, 345
Macadamia-White Chocolate
Dessert, 363
Mint Julep Melon, 339
Orange-Cantaloupe Pops, 341
Orange-Ginger Rhubarb, 353
Peppered Strawberries, 337
Raspberry and Chocolate Tulips, 343
Spiced Cantaloupe, 347
Spicy Baked Oranges, 355
Strawberries with Orange Cream
Dip, 333
Strawberry-Citrus Slush, 365
Tiramisu Cream, 359
Vanilla Cream-Topped
Raspberries, 335

Warm Spiced Peaches, 357
Deviled Eggs with Spicy Crab, 54
Deviled Ham and Cheese Ball, 23
Dijon–Rosemary Roast Leg of Lamb, 375
Dips and spreads
Artichoke Hummus Dip, 307
Bell-Ringer Salsa Cheesecake, 369
Blue Cheese-Walnut Dip, 325
Carrot Hummus, 299
Curried Apple Spread, 330
Deviled Ham and Cheese Ball, 23
Fennel and Onion Dip, 27
Garlic-Feta Cheese Spread, 297
Mediterranean Walnut Spread, 324
Pumpkin Cream Cheese Spread, 371
Roasted Pepper-Cheese Mold, 25
Spanish Olive Spread, 305
Speedy Crab Dip, 29
Spicy Broccoli Spread, 315
Texas Caviar, 306
Tomatillo Guacamole, 296
Double Berry Delight, 361
Down-South Green Beans, 253

E
Easy Citrus Salmon Steaks, 235
Effortless Shrimp Chowder, 65
Eggplant
Broiled Eggplant with Cheese, 257
Thai Lime Custard Soup, 67
Eggs
Deviled Eggs with Spicy Crab, 54
Mushroom-Topped Egg Cups, 373
Endive Leaves with Artichoke Caviar, 39

F
Fast Italian-Style Chicken Soup, 57
Fennel
Fennel and Onion Dip, 27
Warm Asparagus, Fennel, and
Spinach Salad, 83
Feta cheese
Artichoke-Feta Tortilla Wraps, 293
Feta-Stuffed Mushrooms, 319
Garlic-Feta Cheese Spread, 297
Greek-Style Party Pizzettas, 47
Stuffed Turkey Tenderloins, 204
Warm Feta Cheese Dip, 37
Fish
Asian Grilled Salmon Salad, 81

Basil-Buttered Salmon Steaks, 245

Broiled Fish Steaks with Tarragon Cheese Sauce, 209

Citrus Baked Halibut, 217

cooking methods, 16

Easy Citrus Salmon Steaks, 235

Fish Tacos, 215

Ginger-Marinated Sea Bass, 221

Grilled Rosemary Trout with Lemon Butter, 237

Grilled Salmon with Cucumber Salsa, 249

Grilled Salmon with Herb Crust, 211

Grilled Swordfish with Tomato Chutney, 223

Grilled Tuna with Peanut Sauce, 243

Herb-Buttered Fish Steaks, 207

Lemon-Herb Swordfish Steaks, 250

Mustard Jalapeño Salmon, 231

North Sea Chowder, 63

Parmesan Baked Fish, 241

Red Snapper with Fresh Herb-Pecan Crust, 225

Salmon Caesar Salad, 79

Salmon Fillets Bathed in Garlic, 239

Salmon with Fruit Salsa, 219

Sesame-Seared Tuna, 227

Swordfish with Spicy Tomato Sauce, 233

Trout with Mushrooms, 213

Wasabi-Glazed Whitefish with Vegetable Slaw, 229

Fragrant Ginger Cashews, 321

Fruit. See also specific fruits

Fruit-Topped Phyllo Cups, 345

Salmon with Fruit Salsa, 219

G

Garlic

Garlic-Feta Cheese Spread, 297

Garlicky Mushrooms, 273

Garlicky Steak and Asparagus, 91

Garlic-Studded Veal Chops and Asparagus, 121

Salmon Fillets Bathed in Garlic, 239

Thyme and Garlic Chicken Breasts, 185

Ginger-Marinated Sea Bass, 221

Goat cheese

Peppers Stuffed with Goat Cheese, 263

Romas with Chèvre and Basil Pesto, 49

Stuffed Turkey Tenderloins, 204

Summer Squash with Cheese and Sage, 265

Go–With-Anything Tomato Sauté, 287

Grapefruit

Ruby and Gold Grapefruit, 313

Greek-Style Party Pizzettas, 47

Green beans

Down-South Green Beans, 253

Lemon-Marinated Veggies, 277

Greens, salad. See also Spinach

Asian Grilled Salmon Salad, 81

Asparagus with Sorrel Dressing, 259

Balsamic Chicken over Greens, 191

Cabbage and Chicken with Sesame Dressing, 75

Fish Tacos, 215

Grilled Beef, Red Onion, and Blue Cheese Salad, 71

Grilled Chicken and Raspberry Salad, 73

Grilled Lobster with Rosemary Butter, 247

Grilled Pork Chops with Mushroom Stuffing, 127

Grilled Portobellos with Avocado Salsa, 279

Grilled Rosemary Trout with Lemon Butter, 237

Grilled Salmon with Cucumber Salsa, 249

Grilled Salmon with Herb Crust, 211

Grilled Swordfish with Tomato Chutney, 223

Grilled Tuna with Peanut Sauce, 243

Grilled Turkey Piccata, 203

Grilled Turkey Steaks with Sweet Pepper-Citrus Salsa, 199

Grilled Veal Chops with Pesto Mushrooms, 123

Guacamole

Bell-Ringer Salsa Cheesecake, 369

Tomatillo Guacamole, 296

H

Halibut

Citrus Baked Halibut, 217

Herb-Buttered Fish Steaks, 207

Ham

broiling, 12

Deviled Ham and Cheese Ball, 23

Mushroom-Topped Egg Cups, 373

skillet cooking, 11

Herb-Buttered Fish Steaks, 207

Herbed Soy Nuts and Seeds, 304

Herbed Soy Snacks, 320

Herbed Steak, 89

Herbed Tenderloin Steaks and Vegetables, 99

Herbed Top Loin Steak with Balsamic Sauce, 107

Hoisin-Sauced Cornish Hens, 379

Holidays

Asparagus with Citrus Mock Hollandaise, 387

Bell-Ringer Salsa Cheesecake, 369

Chocolate Mousse, 397

Cinnamon-Spiced Pumpkin Soup, 393

Coffee and Cream Dessert, 399

Coriander Turkey Breast, 381

Cranberry Coleslaw, 391

Cranberry Vodka, 395

Crème Fraîche Fool with Berries, 400

Dijon-Rosemary Roast Leg of Lamb, 375

Hoisin-Sauced Cornish Hens, 379

Make-Believe Champagne, 394

Mushroom-Topped Egg Cups, 373

Nut-Crusted Turkey Breast, 377

Oysters Broiled in Blue Cheese Butter, 385

Pear-Chutney Salsa, 383

Pumpkin Cream Cheese Spread, 371

Yam and Peanut Soup, 389

Hot and Sweet Cocktail Weiners, 50

Hot Ribeye Bites, 31

Hummus

Artichoke Hummus Dip, 307

Carrot Hummus, 299
Greek-Style Party Pizzettas, 47

I

Indian Pork Patties, 131
Irish Coffee, 366
Italian Cocktail Meatballs, 51
Italian-Style Chips, 309

K

Keys-Style Citrus Chicken, 181

L

Lamb
broiling, 12
Dijon-Rosemary Roast Leg of
Lamb, 375
direct grilling, 13
Minted Lamb Chops, 160
Orange-Mustard Lamb
Chops, 159
skillet cooking, 11
Lemons
Grilled Rosemary Trout with Lemon
Butter, 237
Lemon Berry Fizz, 327
Lemon-Herb Swordfish
Steaks, 250
Lemon-Marinated Veggies, 277
Lemon-Mustard Chicken, 171
Lemon-Tarragon Vegetables, 271
Lemony Herbed Olives, 303
Limes
Keys-Style Citrus Chicken, 181
Lime-Cilantro Flank Steak, 117
Pepper-Lime Chicken, 177
Lobster
Grilled Lobster with Rosemary
Butter, 247
tails, cooking methods, 17
Low-carb diets
blood sugar levels and, 4–5
breastfeeding and, 7
carbohydrate food sources, 4–5
children and, 6
chronic diseases and, 7
exercise and, 6

family members and, 6
glycemic index and, 5
grocery shopping and, 8
guests and, 7
healthy approach to, 5
kitchen equipment and, 8
low-carb food products and, 7
lunch menus, 18
meal basics, 8–9
pantry ingredients for, 9
pregnancy and, 7
quick cooking methods, 10–17
restaurant meals and, 6–7
snacks and, 9
vacations and, 7
vegetarianism and, 7
weeknight menus, 19–20

M

Macadamias
Macadamia-White Chocolate
Dessert, 363
Savory Nuts, 52
Main dishes (beef and veal)
Beef Steaks with Tomato-Garlic
Butter, 101
Beef Tenderloins with Wine Sauce, 87
Chili-Rubbed Steaks, 109
Coriander-Studded Tenderloin
Steak, 103
Filet Mignon with Portobello
Sauce, 105
Garlicky Steak and Asparagus, 91
Garlic-Studded Veal Chops and
Asparagus, 121
Grilled Veal Chops with Pesto
Mushrooms, 123
Herbed Steak, 89
Herbed Top Loin Steak with
Balsamic Sauce, 107
Herbed Tenderloin Steaks and
Vegetables, 99
Lime-Cilantro Flank Steak, 117
Pepper-Marinated Flank
Steak, 119
Pot Roast with Dill, 115
Round Steak with Herbs, 111
Salsa-Topped Rosemary T-Bones, 93
Sirloin with Mustard and Chives, 95

Steak with Creamy Onion Sauce, 97
Sweet-Pepper Steak, 113
Veal with Apple-Marsala Sauce, 124
Main dishes (lamb and pork)
Broiled Chops with Italian
Vegetables, 141
Country Chops and Peppers, 153
Cumberland Pork Medallions, 135
Dijon-Rosemary Roast Leg of
Lamb, 375
Grilled Pork Chops with Mushroom
Stuffing, 127
Indian Pork Patties, 131
Minted Lamb Chops, 160
Orange-Mustard Lamb Chops, 159
Pecan-Glazed Pork Chops, 143
Peppered Pork with Chive Sauce, 129
Peppery Pork Chops, 151
Pineapple-Glazed Pork, 145
Pork au Poivre with Mustard and
Sage, 133
Pork Chops Dijon, 155
Pork Diane, 137
Pork with Apple Brandy and
Cream, 147
Sherried Pork, 139
Soy and Sesame Pork, 149
Thyme Pork Chops, 157
Main dishes (poultry)
Apple-Glazed Turkey, 197
Balsamic Chicken over Greens, 191
Chicken Alfredo, 189
Chicken and Pea Pods, 167
Chicken with Creamy Chive
Sauce, 183
Chicken with New Mexican–Style
Rub, 173
Chili Powder Nuggets with Cilantro
Cream, 195
Coriander Turkey Breast, 381
Grilled Turkey Piccata, 203
Grilled Turkey Steaks with Sweet
Pepper-Citrus Salsa, 199
Hoisin-Sauced Cornish Hens, 379
Keys-Style Citrus Chicken, 181
Lemon-Mustard Chicken, 171
Middle-Eastern Grilled
Chicken, 175

Mustard Baked Chicken, 165
Nut-Crusted Turkey Breast, 377
Oven–Fried Coconut Chicken, 193
Papaya-Glazed Chicken, 163
Pepper-Lime Chicken, 177
Pesto Chicken Breasts with
    Summer Squash, 187
Plum-Sauced Chicken, 179
Sesame-Ginger Barbecued
    Chicken, 169
Stuffed Turkey Tenderloins, 204
Thyme and Garlic Chicken
    Breasts, 185
Turkey Tenderloins with Cilantro
    Pesto, 201
Main dishes (seafood)
Basil-Buttered Salmon
    Steaks, 245
Broiled Fish Steaks with Tarragon
    Cheese Sauce, 209
Citrus Baked Halibut, 217
Easy Citrus Salmon Steaks, 235
Fish Tacos, 215
Ginger-Marinated Sea Bass, 221
Grilled Lobster with Rosemary
    Butter, 247
Grilled Rosemary Trout with Lemon
    Butter, 237
Grilled Salmon with Cucumber
    Salsa, 249
Grilled Salmon with Herb Crust, 211
Grilled Swordfish with Tomato
    Chutney, 223
Grilled Tuna with Peanut Sauce, 243
Herb-Buttered Fish Steaks, 207
Lemon-Herb Swordfish
    Steaks, 250
Mustard Jalapeño Salmon, 231
Parmesan Baked Fish, 241
Red Snapper with Fresh Herb-
    Pecan Crust, 225
Salmon Fillets Bathed in Garlic, 239
Salmon with Fruit Salsa, 219
Sesame-Seared Tuna, 227
Swordfish with Spicy Tomato
    Sauce, 233
Trout with Mushrooms, 213

Wasabi-Glazed Whitefish with
    Vegetable Slaw, 229
Make-Believe Champagne, 394
Meat. See Beef; Lamb; Pork; Veal
Meatballs
    Italian Cocktail Meatballs, 51
Mediterranean Walnut Spread, 324
Melon
    Mint Julep Melon, 339
    Orange-Cantaloupe Pops, 341
    Spiced Cantaloupe, 347
Mesclun with Olives and Oranges, 84
Middle-Eastern Grilled Chicken, 175
Minted Lamb Chops, 160
Mint Julep Melon, 339
Mozzarella
    Broiled Asparagus and Fresh
        Mozzarella, 283
    Broiled Eggplant with Cheese, 257
    Broiled Fish Steaks with Tarragon
        Cheese Sauce, 209
    Go-With-Anything Tomato Sauté, 287
    Greek-Style Party Pizzettas, 47
Mushroom-Topped Egg Cups, 373
Mushrooms
    Asian Grilled Salmon Salad, 81
    Dancing Mushrooms, 261
    Feta-Stuffed Mushrooms, 319
    Filet Mignon with Portobello
        Sauce, 105
    Garlicky Mushrooms, 273
    Grilled Pork Chops with Mushroom
        Stuffing, 127
    Grilled Portobellos with Avocado
        Salsa, 279
    Grilled Veal Chops with Pesto
        Mushrooms, 123
    Lemon-Marinated Veggies, 277
    Lemon-Tarragon Vegetables, 271
    Mushroom-Topped Egg Cups, 373
    Pork with Apple Brandy and Cream, 147
    Portobello Pizzas, 35
    Pronto Beefy Mushroom Soup, 61
    Saucy Skillet Mushrooms, 255
    Trout with Mushrooms, 213
Mustard
    Dijon-Rosemary Roast Leg of Lamb, 375

Lemon-Mustard Chicken, 171
Mustard Baked Chicken, 165
Mustard Jalapeño Salmon, 231
Orange-Mustard Lamb
    Chops, 159
Pork au Poivre with Mustard and
    Sage, 133
Pork Chops Dijon, 155
Saucy Skillet Mushrooms, 255
Sirloin with Mustard and Chives, 95

N
Napa Cabbage Slaw, 289
Nectarines
    Chili Chicken Appeteasers, 33
    Salmon with Fruit Salsa, 219
North Sea Chowder, 63
Nuts
    Asian-Spiced Pecans, 53
    Blue Cheese-Walnut Dip, 325
    Cheesy Pecan Quesadillas, 295
    Cheesy Spinach Quesadillas, 41
    Down-South Green Beans, 253
    Fragrant Ginger Cashews, 321
    Grilled Tuna with Peanut Sauce, 243
    Herbed Soy Nuts and Seeds, 304
    Herbed Soy Snacks, 320
    Macadamia-White Chocolate
        Dessert, 363
    Mediterranean Walnut Spread, 324
    Nut-Crusted Turkey Breast, 377
    Pistachios with a Kick, 326
    Red Snapper with Fresh Herb-
        Pecan Crust, 225
    Savory Baked Brie, 45
    Savory Nuts, 52
    Teeny Zucchini with Onions, 285
    Toasted Almonds with Rosemary, 323
    Turkey Tenderloins with Cilantro
        Pesto, 201

O
Olives
    Feta-Stuffed Mushrooms, 319
    Greek-Style Party Pizzettas, 47
    Lemony Herbed Olives, 303
    Mesclun with Olives and Oranges, 84

Spanish Olive Spread, 305
Warm Feta Cheese Dip, 37
Onions
    Fennel and Onion Dip, 27
    Grilled Beef, Red Onion, and Blue
        Cheese Salad, 71
    Steak with Creamy Onion Sauce, 97
    Teeny Zucchini with Onions, 285
Oranges
    Easy Citrus Salmon Steaks, 235
    Keys-Style Citrus Chicken, 181
    Mesclun with Olives and Oranges, 84
    Orange-Cantaloupe Pops, 341
    Orange-Ginger Rhubarb, 353
    Orange-Mustard Lamb Chops, 159
    Spicy Baked Oranges, 355
    Strawberries with Orange Cream
        Dip, 333
    Sweet Pepper-Citrus Salsa, 199
Oven-Fried Coconut Chicken, 193
Oysters
    cooking methods, 17
    Oysters Broiled in Blue Cheese
        Butter, 385

P

Papaya-Glazed Chicken, 163
Parmesan
    Artichoke-Feta Tortilla Wraps, 293
    Parmesan Baked Fish, 241
    Roasted Asparagus Parmesan, 267
    Toasted Cheese Tortilla Chips, 311
Peaches
    Chili Chicken Appeteasers, 33
    Salmon with Fruit Salsa, 219
    Warm Spiced Peaches, 357
Peanuts and peanut butter
    Grilled Tuna with Peanut Sauce, 243
    Yam and Peanut Soup, 389
Pear-Chutney Salsa, 383
Peas
    Chicken and Pea Pods, 167
    Wasabi-Glazed Whitefish with
        Vegetable Slaw, 229
Pecans
    Asian-Spiced Pecans, 53
    Cheesy Pecan Quesadillas, 295

Cheesy Spinach Quesadillas, 41
Down-South Green Beans, 253
Pecan-Glazed Pork Chops, 143
Red Snapper with Fresh Herb-
    Pecan Crust, 225
Spicy Baked Oranges, 355
Peppercorns
    cracking, tip for, 133
    Peppered Pork with Chive Sauce, 129
    Peppered Strawberries, 337
    Pepper-Lime Chicken, 177
    Pepper-Marinated Flank
        Steak, 119
    Peppery Pork Chops, 151
    Pork au Poivre with Mustard and
        Sage, 133
Peppers
    Bell-Ringer Salsa Cheesecake, 369
    Broccoli and Peppers, 275
    Broiled Chops with Italian
        Vegetables, 141
    Chicken Alfredo, 189
    chile, handling, 131
    Country Chops and Peppers, 153
    Greek-Style Party Pizzettas, 47
    Hot Ribeye Bites, 31
    Indian Pork Patties, 131
    Lemon-Marinated Veggies, 277
    Mustard Jalapeño Salmon, 231
    Peppers Stuffed with Goat Cheese, 263
    Roasted Pepper-Cheese Mold, 25
    Salmon Caesar Salad, 79
    Salmon with Fruit Salsa, 219
    Sweet Pepper-Citrus Salsa, 199
    Sweet-Pepper Steak, 113
    Swordfish with Spicy Tomato
        Sauce, 233
    Texas Caviar, 306
    Tomatillo Guacamole, 296
Pesto
    Grilled Veal Chops with Pesto
        Mushrooms, 123
    Pesto Chicken Breasts with
        Summer Squash, 187
    Romas with Chèvre and Basil Pesto, 49
    Turkey Tenderloins with Cilantro
        Pesto, 201

Pineapple-Glazed Pork, 145
Pine nuts
    Cheesy Spinach Quesadillas, 41
    Nut-Crusted Turkey Breast, 377
    Savory Baked Brie, 45
Pistachios with a Kick, 326
Pizza
    Greek-Style Party Pizzettas, 47
    Portobello Pizzas, 35
Plum-Sauced Chicken, 179
Popcorn
    Chili Popcorn, 301
    Spiced Popcorn, 302
Pork
    Broiled Chops with Italian
        Vegetables, 141
    broiling, 12
    Country Chops and Peppers, 153
    Cumberland Pork Medallions, 135
    Deviled Ham and Cheese Ball, 23
    direct grilling, 13
    Grilled Pork Chops with Mushroom
        Stuffing, 127
    Hot and Sweet Cocktail Weiners, 50
    Indian Pork Patties, 131
    Mushroom-Topped Egg Cups, 373
    Pecan-Glazed Pork Chops, 143
    Peppered Pork with Chive Sauce, 129
    Peppery Pork Chops, 151
    Pineapple-Glazed Pork, 145
    Pork au Poivre with Mustard and
        Sage, 133
    Pork Chops Dijon, 155
    Pork Diane, 137
    Pork with Apple Brandy and
        Cream, 147
    Sherried Pork, 139
    skillet cooking, 11
    Soy and Sesame Pork, 149
    Teriyaki Pork Salad, 77
    Thyme Pork Chops, 157
Portobello Pizzas, 35
Poultry. See Chicken; Cornish game
    hens; Turkey
Pronto Beefy Mushroom Soup, 61
Pumpkin
    Cinnamon-Spiced Pumpkin Soup, 393

Pumpkin Cream Cheese Spread, 371
Pumpkin seeds
  Herbed Soy Nuts and Seeds, 304

Q

Quesadillas
  Cheesy Pecan Quesadillas, 295
  Cheesy Spinach Quesadillas, 41

R

Radishes
  Wasabi-Glazed Whitefish with
    Vegetable Slaw, 229
Raspberries
  Almond-Sauced Berries, 349
  Grilled Chicken and Raspberry
    Salad, 73
  Raspberry and Chocolate Tulips, 343
  Vanilla Cream-Topped
    Raspberries, 335
Really Hot Iced Coffee, 329
Red Snapper with Fresh Herb-Pecan
  Crust, 225
Rhubarb
  Orange-Ginger Rhubarb, 353
Roasted Asparagus Parmesan, 267
Roasted Pepper-Cheese Mold, 25
Romas with Chèvre and Basil Pesto, 49
Rosemary
  Dijon-Rosemary Roast Leg of
    Lamb, 375
  Grilled Lobster with Rosemary
    Butter, 247
  Grilled Rosemary Trout with Lemon
    Butter, 237
  Salsa-Topped Rosemary T-Bones, 93
  Toasted Almonds with Rosemary, 323
Ruby and Gold Grapefruit, 313

S

Salads
  Asian Grilled Salmon Salad, 81
  Cabbage and Chicken with
    Sesame Dressing, 75
  Cranberry Coleslaw, 391
  Grilled Beef, Red Onion, and Blue
    Cheese Salad, 71

Grilled Chicken and Raspberry
  Salad, 73
Mesclun with Olives and
  Oranges, 84
Napa Cabbage Slaw, 289
Salmon Caesar Salad, 79
Teriyaki Pork Salad, 77
Warm Asparagus, Fennel, and
  Spinach Salad, 83
Salmon
  Asian Grilled Salmon Salad, 81
  Basil-Buttered Salmon
    Steaks, 245
  Broiled Fish Steaks with Tarragon
    Cheese Sauce, 209
  Easy Citrus Salmon Steaks, 235
  Grilled Salmon with Cucumber
    Salsa, 249
  Grilled Salmon with Herb
    Crust, 211
  Herb-Buttered Fish Steaks, 207
  Mustard Jalapeño Salmon, 231
  Parmesan Baked Fish, 241
  Salmon Caesar Salad, 79
  Salmon Fillets Bathed in
    Garlic, 239
  Salmon with Fruit Salsa, 219
Salsa
  Bell-Ringer Salsa Cheesecake, 369
  Grilled Portobellos with Avocado
    Salsa, 279
  Grilled Salmon with Cucumber
    Salsa, 249
  Pear-Chutney Salsa, 383
  Salmon with Fruit Salsa, 219
  Salsa-Topped Rosemary T-Bones, 93
  Sweet Pepper-Citrus Salsa, 199
Saucy Skillet Mushrooms, 255
Sausages
  broiling, 12
  direct grilling, 13
  Hot and Sweet Cocktail Weiners, 50
Savory Baked Brie, 45
Savory Nuts, 52
Sea bass
  Ginger-Marinated Sea Bass, 221
Seafood. See also Fish

cooking methods, 16, 17
Deviled Eggs with Spicy Crab, 54
Effortless Shrimp Chowder, 65
Grilled Lobster with Rosemary
  Butter, 247
Oysters Broiled in Blue Cheese
  Butter, 385
Speedy Crab Dip, 29
Sesame seeds
  Sesame-Ginger Barbecued
    Chicken, 169
  Sesame-Seared Tuna, 227
  Soy and Sesame Pork, 149
Shellfish
  cooking methods, 17
  Deviled Eggs with Spicy Crab, 54
  Effortless Shrimp Chowder, 65
  Grilled Lobster with Rosemary
    Butter, 247
  Oysters Broiled in Blue Cheese
    Butter, 385
  Speedy Crab Dip, 29
Sherried Pork, 139
Shrimp
  cooking methods, 17
  Effortless Shrimp Chowder, 65
Side dishes
  Asparagus with Citrus Mock
    Hollandaise, 387
  Asparagus with Sorrel
    Dressing, 259
  Braised Seasoned Brussels
    Sprouts, 269
  Broccoli and Peppers, 275
  Broiled Asparagus and Fresh
    Mozzarella, 283
  Broiled Eggplant with Cheese, 257
  Cranberry Coleslaw, 391
  Dancing Mushrooms, 261
  Down-South Green Beans, 253
  Garlicky Mushrooms, 273
  Go-With-Anything Tomato Sauté, 287
  Grilled Portobellos with Avocado
    Salsa, 279
  Lemon-Marinated Veggies, 277
  Lemon-Tarragon Vegetables, 271
  Napa Cabbage Slaw, 289

Peppers Stuffed with Goat
  Cheese, 263
Roasted Asparagus Parmesan, 267
Saucy Skillet Mushrooms, 255
Summer Squash with Cheese and
  Sage, 265
Teeny Zucchini with Onions, 285
Vegetables in Spicy Sour Cream, 290
Zucchini alla Romana, 281
Slaws
  Cranberry Coleslaw, 391
  Napa Cabbage Slaw, 289
  Wasabi-Glazed Whitefish with
    Vegetable Slaw, 229
Snacks. See also Appetizers
  Artichoke-Feta Tortilla Wraps, 293
  Artichoke Hummus Dip, 307
  Blue Cheese-Walnut Dip, 325
  Carrot Hummus, 299
  Chai, 328
  Cheesy Pecan Quesadillas, 295
  Chili Popcorn, 301
  Curried Apple Spread, 330
  Feta-Stuffed Mushrooms, 319
  Fragrant Ginger Cashews, 321
  Garlic-Feta Cheese Spread, 297
  healthy, choosing, 9
  Herbed Soy Nuts and Seeds, 304
  Herbed Soy Snacks, 320
  Italian-Style Chips, 309
  Lemon Berry Fizz, 327
  Lemony Herbed Olives, 303
  Mediterranean Walnut Spread, 324
  Pear-Chutney Salsa, 383
  Pistachios with a Kick, 326
  Really Hot Iced Coffee, 329
  Ruby and Gold Grapefruit, 313
  Spanish Olive Spread, 305
  Spiced Popcorn, 302
  Spicy Broccoli Spread, 315
  Texas Caviar, 306
  Toasted Almonds with
    Rosemary, 323
  Toasted Cheese Tortilla Chips, 311
  Tomatillo Guacamole, 296
  Zucchini Bites, 317

Sorrel
  Asparagus with Sorrel Dressing, 259
Soups
  Chilled Avocado Soup, 69
  Cinnamon-Spiced Pumpkin
    Soup, 393
  Corn and Chicken Soup, 59
  Effortless Shrimp Chowder, 65
  Fast Italian-Style Chicken Soup, 57
  North Sea Chowder, 63
  Pronto Beefy Mushroom Soup, 61
  Thai Lime Custard Soup, 67
  Yam and Peanut Soup, 389
Soy and Sesame Pork, 149
Soy nuts
  Herbed Soy Nuts and Seeds, 304
  Herbed Soy Snacks, 320
Spanish Olive Spread, 305
Speedy Crab Dip, 29
Spiced Cantaloupe, 347
Spiced Popcorn, 302
Spicy Baked Oranges, 355
Spicy Broccoli Spread, 315
Spinach
  Cheesy Spinach Quesadillas, 41
  Stuffed Turkey Tenderloins, 204
  Thai Lime Custard Soup, 67
  Warm Asparagus, Fennel, and
    Spinach Salad, 83
Spreads. See Dips and spreads
Squash
  Broiled Chops with Italian
    Vegetables, 141
  Cinnamon-Spiced Pumpkin
    Soup, 393
  Lemon-Tarragon Vegetables, 271
  Pesto Chicken Breasts with
    Summer Squash, 187
  Pumpkin Cream Cheese Spread, 371
  Summer Squash with Cheese and
    Sage, 265
  Teeny Zucchini with Onions, 285
  Vegetables in Spicy Sour Cream, 290
  Wasabi-Glazed Whitefish with
    Vegetable Slaw, 229
  Zucchini alla Romana, 281
  Zucchini Bites, 317

Strawberries
  Almond Cream with Berries, 351
  Double Berry Delight, 361
  Lemon Berry Fizz, 327
  Peppered Strawberries, 337
  Salmon with Fruit Salsa, 219
  Strawberries with Orange Cream
    Dip, 333
  Strawberry-Citrus Slush, 365
Stuffed Turkey Tenderloins, 204
Summer squash. See Squash
Sweet Pepper-Citrus Salsa, 199
Sweet-Pepper Steak, 113
Sweet potatoes
  Yam and Peanut Soup, 389
Swordfish
  Broiled Fish Steaks with Tarragon
    Cheese Sauce, 209
  Grilled Swordfish with Tomato
    Chutney, 223
  Herb-Buttered Fish Steaks, 207
  Lemon-Herb Swordfish
    Steaks, 250
Swordfish with Spicy Tomato
  Sauce, 233

T

Tacos
  Fish Tacos, 215
Tarragon
  Broiled Fish Steaks with Tarragon
    Cheese Sauce, 209
  Lemon-Tarragon Vegetables, 271
Teeny Zucchini with Onions, 285
Teriyaki Pork Salad, 77
Texas Caviar, 306
Thai Lime Custard Soup, 67
Thyme and Garlic Chicken Breasts, 185
Thyme Pork Chops, 157
Tiramisu Cream, 359
Toasted Almonds with Rosemary, 323
Toasted Cheese Tortilla Chips, 311
Tomatillo Guacamole, 296
Tomatoes
  Beef Steaks with Tomato-Garlic
    Butter, 101
  Broiled Chops with Italian
    Vegetables, 141

Go-With-Anything Tomato
Sauté, 287
Grilled Beef, Red Onion, and Blue
Cheese Salad, 71
Grilled Portobellos with Avocado
Salsa, 279
Grilled Rosemary Trout with Lemon
Butter, 237
Grilled Swordfish with Tomato
Chutney, 223
Herbed Tenderloin Steaks and
Vegetables, 99
Lemon-Marinated Veggies, 277
North Sea Chowder, 63
Romas with Chèvre and Basil
Pesto, 49
Salsa-Topped Rosemary T-Bones, 93
Swordfish with Spicy Tomato
Sauce, 233
Tomatillo Guacamole, 296
Tortillas
Artichoke-Feta Tortilla Wraps, 293
Cheesy Pecan Quesadillas, 295
Cheesy Spinach Quesadillas, 41
Fish Tacos, 215
Greek-Style Party Pizzettas, 47
Homemade Low-Carb Chips, 37
Italian-Style Chips, 309
Toasted Cheese Tortilla Chips, 311
Trout
Grilled Rosemary Trout with Lemon
Butter, 237
Trout with Mushrooms, 213
Tuna
Broiled Fish Steaks with Tarragon
Cheese Sauce, 209
Grilled Tuna with Peanut Sauce, 243
Sesame-Seared Tuna, 227
Turkey
Apple-Glazed Turkey, 197
broiling, 14
Coriander Turkey Breast, 381
Grilled Turkey Piccata, 203
Grilled Turkey Steaks with Sweet
Pepper-Citrus Salsa, 199
microwaving, 15
Nut-Crusted Turkey Breast, 377

Stuffed Turkey Tenderloins, 204
Turkey Tenderloins with Cilantro Pesto, 201

V
Vanilla Cream-Topped
Raspberries, 335
Veal
broiling, 12
direct-grilling, 13
Garlic-Studded Veal Chops and
Asparagus, 121
Grilled Veal Chops with Pesto
Mushrooms, 123
skillet cooking, 11
Veal with Apple-Marsala Sauce, 124
Vegetables. See also specific
vegetables
Broiled Chops with Italian
Vegetables, 141
Herbed Tenderloin Steaks and
Vegetables, 99
Lemon-Marinated Veggies, 277
Lemon-Tarragon Vegetables, 271
Vegetables in Spicy Sour Cream, 290
Wasabi-Glazed Whitefish with
Vegetable Slaw, 229

W
Walnuts
Blue Cheese-Walnut Dip, 325
Mediterranean Walnut Spread, 324
Savory Nuts, 52
Teeny Zucchini with Onions, 285
Turkey Tenderloins with Cilantro
Pesto, 201
Warm Asparagus, Fennel, and
Spinach Salad, 83
Warm Feta Cheese Dip, 37
Warm Spiced Peaches, 357
Wasabi-Glazed Whitefish with
Vegetable Slaw, 229
Whitefish
Wasabi-Glazed Whitefish with
Vegetable Slaw, 229

Y
Yam and Peanut Soup, 389

Yogurt
Artichoke-Feta Tortilla Wraps, 293
Indian Pork Patties, 131
Middle-Eastern Grilled
Chicken, 175
Orange-Cantaloupe Pops, 341
Vanilla Cream-Topped
Raspberries, 335
Yogurt-Chive Sauce, 293

Z
Zucchini
Broiled Chops with Italian
Vegetables, 141
Endive Leaves with Artichoke
Caviar, 39
Lemon-Tarragon Vegetables, 271
Pesto Chicken Breasts with
Summer Squash, 187
Teeny Zucchini with Onions, 285
Vegetables in Spicy Sour Cream, 290
Wasabi-Glazed Whitefish with
Vegetable Slaw, 229
Zucchini alla Romana, 281
Zucchini Bites, 317

METRIC INFORMATION

The charts on this page provide a guide for converting measurements from the U.S. customary system, which is used throughout this book, to the metric system.

Product Differences

Most of the ingredients called for in the recipes in this book are available in most countries. However, some are known by different names. Here are some common American ingredients and their possible counterparts:

- Sugar (white) is granulated, fine granulated, or castor sugar.
- Powdered sugar is icing sugar.
- All-purpose flour is enriched, bleached or unbleached white household flour. When self-rising flour is used in place of all-purpose flour in a recipe that calls for leavening, omit the leavening agent (baking soda or baking powder) and salt.
- Light-color corn syrup is golden syrup.
- Cornstarch is cornflour.
- Baking soda is bicarbonate of soda.
- Vanilla or vanilla extract is vanilla essence.
- Green, red, or yellow sweet peppers are capsicums or bell peppers.
- Golden raisins are sultanas.

Volume and Weight

The United States traditionally uses cup measures for liquid and solid ingredients. The chart below shows the approximate imperial and metric equivalents. If you are accustomed to weighing solid ingredients, the following approximate equivalents will be helpful.

- 1 cup butter, castor sugar, or rice = 8 ounces = ½ pound = 250 grams
- 1 cup flour = 4 ounces = ¼ pound = 125 grams
- 1 cup icing sugar = 5 ounces = 150 grams

Canadian and U.S. volume for a cup measure is 8 fluid ounces (237 ml), but the standard metric equivalent is 250 ml.

1 British imperial cup is 10 fluid ounces.

In Australia, 1 tablespoon equals 20 ml, and there are 4 teaspoons in the Australian tablespoon.

Spoon measures are used for smaller amounts of ingredients. Although the size of the tablespoon varies slightly in different countries, for practical purposes and for recipes in this book, a straight substitution is all that's necessary. Measurements made using cups or spoons always should be level unless stated otherwise.

Common Weight Range Replacements

Imperial / U.S.	Metric
½ ounce	15 g
1 ounce	25 g or 30 g
4 ounces (¼ pound)	115 g or 125 g
8 ounces (½ pound)	225 g or 250 g
16 ounces (1 pound)	450 g or 500 g
1¼ pounds	625 g
1½ pounds	750 g
2 pounds or 2¼ pounds	1,000 g or 1 Kg

Oven Temperature Equivalents

Fahrenheit Setting	Celsius Setting*	Gas Setting
300°F	150°C	Gas Mark 2 (very low)
325°F	160°C	Gas Mark 3 (low)
350°F	180°C	Gas Mark 4 (moderate)
375°F	190°C	Gas Mark 5 (moderate)
400°F	200°C	Gas Mark 6 (hot)
425°F	220°C	Gas Mark 7 (hot)
450°F	230°C	Gas Mark 8 (very hot)
475°F	240°C	Gas Mark 9 (very hot)
500°F	260°C	Gas Mark 10 (extremely hot)
Broil	Broil	Grill

*Electric and gas ovens may be calibrated using celsius. However, for an electric oven, increase celsius setting 10 to 20 degrees when cooking above 160°C. For convection or forced air ovens (gas or electric) lower the temperature setting 25°F/10°C when cooking at all heat levels.

Baking Pan Sizes

Imperial / U.S.	Metric
9×1½-inch round cake pan	22- or 23×4-cm (1.5 L)
9×1½-inch pie plate	22- or 23×4-cm (1 L)
8×8×2-inch square cake pan	20×5-cm (2 L)
9×9×2-inch square cake pan	22- or 23×4.5-cm (2.5 L)
11×7×1½-inch baking pan	28×17×4-cm (2 L)
2-quart rectangular baking pan	30×19×4.5-cm (3 L)
13×9×2-inch baking pan	34×22×4.5-cm (3.5 L)
15×10×1-inch jelly roll pan	40×25×2-cm
9×5×3-inch loaf pan	23×13×8-cm (2 L)
2-quart casserole	2 L

U.S. / Standard Metric Equivalents

⅛ teaspoon = 0.5 ml	
¼ teaspoon = 1 ml	
½ teaspoon = 2 ml	
1 teaspoon = 5 ml	
1 tablespoon = 15 ml	
2 tablespoons = 25 ml	
¼ cup = 2 fluid ounces = 50 ml	
⅓ cup = 3 fluid ounces = 75 ml	
½ cup = 4 fluid ounces = 125 ml	
⅔ cup = 5 fluid ounces = 150 ml	
¾ cup = 6 fluid ounces = 175 ml	
1 cup = 8 fluid ounces = 250 ml	
2 cups = 1 pint = 500 ml	
1 quart = 1 litre	